"By denaturalizing the war economy through a gendered political economy lens, Hozić and True offer analysis and alternatives to the devastating turn towards militarization. This work is urgent and necessary."

**Mona Ali**, *Associate Professor, Department of Economics, State University of New York, New Paltz, NY, USA*

"*War Economy: Gendered Circuits of Violence and Capital* holds up a feminist mirror to today's capital and state led economies of war and politics of violence to show how these gendered circuits enmesh international and national conflicts and crisis with the everyday economies of social reproduction. This approach is urgently needed for our thinking about today's crisis ridden world."

**Shirin Rai**, *Distinguished Research Professor, SOAS, University of London*

"This impressive, wide-ranging volume interrogates the deadly interplay of capital, bodies, weapons and militarized technologies in wars and conflicts. Individually and together, the chapters offer the reader much-needed feminist insights into the rapid and complex changes unfolding in the global political economy."

**Srdjan Vucetic**, *Professor at the Graduate School of Public and International Affairs, University of Ottawa, USA*

AF739670

# WAR ECONOMY

*War Economy: Gendered Circuits of Violence and Capital* examines the war economy from feminist perspectives, bringing fresh thinking in the context of heightened geopolitical tensions.

This book challenges the common understanding of war economy as a state-driven, top-down project necessitated by a conflictual international order. It introduces the concept of gendered circuits of violence – different types of violence across space and time – to conceptually and empirically link crises and wars through flows of capital, bodies, weapons, and militarised technologies. It deals with real-world conflicts, including in Gaza and Russia/Ukraine as well as Bosnia and Herzegovina, Iran, Liberia, and Mexico. With increasing calls for the development of a war economy, especially in Europe, and broad acceptance that the global political economy is rapidly being primed for war, this book's feminist political economy analysis and alternatives are vital and urgent.

*War Economy* will appeal to students, scholars, and policymakers in the areas of International Political Economy, Politics and International Relations, Gender Studies, Security Studies, and War, Peace, and Conflict Studies.

**Aida A. Hozić** is Associate Professor of International Relations at the University of Florida. Her research is situated at the intersection of political economy, cultural studies, and international security.

**Jacqui True** is Professor of International Relations and Director of the Australian Research Council (ARC) Centre of Excellence for the Elimination of Violence against Women (CEVAW). Her research is focused on the political economy of violence against women, conflict-related gender-based violence, and feminist foreign policy analysis.

## RIPE Series in Global Political Economy

Series Editors: Susanne Soederberg *(Queen's University, Canada)*,
Adrienne Roberts *(The University of Manchester, UK)*,
Samuel Knafo *(University of Sussex, UK)* and
Naná de Graaff *(Vrije Universiteit Amsterdam, the Netherlands)*.

For almost two decades now, the *RIPE Series in Global Political Economy* published by Routledge has been an essential forum for cutting-edge scholarship in International Political Economy, which we understand to be a broadly defined area of research that may cut across other disciplines. The series brings together new and established scholars working in critical, cultural and constructivist political economy. Books in the *RIPE Series* typically combine an innovative contribution to theoretical debates with rigorous empirical analysis.

The *RIPE Series* seeks to cultivate:

- Field-defining theoretical advances in International Political Economy.
- Novel treatments of key issue areas, such as global finance, trade, and production, both historical and contemporary.
- Analyses that explore the political economic dimensions of relatively neglected topics, such as the environment, gender, race, and colonialism from both Western and non-Western perspectives.
- Accessible work that will inspire advanced undergraduates and graduate students in International Political Economy.

**The Politics of Late Urban Entrepreneurialism**
The Innovation District
*Greig Charnock, Jose Mansilla and Ramon Ribera-Fumaz*

For more information about this series, please visit: www.routledge.com/RIPE-Series-in-Global-Political-Economy/book-series/RIPE

# WAR ECONOMY

## Gendered Circuits of Violence and Capital

*Edited by*
*Aida A. Hozić and Jacqui True*

Routledge
Taylor & Francis Group
LONDON AND NEW YORK

Designed cover image: Imperial War Museum

First published 2026
by Routledge
4 Park Square, Milton Park, Abingdon, Oxon OX14 4RN

and by Routledge
605 Third Avenue, New York, NY 10158

*Routledge is an imprint of the Taylor & Francis Group, an informa business*

© 2026 Aida A. Hozić and Jacqui True

The right of Aida A. Hozić and Jacqui True to be identified as authors of this work has been asserted in accordance with sections 77 and 78 of the Copyright, Designs and Patents Act 1988.

With the exception of Chapter 1, no part of this book may be reprinted or reproduced or utilised in any form or by any electronic, mechanical, or other means, now known or hereafter invented, including photocopying and recording, or in any information storage or retrieval system, without permission in writing from the publishers.

Chapter 1 of this book is freely available as a downloadable Open Access PDF at http://www.taylorfrancis.com under a Creative Commons Attribution-Non Commercial-No Derivatives (CC BY-NC-ND) 4.0 International license.

Any third party material in this book is not included in the OA Creative Commons license, unless indicated otherwise in a credit line to the material. Please direct any permissions enquiries to the original rightsholder.

This research was supported (partially) by the Australian Government through the Australian Research Council's Centre of Excellence for the Elimination of Violence Against Women (Project number CE230100004).

For Product Safety Concerns and Information please contact our EU representative GPSR@taylorandfrancis.com. Taylor & Francis Verlag GmbH, Kaufingerstraße 24, 80331 München, Germany.

*Trademark notice*: Product or corporate names may be trademarks or registered trademarks, and are used only for identification and explanation without intent to infringe.

*British Library Cataloguing-in-Publication Data*
A catalogue record for this book is available from the British Library

ISBN: 9781032946108 (hbk)
ISBN: 9781032935591 (pbk)
ISBN: 9781003571667 (ebk)

DOI: 10.4324/9781003571667

Typeset in Times New Roman
by codeMantra

# CONTENTS

# IMAGE AND TABLE

**Image**



**Table**

# CONTRIBUTORS

**Asma Abdi** is an ESRC Postdoctoral Fellow at the Institute of Arab and Islamic Studies, University of Exeter. Her research focuses on the intersections of global political economy, feminist theory, and post/decolonial approaches in the Global South, with a particular focus on the Middle East and Iran.

**Vesna Bojicic-Dzelilovic** is a Senior Research Fellow with LSE IDEAS, London School of Economics and Political Science and an Associate Research Fellow with LSEE, LSE Research Unit on Southeast Europe. She specialises in the political economy of development with a particular interest in conflict–informality nexus and international aid to post-war recovery in the Western Balkans where she has been conducting fieldwork for over 30 years.

**Carol Cohn** is the founding Director of the Consortium on Gender, Security and Human Rights at the University of Massachusetts Boston. She works across scholarly, policy, and activist communities to create the multidimensional, feminist-gendered analyses that are imperative to finding sustainable and just solutions – not only to wars, but also to the structural inequalities and environmental crises that underlie them.

**Elliot Dolan-Evans** is a Lecturer in the Faculty of Law, Monash University. His research focuses on the political economy of peacebuilding, the International Financial Institutions, and questions of capitalism and health. His first solo book, *Making War Safe for Capitalism: The World Bank, IMF and the Conflict in Ukraine*, is published in 2025.

**Claire Duncanson** is a Professor of International Relations at the University of Edinburgh. She has published widely on issues related to gender, peace, and security, with a particular focus on gender and peacebuilding. Her current work aims to bring a feminist analysis to the political economy of building peace.

**Raksha Gopal** is a PhD candidate in International Relations/Political Science at the Geneva Graduate Institute and a researcher at the Gender Centre. She is part of the *Gendering Survival from the Margins* project, funded by the Swiss National Science Foundation (SNSF) and a member of the Borders, Race, Ethnicity and Migration (BREM) Network at the University of Warwick.

**Marsha Henry** is the Secretary Hillary Rodham Clinton Chair in Women, Peace, Security and Justice at the Mitchell Institute. Professor Henry's research focuses on gender, peace, and security; gender and militarisation; gender and development; and intersectional feminist methodologies.

**Denisa Kostovicova** is Professor of Global Politics at the European Institute and Lead of the LSEE Research on South East Europe Programme at the Hellenic Observatory, both at the London School of Economics and Political Science (LSE). She is a leading scholar of conflict and peace processes with a particular interest in post-conflict politics, reconstruction, and security in the Balkans.

**Daniela Lai** is a Senior Lecturer in International Relations at Royal Holloway, University of London. Her research draws on feminist IPE and IR and looks at questions of violence and justice and their intersection with political economy, with a particular focus on conflict-affected countries. Her book *Socioeconomic Justice: International Intervention and Transition in Post-War Bosnia and Herzegovina* was published in 2020.

**Luisa Lupo** is a PhD candidate in International Relations/Political Science at the Geneva Graduate Institute and a researcher at the Gender Centre, where she is part of the project *Gendering Survival from the Margins*, funded by the Swiss National Science Foundation (SNSF). She is also an affiliate of the Institute's Centre on Conflict, Development and Peacebuilding (CCDP).

**Jennifer G. Mathers** is a Senior Lecturer in the Department of International Politics at Aberystwyth University. Her research expertise spans area studies (Ukraine and Russia) and gender, conflict, and security. She has published on militarisation, protest politics, and gender and war, and is currently writing a book that examines Russia's war in Ukraine from the perspective of feminist security studies.

**Iratxe Perea Ozerin** is a Lecturer in International Relations at the University of the Basque Country (UPV/EHU) since 2015. She is also a member of the consolidated research group of the Basque university system "Basque Country, Europe and America: Atlantic Links and Relations." Her research interests are in the areas of feminist international political economy and the connections between gender violence, (in)security and austerity, and transnational social movements, revolutions, and Latin America and the Caribbean.

**Daniela Philipson Garcia** is a PhD candidate at Monash University. Her research focuses on the effects of militarisation on gender-based violence from a feminist political economy lens. She is a Fulbright-García Robles Scholar with a Master's in Public Policy from Harvard University.

**Elisabeth Prügl** is a Professeure honoraire at the Geneva Graduate Institute and Founding Director of the Institute's Gender Centre. Her research focuses on feminist international relations and gender politics in international governance. She has written on the international regulation of atypical forms of women's labour, such as industrial homework and agricultural labour, and on gender mainstreaming and gender expertise in international governance.

**Anna Stavrianakis** is Professor of International Relations at the University of Sussex and Director of Research and Strategy at Shadow World Investigations. She researches and teaches on the global arms trade, arms control, militarism, and global (in)securities. She works with activists, campaigners, journalists, lawyers, organisers, parliamentarians, and researchers in pursuit of accountability for the harms caused by the arms trade.

# ACKNOWLEDGEMENTS

This edited volume builds upon and expands a special issue of *Review of International Political Economy* (RIPE) (27:6, 2020) entitled "International Financial Institutions (IFIs) and Gendered Circuits of Labour and Violence," edited by Aida A. Hozić and Jacqui True. In the period between 2020 and 2025, we have seen an acceleration in the crises facing the global political economy with the COVID-19 pandemic, Russia's invasion of Ukraine, and the conflict in Gaza, among other wars, especially in Africa and Asia, that have wider ramifications for stability and peace. We therefore felt that the focus on gendered circuits of violence and capital, which was the theme of the original special issue, needed to be revisited. We wanted to highlight not merely the role of IFIs but of states themselves and their political economies primed for war.

Two chapters in this volume (by Carol Cohn & Claire Duncanson, and by Daniela Lai) were originally published in that special issue. They have been, respectively, shortened and lightly edited, and updated and substantively transformed for inclusion in this book. The chapter by Vesna Bojicic-Dzelilovic, Denisa Kostovicova, and Marsha Henry is a significantly revised version of their previously published article "Drawing on the continuum: a war and post-war political economy of gender-based violence in Bosnia and Herzegovina," *International Feminist Journal of Politics* (22:2, 2020). All other chapters have been specifically developed for this volume. They rely on the concept of gendered circuits of violence, first articulated in the special issue of RIPE, adapting it to illuminate the global move to state-led war economy. We are grateful to our colleagues for engaging with this concept to address the most pressing political emergencies of our time by making the connection between crises of social reproduction and conflict as priorities and budgets shift towards war production and defence.

This book was developed in the spring of 2024, when Aida A. Hozić was a Fulbright Distinguished Scholar at Pembroke College and the Department of Politics and International Relations, Oxford University, United Kingdom. She is thankful to all the scholars, including Jacqui True, who participated in the lecture series on feminist political economy of war and peace that she organized at Pembroke. Aida wishes to thank the UK Fulbright Commission, Professor Stephen Whitefield, Humeyra Biricik, DPhil, Vanessa Gouws, Operations Bursar, and the Pembroke community for their help and warm welcome in the chilling political times.

During this time, Jacqui True led a successful bid for an Australian Research Council (ARC) Centre of Excellence, the first to be focused on the elimination of violence against women in the Indo-Pacific region. As a result, her contribution to this volume has been supported by the Australian Government through the ARC's CEVAW (Project number CE2301100004) established in 2024.

The image on the cover is of women workers at the Chilwell filling factory in Nottinghamshire, UK, in 1917. They were known as "canary girls" as they worked with the highly toxic TNT, which turned their skin orange-yellow, like the caged birds. The image perfectly captures the unresolved contradiction between women's participation in the labour force, including in war economies, and the price they pay for their inclusion. This volume speaks to that tension, which, in our view, defines the contemporary global political economy in its haste to yet another World War.

# 1

# TOWARDS A FEMINIST THEORY OF WAR ECONOMY

*Aida A. Hozić and Jacqui True*

We face an uncertain global context in which it is vital to understand the relationship between war and economic crises. New major wars have broken out, and conflict deaths are at their highest level since World War II. Sexual violence and gender-based targeting have become a crucial facet of 21st-century war fighting. They are manifest in explicit attacks on all aspects of social and sexual reproduction as well as bodies with the intent to oppress the enemy group (UN Security Council 2024).[1] Total global military expenditure reached $2,443 billion in 2023, an increase of 6.8% in real terms from 2022. This was the steepest year-on-year increase since 2009.[2] The global political economy is increasingly becoming a *war economy* wherein economic growth, employment and political consensus depend on defence spending and military buildup.

The US military-industrial complex is alive and well stimulated by Russia's war in Ukraine, the Israel/Palestine conflict, deterrence in the Indo-Pacific region and in the latter context, and the de-risking of security-sensitive economic sectors. In Europe, calls for a pre-emptive war economy have come from the highest-ranking European Union (EU) politicians. The economies of Russia and Ukraine *de facto* operate as war economies with Russia's economy arguably resilient even in the face of wide-ranging sanctions (Fenton and Kolyandr 2025).[3] Israel has been characterised as a techno-military marvel, exporting its defence and surveillance technologies to the rest of the world (Loewenstein 2023), while China has also expanded its range of dual-use technologies and bolstered defence research and innovation capacity. The development of autonomous weapons represents a qualitative departure and transcendence of the limits of previous wars (Bode and Huelss 2018). Contemporary war zones and their targets are increasingly sites of experimentation and (machine) learning. Both Ukraine and Gaza have been described as laboratories of future warfare because of their reliance on new generations of

DOI: 10.4324/9781003571667-1
This chapter has been made available under a CC BY-NC-ND 4.0 license.

drones and AI targeting, respectively (Abraham 2023; Sukman 2024; Entous 2025; Frenkel and Odenheimer 2025). The weapons and algorithms they are generating now will make prospective wars even easier to fight as well as serve as a new source of economic growth and innovation (Shah and Kirchhoff 2024).

Alongside these innovations in warmaking, we are witnessing the exodus of families from war zones and the destruction of social and health infrastructure. According to UNHCR (2024), there were 122.6 million displaced persons in the world in mid-2024, more than six times as many as in the early 1990s. Most of the displaced are women and children. The gendered distribution of harm is notable in Ukraine (Mathers 2020, this volume), in the targeting of hospitals and education institutions in Gaza (ni Aolain 2024) and in the wilful institutionalisation of "gender apartheid" in Afghanistan (True and Akbari 2024). The mass displacement and migration from the current and former war zones is funnelled into low-cost labour markets and global care chains (Hozić 2024a, 2024b), and various forms of lucrative gendered violence and exploitation including human trafficking and slavery (Caruana et al. 2020). These human processes are constitutive of the war economy.

Despite all this evidence of the connection between war and the economy, the reorientation of the global political economy around war has hardly been observed by scholars. Academic amnesia continues to hide the roots of capitalism in war finance (Sonenscher 2022). Unsurprisingly, perhaps, International Political Economy (IPE) and International Relations (IR) have not paid attention to shifts in economic production and social reproduction sectors to support war preparedness. Mona Ali (2023) has aptly called the reorientation of production and reproduction around war, "militarized adaptation." Rather than analysing how war and the global economy are transforming one another, scholars have focused on conventional areas of research related to the war machine – industrial policy, green transition, technological change, and competition. Political economy analyses addressing the causes of violent conflict and insecurity, and international security analyses considering economic drivers and implications are still rare (True and Hozić 2020: 1195). Thus, IR and IPE disciplines continue to reinforce the outdated binary dichotomy between security and economic dynamics in their analysis of global politics (Kirshner 1998). Scholars of historical materialism have recognised the war economy as endogenous to capitalism, including its effects on the social reproduction usually associated with women's unpaid or devalued labour (Bieler and Morton 2018). However, they tend to see Marx's "hidden abode" as derivative of and subordinate to capitalist accumulation (Cammack and Gimenez 2024).

From a feminist perspective, there is an acute crisis of social reproduction exacerbated by rising geopolitical tensions previously related to the global financial crisis and now to globalised conflict and war preparedness (see also Hozić & True 2016).[4] The crisis is rooted in women's bodies and work and is not simply an epiphenomenon of capitalism's perpetual crises. Social reproduction refers to the work in the family-household, market and state that is essential to maintaining and reproducing life (including biological reproduction, care work, and the reproduction of communities and culture) (see Rai et al. 2013). The post-pandemic global political economic environment together with the wars in Ukraine and Gaza has led to volatility and uncertainty in global supply chains producing a cost-of-living crisis in many high-income countries. The remedies – the high interest rates, which have increased loan servicing, as well as the sanctions and war-induced food crises – have had a major impact on the global South. Their compound effect has aggravated the crisis of social reproduction, which manifests itself not only in diminishing growth (Baccaro et al. 2022) but also in declining birth and marriage rates, ageing populations and extreme labour shortages in the care sector across the world.[5] This situation has given rise to extremist politics – advocating pro-natalist, anti-gender equality policies restricting women's reproductive rights to shore up economic growth and future taxpayers, and anti-immigration and foreign aid policies as a response to domestic housing and other social infrastructure shortages (see Kuhar & Paternotte 2017).

Feminist political economists view the tensions between capitalist accumulation and social reproduction as co-constitutive, threatening the very ability of the world to sustain itself (Le Baron and Roberts, 2010). They observe how austerity policies and violent attacks on social reproduction and available infrastructure for social reproduction depend on location in the global political economy and have disproportionate effects on women and minoritised groups (Mezzadri et al. 2022; Hozić and True 2017). Moreover, they argue that these attacks have led to the depletion of social reproduction in many contexts referring to the harm caused when the outflow of resources for care work and maintaining life "exceeds the inflow of resources available to those engaged in it." Such depletion is not simply a consequence of crisis but as Shirin Rai (2024) argues, it can be anticipatory, produced and aggravated by expectations of multiple, prospective environmental challenges and "man-made" disasters.

Feminist scholars of social reproduction are aware that a resolution to the crisis demands more extreme forms of state responses, such as incarceration (Le Baron and Roberts, 2010). However, they have not thus far analysed the war economy and role of state-led violence in the destruction – and regeneration – of the capacity for the social reproduction of life. Recent scholarly efforts to pluralise social reproduction only mention war and conflict in passing (Mezzadri et al. 2025). To address these gaps, this volume centres the role of war economies and peripheral wars in contemporary capitalism, both building on and expanding social reproduction theory.

In this chapter, we theorise the war economy from a feminist perspective, connecting scholarship on global political economy and social reproduction of life (Elias and Rai 2019) with that on war and gendered violence (True 2012). First, we explore conventional typologies of "war economy" and how the concept has evolved across various contexts and scholarly literatures. Second, we advance a theoretical framework for investigating and explicating the war economy as a manifestation of temporal, spatial, and scalar gendered circuits of violence and capital in and outside recognised "war/conflict zones" (True and Hozić 2020). We explain why we highlight circuits of violence and capital and illustrate the analytical utility of the theory through its application to contemporary situations where conflict and crises of social reproduction collide. We stress the interconnected nature of war economies within and across global regions and situations of militarisation, conflict, and negative peace. Third, extending our theoretical argument, we propose that feminist methodologies are essential for studying the war economy and its widespread circuits, providing some examples from the following chapters. Finally, we outline the structure of the volume and its contribution to scholarship that seeks to understand as well as support social change in the world.

## Defining war economy

There are varying definitions of "war economy." Simply put, it is defined as all economic activity occurring during war or any situation where an entire society is organised for war with all its socio-economic goals and activity subordinated to fighting war. The term has existed since the 1930s and was prevalent during the Cold War. At this time, "military Keynesianism" became a "colossal balancer," the preferred solution to the inherent instability of private investment (Barker 2022). Discussion of the war economy declined in the period of anticipated post-Cold War peace dividend but resurfaced in face of the 9/11 attacks in the United States. In the aftermath of 9/11, James K. Galbraith (2001, 2004) argued that the deleterious economic impact of the terror attacks and the security response on the US economy made the situation akin to a wartime economy.[6] As the global "War on Terror" expanded, there were occasional references to the United States as a permanent war economy (Duncan and Coyne 2013), a concept originally developed by Edward Sard in the 1940s (van der Linden 2018). Another major uptick in mentions of "war economy" occurred in 2015 with the civil war in Syria and the rise of Islamic State, and then again starting in 2020, prompted by Russia and its military buildup. Parallels with a war economy were also observed during the COVID-19 pandemic when states used emergency "war powers" to procure protective gear, secure lockdowns and maintain essential workers (Gibson-Fall 2021). In the last several years, political leaders from France to Egypt and Argentina have been discussing the war economy to address the post-pandemic economic crisis and security threats by advocating for greater defence investment. Alex de Waal (2025) has linked the resurgence of contending war economies, especially in BRICS countries, to the return of famines. Europe's plans for Ukraine's recovery are linked to the idea that the country should be armed to its teeth and turned into a "steel porcupine" (Economist 2025), a metaphor that seems to capture the aspirations of most global leaders concerned about rising global instability.

Scholars commonly distinguish between two types of war economy: State-led war economies often associated with great powers and anti-state or non-state "warzones" frequently located in the periphery where states are either re-made or destroyed. The first type of a war economy is a state-driven top-down project that subordinates economic activity – especially in manufacturing, research and development – to military needs. Usually conceived as government-supported production for military defence/victory, today's calls for revitalising war economies mostly look to the precursors of the World War II military buildup or the development of the military-industrial complex during the Cold War. Both examples are closely related to the already mentioned "military Keynesianism" since state expenditure on defence sector could also stimulate demand. Conceptually, there are some affinities between analyses of state-led war economy and critical analyses of the role of the state in capitalism (Babić 2023; Alami and Dixon 2024), including its increasingly coercive and repressive practices associated with authoritarian neoliberalism (Bruff and Tansel 2020) and carceral state (Le Baron and Robinson 2010).

The second type of "war economy" or "warzone economy" associates it with the criminal and illegal practices of non-state armed actors in times of war when lawlessness and disorder prevail (Bojicic-Dzelilovic and Turkmani 2018: 54). The wars in the 1990s – especially in the former Yugoslavia and in central Africa – generated major academic and policy debates about "new wars" and their economic models (Kaldor 1999, 2013). These peripheral war economies can encompass the extractive, coercive strategies of non-state armed groups, and the coping strategies of civilians. Civilians too may use violence since it often becomes an entrenched way of allocating and distributing resources during war.

Critics of war economy note its propensity to create distortions in the marketplace. Through its economically parasitic output, the war economy generates inflationary pressures (Melman 1972). It diverts resources from other uses that could improve the general standard of living (Duncan and Coyne 2013). By contrast, supporters of a war economy highlight its positive economic externalities. They include employment guarantees, state investment and subsidies, and stabilisation of production via assured domestic demand. In principle, states aim to avoid trading off between guns and butter seeking instead to bolster economic activity via the use of their military power (Poast 2019). "Bidenomics," the US turn towards industrial policy and infrastructure building under President Jospeh Biden (2020–2024), took a decisive turn towards war economy once it ran into political roadblocks, especially on social spending (Elrod 2024; Tooze 2024). Even in peripheral conflicts, researchers have noted that a war economy can create opportunities for profit-making via illicit activities but also stimulate development of novel coping strategies by different local actors (Bojicic-Dzelilovic and Turkmani 2018).

Departing from either type of war economy, it is important to highlight that gender relations have always been deeply and causally implicated in the evolution and entrenchment of war economies. Historically, state-led war economies were closely related to protectionism and mercantilism, and pro-natalist family policies (Federici 2012; Feinberg 2006). Any discussion of guns vs (or and) butter cannot but have consequences for expenditures on services that crucially affect women's roles and demands for their (unpaid) labour. Wars and war economy redistribute resources, sometimes drawing women into the labour force in greater numbers. Not surprisingly, contemporary media commentaries on emerging war economies in Europe and the United States allude to the return of Rosie the Riveter (Roussi, Politico 2023). And yet gender is hardly ever explicitly mentioned in discussions about the transformation of national and global economies to prepare for or sustain war.

## Feminist perspectives on war economy

Feminist approaches capture a broader phenomenon of "war" than the two dominant definitions, although they have rarely engaged with the concept of war economy directly despite its significant – and varied – gendered effects. A notable exception is V. Spike Peterson (2008, 2016) whose taxonomy of coping, combat, and criminal/informal economies has informed several chapters in this volume. Similarly, Cynthia Enloe, in her multiple works, has always insisted on conceptualising war as encompassing social and economic activity outside of – as well as during – conflict, highlighting militarisation as an everyday social process fuelling war (Enloe 1990, 2000).

These feminist conceptualisations provide an entry point for a gendered analysis of the war economy. Material and ideological preparations for war are marked by the quest for "hard" rather than human security. They tend to reinforce gender hierarchies by promoting militarised masculinities, leading to the erasure of women and devaluation of any activities considered "feminine" (Peterson 2008). Gendered divisions of labour and social reproduction sustain and mobilise fighters in civil conflicts (Davies and True 2024; Hedstrom 2017). And as feminist political scientists have observed, war can be a rupture and catalyst for expanding women's rights and political agency due to "changes in the political elite and dominant economic interests" (Tripp 2023: 926; Hughes 2009). In the African continent, Aili Tripp (2015) argues that women's political representation worldwide has expanded more rapidly after conflict, crisis and revolution, especially after decolonial wars of independence. As a result, in some contexts women have been empowered by war and the war economy.[7] But contingency has always played a role in women's improved representation, which has not usually endured.

In this volume, we centre the war economy as the turn to and/or acceptance of war to address political and economic crises. Our innovation is basic – we theorise war + economy to expose how war production and gendered circulation of violence are increasingly viewed as solutions to stagnant economic and population growth. But we also highlight how crises of social reproduction, especially in the world's largest economies, drive the current push towards the development and entrenchment of state-led and/or state-sanctioned war economies.

There is no doubt that the quest for economic domination is driving war and conflict in many contexts worldwide. Finance capital scrambles for resources through "shock doctrine" military intervention and rebuilding of former war zones. As we have seen in previous wars in Iraq and Afghanistan, there is a massive benefit to private capital including defence contractors from war activity.[8] Yet, from a feminist perspective, we also observe that the years of austerity politics and the shock of the COVID pandemic, have brought the global care economies – and their providers – to the breaking point (Mezzadri, 2022; Tanyag, 2025). Deeply unequal and gendered care labour tends to depend on women and immigrants (Hozić and True 2017; Dowling 2021). Peripheral wars and climate change-related disasters have been washing refugees up on the shores of the world's wealthiest economies, creating a reserve labour army while feeding anti-immigrant sentiments. Combined, demographic decline and dependence on migrant labour and care feed grievances that are fanned by anti-gender and anti-immigration populist movements. These political dynamics strengthen conservative and far-right political forces, which revolve around the "great replacement theory." They inadvertently weaken the social reproduction model, which has for decades been reliant on surplus population displaced by wars fought elsewhere.

We recognise that the war economy has many guises and may look different in diverse contexts at different levels of "preparedness." It differs in countries that fight wars at a distance and those that are currently war zones, compared with others that are in a constant state of "readiness." It includes activities supporting war in other continents such as "proxy wars" as well as the "war on drugs" in the context of US foreign policy and the deployment of militaries domestically for public order/security as in cases in Latin America, and, under Trump administration, in the US. Feminist analysis aims to connect these sites theoretically and empirically, eschewing the methodological nationalism that persists in IR and IPE (Hozić and True 2016). It shows how combat and coping, formal and shadow economies are part of the same war economy (Peterson 2008, 2016; Nordstrom 2004). These frontline economies involve labour supporting the war effort. While men are often most of the fighters, the context of war and violence intensifies the depletion of women's lives as they labour to meet the needs of their households and communities (Rai et al. 2019). Such depletion heightens women's vulnerability to gender-based violence in conflict situations and erodes their coping capacities. For example, in Russia's war in Ukraine, "continued shelling fosters an environment of emotional exhaustion, prolonged stress and displacement," all of which contribute to increased gender-based violence (UNFPA 2025). War economy as a concept brings together all these varying types of war activity not only production through arms and the defence industry but also through people, care economy, peacekeeping and humanitarian industry, energy sector, and so on (Jennings 2014).

Much of IR scholarship views recent wars as isolated events that the international community has benevolently sought to contain and resolve. It does not examine these conflict-resolution efforts as part of an economy sustained by persistent wars. Ironically, building the international legal scaffolding to safeguard civilians has humanised wars while also making them more acceptable and more lucrative for some (Moyn 2021). These wars have also become the terrain for various protections of civilians and normative policy agendas, such as the Responsibility to Protect (R2P) and Women, Peace and Security (WPS). Such agendas seek to ensure the inclusivity of protection, while falling short of challenging war production in the world's major powers and providing alternatives to arms exporting.

While not simply an agenda in service of great powers or interventions, WPS is a contested and evolving result of a bargain between states, both liberal and global South states, and feminist movements. However, its often top-down implementation has tended to address the humanitarian consequences of wars, but not their root causes (Meger 2016). WPS has also failed in its strategy to advance women's participation in peace processes to expedite war endings (Akbari and True 2024; Olivius et al. 2022). Efforts to build protections for women and address gendered insecurities are increasingly ineffective as we see, for instance, in the upward trend in sexualised violence perpetrated against civilians in the face of 15 years of international efforts to prohibit its use as a 'weapon of war'.[9] Moreover, when it comes to economic recovery after wars, women are frequently not deemed essential to be included, compensated or resourced for their peacebuilding efforts (Duque et al. 2023; Davies and True 2022).

In the next part, we introduce the framework of gendered circuits of violence and capital to further develop our feminist approach to war economy, examining how it operates in diverse settings, both in war zones and zones of apparent peace and stability.

## The framework of gendered circuits

The framework of gendered circuits draws on feminist political economy and security studies analysis to make visible the gendered connections between economic change and wars that are neglected in conventional approaches to conflicts and post-conflict recovery. As we argued in the previous section, there is literally no mention of gender in discussions about the state-driven war economies although women may be mentioned in peripheral war economies but usually only as victims of the criminalised networks that run them rather than as potential builders of sustainable peace (Chinkin and Kaldor, 2013). Gendered circuits of violence highlight the dynamic relation between plural locales through the violent circulation of people and capital. Historically, as mentioned above, peripheral wars produced surplus populations who filled the ranks of the much-needed care workers and contributed to the population growth in stagnant "First World" economies. That model is now reaching its political limits and is being replaced by state-led war economies. By focusing on the feminised and racialised bodies that move because of displacement from conflict and gendered violence and circuits of capital investment, we can demonstrate complex interconnections between these different models of war economies.

Gendered circuits capture three dimensions of the patterns of violence, highlighted by feminist analysis: First, the circuit that connects different types of violence including physical, economic, psychological and discursive or symbolic violence that may co-occur and compound each other, especially in situations of armed conflict and war production. Second, the circuit of violence across temporalities – from the precursors of war in everyday, normalised violence to the outbreak of war, and in transitions from conflict to peace and beyond. Third, the circuits of capital across territories at war or not – from households, factories and supply chains to borderlands to war zones.

The first and second circuits are often referred to in feminist conflict and sociological studies as a "continuum of violence." Such a continuum of sexual and gender-based violence has been found to exist across the life course of women and girls as well as before, during and after conflict (Kelly 1987; Cockburn 2004). With the circuits concept, we aim to incorporate these observations of continuities in the patterns of violence. However, we also seek a framework that analyses how different experiences of violence are materially connected through the social relations of production and reproduction or along global supply and care chains that connect high-, middle- and low-income countries and regions, and fragile, conflict-affected and stable, prosperous settings.

Our approach to gendered circuits cuts across and dynamically relates the two types of war economy: both powerful and/or strong states invested in defence and extractivism, and fragile states dependent on the production stimulated by war and illicit trade. With the circuits concept, we seek to break down binary understandings of war and peace, conflict and post-conflict, global North and South to investigate how the violence of armed conflict and war are enabled by the violence of structural inequality embedded in movements of arms/weapons, capital, technology, and people through both migration and humanitarianism.

Documenting and analysing gendered circuits exposes the global reliance on war not only through state-led military-industrial complexes or the financialisation of military endeavours but through processes of social reproduction, and on (women's) bodies that labour. The multi-scalar war economy depends on circuits of physical and structural violence linking the centres and margins of the global political economy. The destruction of non-capitalist societies through war, for example, provides new territory for capitalist expansion and investment. The war economy drains resources from social reproduction of life and labour through targeted cuts to education, health, and care sectors and informal household economies with the aim of expanding markets for efficiency and capital gain.

Mediated by sanctions, militarisation, geopolitical pressures, and aspirations, war economies anchor and amplify existing austerity policies as well as measures aimed at subordinating women to traditional family values, household work, and motherhood. Pro-natalist politics also lurk in the background of re-nationalised growth models and militarised techno-fantasies (Slobodian, 2024). In former and contemporary war zones such as Bosnia and Herzegovina, Liberia and Guatemala, and Ukraine and Gaza, war economies extend backwards and forwards in time, with control over resources, material and institutional, enabling violent masculinities and extreme forms of population governance and/or extermination.

By following the bodies that labour in the sites of global capitalism's expansion, in this volume, we seek to expose the gendered dynamics of these circuits of violence and capital that prime societies for conflict (Hozić 2021). We can see, for example, how circuits of violence are manifest through the growth and diffusion of this security industry worldwide. Mostly male soldiers trained for warfighting who morph into peacebuilders in fragile settings and then become part of the massive, growing private security industry (Kruck and Schneiker 2017). Similarly, logistics networks and civilian workers who sustain daily operations of overseas military interventions link the geopolitical manoeuvres of great powers to the intimate politics of transnational households (Chua et al. 2018; Moore 2019; Khalili 2021). Gendered structural inequality is produced and reinforced through these circuits of capital and labour across zones of war and relative peace.

We argue that the upshot of the war economy is the continual generation of new forms of feminised poverty during and after war. Feminised poverty is pervasive in Ukraine because of Russia's invasion, in Taliban-led Afghanistan after the withdrawal of Western powers and the institutionalisation of gender apartheid, and in Myanmar and Gaza, where widespread military bombing of hospitals and education institutions has disproportionately harmed women and children, to name just a few examples. In the next part, we suggest that studying state-led or peripheral war economy in myriad contexts requires feminist methodologies.

## Feminist methodologies for studying the war economy

Feminist ways of knowing have foresight and criticality when it comes to violence, conflict, and war. In many conflict-affected settings, we notice the ability of women to literally see the wars coming since they are often responsible for everyday survival in families and communities. Women are hyper-alert to events on the ground and pick up signals through neighbourhoods and community networks that others (including those in power) ignore. Early warning signs are virtually built into feminist perspectives on war and security (Enloe 2000). Ontologically, we seek to break down boundaries between war and peace. We aim to demonstrate how gendered violence is a pattern and a lived experience across different economies, conflict zones, and through time. Such an approach to building knowledge contrasts with the usual presentation of economic and/or contemporary wars as discrete events, caused by site-specific vulnerabilities and institutional weaknesses within or between states (Sylvester 2013; Clift et al. 2025). Moreover, feminist political economy analysis aims to reveal the "invisible" aspects of contemporary capitalism including its dependence on perpetual crises and wars. While this perspective may be shared with scholars influenced by theories of uneven and combined development (Bieler and Morton 2018), feminist political economy is less wedded to the state as an object of analysis. We emphasise the cascading nature of wars and crises in the post-Cold War period by demonstrating their interconnectedness through weapon, technology, and people flows.

This volume includes feminist perspectives on war economy, adopting different methodological approaches. The chapters are case studies, which rely on ethnographic, qualitative research and/or interpretive methods, but all are guided by the key principles of feminist methodology to make the invisible visible and to highlight gendered and racialised structures that perpetuate violence across time and space. The chapters eschew methodological nationalism in studying war economy. They emphasise instead its relational and intersectional aspects, which connect war + economy and zones of war and peace: This feminist analysis interrogates the subordination of social reproduction to war production in myriad contexts and its deleterious effects on people of different age, gender, ethnic and racial backgrounds, employment, and socio-economic status.

### *Outline of the volume*

In this book, we aim to develop and advocate for feminist perspectives on war economies. The volume is thematically organised around circuits of violence – their different types, their protracted time horizon, and their spatially expansive reach. The case studies connect to the wider global political economy in line with the concept of gendered circuits, which captures the patterns of individual, structural, and political violence as well as the transnational and temporal continuities of violence in the war economy. Parts I–III of the book are structured as follows:

1 *Gendered circuits: Continuums*

The first part of the volume explores continuums of individual, structural, and political violence. The case studies in this part show how different types of violence and geopolitical tensions and pressures co-occur and compound each other in war economy settings. In the opening chapter, Chapter 2, Anna Stavrianakis makes the case for increased scholarly attention to arms trade as a key node in global circuits of violence and vector of global war economies. By connecting the economy of war preparation to violence in war zones and asymmetries in the global arms trade, she seeks to make connections between violence within and between societies as well as the connections between economic and physical violence. In Chapter 3, Daniela Philipson Garcia addresses the case of Mexico, where militarisation drives criminal wars, also known as the "war on drugs," and at the same time intensifies human rights violations, gendered inequalities, and gendered violence. Her chapter shows the continuum of inter-personal, structural and state violence and how war economy policies dismantle social infrastructure, further exacerbating the violence against women and marginalised Indigenous communities including widespread femicide and disappearances of women. In Chapter 4, Asma Abdi analyses the way Iranian state pursues war and militarisation – under the label of "resistance economy" – as solutions to overlapping political, economic, and geopolitical crises induced by the US sanctions. The chapter bridges temporally and spatially different forms of gendered violence that occur in the shadow of mutually reinforcing regimes of international sanctions and the Iranian state's war economy. Abdi highlights how reproductive economies bolster a patriarchal gendered division of labour. As a result, Abdi argues that matters of social reproduction, such as the age of marriage, women's productive and reproductive roles, and biological reproduction, have emerged as key sites of the state's coercion.

2 *Gendered circuits: Temporalities*

The second part of this book is focused on circuits of violence as they travel through time, across different temporalities before, during, and after wars. The case studies in this part show the continuity between precursors of war in everyday, normalised violence enabled by the war economy to the outbreak of war – and vice versa – as gendered violence persists in transitions to and from war and peace and beyond. Thus, in Chapter 5, Vesna Bojicic-Dzelilovic, Denisa Kostovicova, and Marsha Henry analyse the epidemic of gender-based violence in Bosnia and Herzegovina, where decades after the war's end, the entrenched war economy still finds its outlet. Their chapter challenges the distinctions often made between war and post-war economies, highlighting instead the ongoing re-ordering of economy and society through violent extraction and control over resources, which then perpetuates gendered circuits of violence and manifests itself in femicide. In Chapter 6, Jenny Mathers investigates Ukraine and the contradictions inherent to the war effort, considering Russia's invasion and demands of international donors to privatise the economy and relinquish control to foreign interests. By drawing on insights from feminist security studies and feminist political economy, Mathers explores how these contradictory pressures undermine the state's support for the very women's health and community workers upon whom the state relies in its continued war effort. In Chapter 7, Iratxe Perea Ozerin explores the long shadow of the Global Financial Crisis and austerity politics in Southern Europe and the ways that austerity is being securitised through militarisation, defence spending and emerging war economies. In Chapter 8, Carol Cohn and Claire Duncanson question the role of International Financial Institutions (IFIs) in post-war settings. The IFIs, as Cohn and Duncanson demonstrate, stimulate recovery of economy rather than recovery of societies after wars, frequently anchoring that recovery in extractivism of local resources and thus exacerbating the crisis of social reproduction. An alternative approach to economic recovery, one that would privilege care – and the infrastructure that supports it – could much more effectively rebuild lives damaged by war and create conditions for sustainable peace.

3 *Gendered circuits: Movements*

The third part of this book explores the violence and capital movements across territories from households to borderlands to conflict zones. The chapters in this part highlight how various spaces of social reproduction in different settings are drawn into the same global circuits of violence. Daniela Lai, in Chapter 9, revisits Bosnia and Herzegovina, where the neglect of gendered justice continues to produce insecurities in households and across the region. The gendered circuits of violence produced by neoliberal economic reforms and still connected to wartime political economy are now extended into the post-pandemic crisis of care and livelihoods, compounded by ecological and geopolitical crises. In Chapter 10, Eliott Dolan-Evans simultaneously confronts the conflicts in Ukraine and Gaza. Deploying everyday feminist political economy analysis, Dolan-Evans focuses on energy as a resource that is being fought over in wars but also as a resource used to manage (and extinguish) entire populations. Finally, in Chapter 11, Elisabeth Prügl, Raksha Gopal, and Luisa Lupo re-conceptualise the relationship between social reproduction and violence in the context of the emerging war economies. By analysing the multiple meanings of gendered circuits of violence, they follow the flows and movements of violence through different arteries, focusing more specifically on those of global capitalism, transnational biopolitics and colonial epistemes of mastery. They conclude by arguing that social reproduction is a powerful lens for "identifying and interpreting often ambivalent experiences of people living in war economies." Their chapter enables us to acknowledge that the war economy involves "both life-making and reproducing violence."

## Conclusion

The feminist conceptualisation of the war economy as a product of economic and security crises is unique. In this chapter that frames the volume on war economy, we argue that gendered circuits of violence and capital are organising principles of the contemporary global political economy. War and conflict are no longer in abeyance but are increasing globally. Feminist political economy analysis, focusing on gendered circuits, dispels the hope that conflict can be contained in the periphery of the global political economy. Feminist analysis in this chapter and this volume addresses the world's current predicament, connecting increasing conflicts, disruptions to supply chains, trade, and sustainable economies and their harmful impacts on everyday life and human security within and across regions. Countries depend on migrant workers for care and life support, while global trade and production networks depend on the unfettered circulation of bodies that labour and do not just supply parts. Ending war and breaking down gendered circuits of violence and capital therefore does not mean stopping the flow of bodies but rather ensuring their safety and dignity everywhere.

Alternatives to the current war economy-primed international order are vital. Demilitarising economies will be essential for delivering economic and social justice for the world's peoples, especially for women. Austerity and pro-natalist policies associated with the turn to war economy have been shown to negatively impact women's economic livelihoods while attacking their human rights to bodily integrity, to employment, to freedom of speech and association, among others. Throughout the 'developing world', changes in consumption patterns in the global North and disruptions in global supply chains have deepened existing gender inequalities. In the 'developed world' Women are no longer willing to become unpaid family workers or housewives despite the far-right "trad wives" trend. Probably the most significant trend over the last half-century is the political and economic empowerment of women. Demographic decline in some parts of the world is a reproductive strike by women who refuse to be mothers and reject marriage and the subservience that it often comes with. Although women are not a homogeneous group, they are among the most educated worldwide and have entered most professions and institutions holding power across regions and countries, including the military. To promote recovery from war and the prevention of future conflict, societies must harness both women's and men's human capacities. Yet economic policies around the world typically privilege marketisation and privatisation of natural resources, physical infrastructure and foreign investment opportunities that overall benefit men's jobs, incomes, and assets more than women's. Countries need to invest in wellbeing economies that prioritise the replenishment of social, health, and care infrastructure and education to support inclusive, gender-equal, and knowledge-based economies that can integrate immigrants, displaced people, and war veterans.

## Notes

1 In 2024, the UN Secretary-General's Security Council report showed a 50% increase in the use of conflict-related sexual and gender-based violence (CRSV) by conflict parties.
2 https://www.sipri.org/media/press-release/2024/global-military-spending-surges-amid-war-rising-tensions-and-insecurity
3 Both Russia and Ukraine have been secretive in reporting of their losses, and the impact of the war on Russian economy is very difficult to estimate. Some analysis indicates that economic downturn is quite severe. See Cooper (2025).
4 With important exceptions, Abrahamsen & Williams 2007; Blanchard et al. 1999; Homolar 2010.
5 McKinsey (2025) published an exceptionally alarming demographic report, predicting that populations in some major economies will fall 20–50% by 2100.
6 The events of 9/11 had a negative impact on economic sectors related to travel and leisure and led to a decline in consumer spending at the same time as defence/security spending increased.
7 For instance, in the communist Soviet Union, which suffered massive losses of men during World War II, women continued to be included in the post-war recovery and Cold War economy (see Alexievich 2018).
8 The Cost of War Project (2023), which started with Iraq war and then continued with Afghanistan war, counted the cost of war to the American public, but not its benefit to the American private sector.
9 The UN Secretary-General's report to the UN Security Council (2024) report showed a 50% increase in the use of conflict-related sexual and gender-based violence by conflict parties.

## References

Abraham, Y. (2023) "A mass assassination factory': Inside Israel's calculated bombing of Gaza', *+972 Magazine*, November 30. Available at https://www.972mag.com/mass-assassination-factory-israel-calculated-bombing-gaza/. Accessed on May 6, 2026.

Abrahamsen, R., & Williams, M. C. (2007). Selling security: Assessing the impact of military privatization. *Review of International Political Economy*, 15(1): 131–146. https://doi.org/10.1080/09692290701751332

Akbari, F. & True, J. Bargaining with Patriarchy in Peacemaking: The Failure of Women, Peace, and Security in Afghanistan, *Global Studies Quarterly*, 4 (1), ksae004, https://doi.org/10.1093/isagsq/ksae004

Alami, I., & Dixon, A. D. (2024) *The spectre of state capitalism*. Oxford University Press.

Alexievich, S. (2018) *The unwomanly face of war.* Penguin.

Ali, M. (2022) 'Between tragedy and techno-optimism: The new climate realpolitik', *Green*, *2*(1): 25–30. https://shs.cairn.info/journal-green-2022-1-page-25?lang=en.

Babić, M. (2023) *The rise of state capital: Transforming markets and international politics* (p. 184). Agenda Publishing Limited.

Baccaro, L., Blyth, M., & Pontusson, J. eds. (2022). *Diminishing returns: The new politics of growth and stagnation.* Oxford University Press.

Barker, T. (2022) *Cold war capitalism: The political economy of American military spending, 1947–1990* (Doctoral dissertation, Harvard University).

Bieler, A., & Morton, A. D. (2018) *Global capitalism, global war, global crisis*. Cambridge University Press.

Blanchard, Jean-Marc F., Edward D. Mansfield and Norrin M. Ripsman (1999) "The political economy of national security: Economic statecraft, interdependence, and international conflict." *Security Studies*, 9(1–2), 1–14.

Bode, I., & Huelss, H. (2018) 'Autonomous weapons systems and changing norms in international relations', *Review of International Studies, 44*(3): 393–413. doi:10.1017/S0260210517000614.

Bojicic-Dzelilovic, V., & Turkmani, R. (2018) 'War economy, governance and security in Syria's opposition-controlled areas', *Stability: International Journal of Security and Development*, *7*(1): 1–17.

Bruff, I., & Tansel, C. B. eds. (2020) 'Authoritarian neoliberalism: Trajectories of knowledge production and praxis', In *Authoritarian Neoliberalism: Philosophies, Practices, Contestations* (1st ed.) (pp. 1–12). Routledge. https://doi.org/10.4324/9780429355028

Caruana, R., Crane, A., Gold, S., & LeBaron, G. (2020) 'Modern slavery in business: The sad and sorry state of a non-field', *Business & Society*, *60*(2): 251–287. https://doi.org/10.1177/0007650320930417 (Original work published 2021)

Chua, C., Danyluk, M., Cowen, D., & Khalili, L. (2018) 'Introduction: Turbulent circulation: Building a critical engagement with logistics', *Environment and Planning D*, *36*(4): 617–629. https://doi.org/10.1177/0263775818783101 (Original work published 2018)

Cockburn, C. (2004) 'The continuum of violence: A gender perspective on war and peace', In *Sites of violence: Gender and conflict zones*, edited by W. Giles and J. Hyndman (pp. 24–44). University of California Press. https://doi.org/10.1525/9780520937055-004

Cooper, J. (2025) 'Russia's economy is stagnating – but that won't force it to end the war', March 10, Available at https://theconversation.com/russias-economy-is-stagnating-but-that-wont-force-it-to-end-the-war-251296

Costs of War Project. (2023) 'The human and financial costs of the Afghanistan war', Watson Institute of International and Public Affairs, Brown University, USA.

Davies, S. E., & True, J. (2024) *Hidden wars: Gendered violence in Asia's civil conflicts.* Oxford University Press.
de Waal, A. (2025) 'Hunger in global war economies: Understanding the decline and return of famines', *Disasters*, *49*(1), e12661. https://doi.org/10.1111/disa.12661
Dowling, E. (2022) *The care crisis: What caused it and how can we end it?* Verso Book.
Duncan, T. K., & Coyne, C. J. (2013) 'The origins of the permanent war economy', *The Independent Review*, *18*(2), 219–240
Duque-Salazar, J., Forsberg, E., & Olsson, L. (2023) 'Implementing Gender Provisions: A Study of the Comprehensive Agreement on the Bangsamoro in the Philippines', *International Negotiation*, *28*(2), 306–337.
Economist, The. (2025) 'How Europe hopes to turn Ukraine into a 'steel porcupine'', *The Economist*, April 6. Available at https://www.economist.com/europe/2025/04/06/how-europe-hopes-to-turn-ukraine-into-a-steel-porcupine. Accessed on May 6, 2025.
Elias, J., & Rai, S. M. (2019) 'Feminist everyday political economy: Space, time, and violence', *Review of International Studies*, *45*(2): 201–220. doi:10.1017/S0260210518000323
Elrod, A. Y. (2024) 'What was Bidenomics?', *Phenomenal World*. September 26. Available at https://www.phenomenalworld.org/analysis/what-was-bidenomics/ Accessed May 7, 2025.
Enloe, C. (1990) *Bananas, Beaches and Bases: Making Feminist Sense of International Politics*, 1st edn. University of California Press.
Enloe, C. (2000) *Manoeuvres: The international politics of militarizing women's lives*. University of California Press.
Entous, A. (2025) 'The secret history of the war in Ukraine', *New York Times*, March 29. Available at https://www.nytimes.com/interactive/2025/03/29/world/europe/us-ukraine-military-war-wiesbaden.html. Accessed on May 6, 2025.
Federici, S. (2012) *Revolution at point zero: Housework, reproduction and feminist struggle*. PM Press.
Feinberg, M. (2006) *Elusive equality: Gender, citizenship, and the limits of democracy in Czechoslovakia, 1918–1950*. University of Pittsburgh Press.
Frenkel, S., & Odenheimer, N. (2025) 'Israel's A.I. experiments in Gaza Raise ethical concerns', *New York Times*, April 25. Available at https://www.nytimes.com/2025/04/25/technology/israel-gaza-ai.html. Accessed on May 6, 2025.
Galbraith, J. K. (2001). The meaning of a war economy. *Challenge, 44*(6), 5–12. http://www.jstor.org/stable/40722105
Galbraith, J. K. (2004) 'The worldly philosophers and the war economy', *Social Research: An International Quarterly*, *71*(2): 293–304.
Gibson-Fall, F. (2021) 'Military responses to COVID-19, emerging trends in global civil-military engagements', *Review of International Studies*, *47*(2): 155–170. https://doi.org/10.1017/S0260210521000048.
Hedstrom, J. (2017) 'The political economy of the Kachin revolutionary household', *The Pacific Review*, *30*(4): 581–595.
Homolar, A. (2010). The political economy of national security. Review of International Political Economy, 17(2): 410–423. https://doi.org/10.1080/09692291003623682
Hozić, A. A. (2021) "Follow the bodies: Global capitalism, global war, global crisis and feminist IPE." *International relations*, *35*(1): 173–177.
Hozić, A. A. (2024a) 'Financial crisis and security', In *Security Studies: An Applied Introduction*, (pp. 375–395) edited by N. Rossi & M. Riemann. SAGE Publications Limited.
Hozić, A. A. (2024b) 'Insecurities and Economies of Care', in *The Western Balkans 2024: Assessment of the Current Security Posture and Geopolitical Challenges*. New

Lines Institute. Available at https://newlinesinstitute.org/political-systems/insecurity-and-economies-of-care/. Accessed on October 5, 2025.

Hozić, A. A., & True, J. eds. (2016) *Scandalous economics: Gender and the politics of financial crises*. Oxford University Press.

Hozić, A. A., & True, J. (2017) 'Brexit as a scandal: Gender and global trumpism', *Review of International Political Economy*, *24*(2): 270–287.

Jennings, K. M. (2014) 'Service, sex, and security: Gendered peacekeeping economies in Liberia and the Democratic Republic of the Congo', *Security Dialogue*, *45*(4): 313–330.

Kelly, L. (1987) 'The continuum of sexual violence', In *Women, Violence and Social Control. Explorations in Sociology*, edited by J. Hanmer and M. Maynard. Palgrave Macmillan.

Khalili, L. (2021). *Sinews of war and trade: Shipping and capitalism in the Arabian Peninsula*. Verso Books.

Kruck, A., & Schneiker, A. eds. (2017) *Researching non-state actors in International Security Theory and Practice*. Routledge.

Kuhar, R., & Paternotte, D. eds. (2017) *Anti-gender campaigns in Europe: Mobilizing against equality*. Rowman & Littlefield International, Ltd.

LeBaron, G., & Roberts, A. (2010) 'Toward a feminist political economy of capitalism and carcerality', *Signs: Journal of Women in Culture and Society*, *36*(1): 19–44. https://doi.org/10.1086/652915.

Lessing, B. (2015). Logics of Violence in Criminal War. *Journal of Conflict Resolution, 59*(8), 1486–1516. https://doi.org/10.1177/0022002715587100 (Original work published 2015)

Loewenstein, A. (2023). *The Palestinian laboratory: How Israel exports the technology of occupation around the world*. Verso.

McKinsey Global Institute (2025), Dependency and depopulation? Confronting the consequences of a new demographic reality, January 15, 2025. Available at https://www.mckinsey.com/mgi/our-research/dependency-and-depopulation-confronting-the-consequences-of-a-new-demographic-reality. Accessed on October 5, 2025.

Melman, S. (1972) 'Ten propositions on the war economy', *The American Economic Review*, *62*(1/2): 312–318.

Mezzadri, A. (2022) 'Social reproduction and pandemic neoliberalism: Planetary crises and the reorganisation of life, work and death', *Organization*, *29*(3): 379–400. https://doi.org/10.1177/13505084221074042.

Mezzadri, A., Newman, S., & Stevano, S. (2022) 'Feminist global political economies of work and social reproduction', *Review of International Political Economy*, *29*(6): 1783–1803.

Mezzadri, A., Rai, S. M., Stevano, S., Alessandrini, D., Bargawi, H., Elias, J., & Wöhl, S. (2025). Pluralizing social reproduction approaches. *International Feminist Journal of Politics*, *27*(1): 6–33. https://doi.org/10.1080/14616742.2024.2447594

Moore, A. (2019) *Empire's labor: The global army that supports US Wars* (p. 264). Cornell University Press.

Moyn, S. (2021) *Humane: How the United States abandoned peace and reinvented war*. Farrar, Straus and Giroux.

Ni Aolain, F. (2024) 'A Zone of Silence: Obstetric violence in Gaza and beyond', *Just security,* February 21, https://www.justsecurity.org/92562/a-zone-of-silence-obstetric-violence-in-gaza-and-beyond/

Nordstrom, C. (2004) *Shadows of war: Violence, power and International profiteering in the twenty-first century*. University of California Press.

Olivius, E., Hedstrom, J., & Phyu, Z. Z. (2022) 'Feminist peace or state cooperation?', *European Journal of Politics and Gender, 5*(1): 25–43.

Peterson, V. S. (2008). "New wars" and gendered economies. *Feminist Review*, *88*, 7–20.

Peterson, V. S. (2016) Gendering insecurities, informalization and war economies', In *The Palgrave Handbook of Gender and Development: Critical Engagements in Feminist Theory and Practice* (pp. 441–462) edited by W. Harcourt. Palgrave Macmillan UK.

Poast, P. (2019) 'Beyond the "Sinew of War": The political economy of security as a subfield', *Annual Review of Political Science*, *22*(1): 223–239. https://doi.org/10.1146/annurev-polisci-050317-070912.

Rai, S. M. (2024). *Depletion: The human costs of caring*. Oxford University Press.

Rai, S. M., Hoskyns, C., & Thomas, D. (2013) 'Depletion: The cost of social reproduction', *International Feminist Journal of Politics*, *16*(1): 86–105. https://doi.org/10.1080/14616742.2013.789641

Roussi, A. (2023) 'EU industry chief: We need to switch to 'war economy mode'', *Politico*, May 11. Available at https://www.politico.eu/article/thierry-breton-eu-needs-war-economy-mode-on-defense-production/

Shah, R. M., & Kirchhoff, C. (2024) *Unit X: How the pentagon and silicon valley are transforming the future of war*. Simon and Schuster.

Sonenscher, M. (2022) *Capitalism: The story behind the word*. Princeton University Press. https://doi.org/10.2307/j.ctv2f9xt1s

Slobodian, Q. (2024) 'Elon Musk wants us to have more children', *New Statesman*. July 29. Available at https://www.newstatesman.com/ideas/2024/07/elon-musk-wants-us-have-more-children-demography-will-macaskill. Accessed on May 7, 2025.

Sukman, D. (2024) 'Something old and something new lessons from the Ukraine-Russia war', *Military Review*. Available at https://www.armyupress.army.mil/Journals/Military-Review/Online-Exclusive/2024-OLE/Lessons-Ukraine-Russia-War/ Accessed on May 6, 2025

Sylvester, C. (2013) *War as experience: Contributions from international relations and feminist analysis*. Routledge.

Tooze, A. (2024) 'Great power politics', *London Review of Books*, *46*: 21. November 7. Available at https://www.lrb.co.uk/the-paper/v46/n21/adam-tooze/great-power-politics. Accessed on May 7, 2025.

Tripp, A. M. (2015) *Women and power in postconflict Africa*. Cambridge University Press.

Tripp, A. M. (2023) 'War, revolution, and the expansion of women's political representation', *Politics & Gender*, *19*(3): 922–927.

True, J. (2012) *The political economy of violence against women*. Oxford University Press.

True, J., & Akbari, F. (2024) 'Geopolitical narratives of withdrawal and the counter-narratives of women's rights activism in Afghanistan', *Global Studies Quarterly*, *4*: 3. https://doi.org/10.1093/isagsq/ksae051

True, J., & Hozić, A. A. (2020) 'Don't mention the war! International financial institutions and the gendered circuits of violence in post-conflict', *Review of International Political Economy*, *27*(6): 1193–1213. https://doi.org/10.1080/09692290.2020.1732443

UNFPA. (2025) *Voices from Ukraine: Assessment, findings and recommendations.* UN Population Agency, March, https://ukraine.unfpa.org/en/publications/voices-ukraine-pilot

UNHCR. (2024) Mid-year trends. Available at https://www.unhcr.org/mid-year-trends. Accessed on May 7, 2025.

UN Security Council. (2024) Conflict-related sexual violence. *Report of the Secretary-General*, S/2024/292, April 4, https://docs.un.org/en/S/2024/292

# PART I

# Gendered Circuits (I)

## Continuums

# 2

# THE ARMS TRADE, WAR ECONOMIES, AND GLOBAL CIRCUITS OF VIOLENCE

*Anna Stavrianakis*

Catastrophic violence in Gaza, Ukraine, Syria, Yemen, and elsewhere is drawing increased attention to the arms trade as a primary means of violence. Armed violence is at historically high levels quantitatively (Davies et al. 2024) with fatalities from organised violence in 2022 making it the deadliest year since the Rwandan genocide (Davies et al. 2023). And yet attention to war and violence is unevenly distributed: the Tigray war has been more deadly than the Russia-Ukraine war but far less visible to western eyes and on the international diplomatic scene. The Internal Displacement Monitoring Center reports that at the end of 2023, 68.3 million people were internally displaced because of conflict – a 49% increase over the last five years (IDMC 2024).

Simultaneously, responses to the world's political, economic, and social challenges are becoming increasingly militarised. Global military spending has never been higher, at over \$2.7 trillion, and representing a growing share of states' expenditure overall (SIPRI 2025a). The volume of international arms transfers has fluctuated over recent years, but there has been an upward trend in the 2000s, dashing liberal hopes of a peace dividend at the end of the Cold War (SIPRI 2025b). The Russian invasion of Ukraine and Israel's genocidal war on Gaza have boosted arms company profits, sending order books to record levels. Assisting Ukraine's self-defence and Israel's genocide have not only proved an economic boon to the arms industry but are also being mobilised in a key step change in Western re-militarisation and investment in, and legitimation of, war economies.

This chapter makes the case for increased scholarly attention to the arms trade as a key node in global circuits of violence and vector of global war economies. It does so by connecting the harm to human rights caused by weapons to the wider economic, political, and social harms that are facilitated by the *production* of weapons. Further, it foregrounds the global character of war economies and circuits of

DOI: 10.4324/9781003571667-3

violence, emphasising the transnational and asymmetrical dynamics of arms production, circulation, and use. Connecting the political economy of war preparation to the conduct of violence in these ways allows us to better understand the connections between violence *within* as well as *between* societies as well as the connections between *economic* and *physical* violence.

The chapter proceeds as follows. First, I give an overview of how feminist political economy and security studies have theorised war and violence, with a focus on key concepts that can help frame analysis of the arms trade. Then, I turn to gendered circuits of the war economy, examining the political economy of the arms trade and briefly illustrating how they play out in the war in Ukraine and genocide in Gaza. The chapter then explores the gendered, racialised, and classed dynamics of arms production, with a focus on the United States and the United Kingdom. It closes with a reflection on the demands placed on feminist political economy and security studies by the global arms trade.

## Gendering war and violence: feminist IR, IPE, and security studies

As an empirical phenomenon, the arms trade cuts across many of the conceptual debates in feminist security studies, feminist IPE and feminist International Relations (IR) more widely. Key feminist interventions include critiques of the public/private distinction, of the separation between the domestic and the international, and between the political and economic. Feminists have highlighted the variety of and connections between forms of violence as part of their critique of the binary distinction between war and peace. Nonetheless, there is surprisingly little literature specifically on weapons or the arms trade that situates it in these wider feminist debates.

There are a range of feminist studies of specific weapons technologies, from low-tech small arms (e.g. Farr et al. 2009; Frey 2017; Mutimer 2006) to high-tech drones (e.g. Clark 2022; Jackman and Brickell 2022; Wilcox 2017), but there are fewer examples of systemic analysis of the arms trade that foregrounds the wider range of weapons and integrate political economy as well as (in)security (c.f. Acheson 2022; Stavrianakis 2019). Analysis of the arms trade requires us to focus on the discursive and material dimensions of violence, its political and economic dimensions, and the construction of masculinities as well as femininities, all of which are also always racialised as well as gendered. Here I select four key feminist themes that can help frame analysis of the arms trade: the ongoing emphasis on militarism; the continuum of violence; circuits of violence; and (the uncertain demand of) disarmament.

Feminists have paid sustained attention to militarism even as the concept fell out of fashion elsewhere in IR. They mobilised it to indicate that "it is not quite so easy to set aside 'ordinary' aggression, force or violence as 'not war'" (Cockburn 2010:146), especially when we pay attention to the experience of violence in the global South (Cockburn and Enloe 2012). In this, feminist approaches resonate with post- and anti-colonial scholarship that understands war as a structure rather than an event, generative as well as violent, and central rather than exceptional to global order (Khayyat 2023:117). And it troubles the state-centric ontology of war, violence, and militarism. As Laura Sjoberg and Sandra Via put it, "absolutely distinguishing between the personal, national and international level of war and militarism lacks conceptual and empirical rigor at best" (2010:231–4).

Feminist accounts of militarism, by extension, also help illuminate the continuum of violence (e.g. Kostovicova et al. 2020; Yadav and Horn 2021). Gender "links violence at different points on a scale reaching from the personal to the international, from the home and the back street to the maneuvers of the tank column and the sortie of the stealth bomber" (Cockburn 2004:43). Feminists have long been articulating the idea of war and militarism as a spectrum or a system, in which the forms, intensities, and characteristics may vary, but the gendered basis of violence is central (Cockburn 2010; Gray 2016; True 2012). The concept of the continuum has temporal and spatial dimensions (Wibben 2020), and a variety of types of weapons technology are used at different points on the continuum.

This is where the concept of gendered circuits of violence (True and Hozić 2020) comes in: to help us see the connections not only between points on the continuum but also the way they are internationalised. True and Hozić use the idea of circuits to capture the different types, temporalities, and spatiality of violence, and they pick out the global arms trade as one of the ways in which "violence and harm are exacerbated through the global economy" (True and Hozić 2020:1197). Using circuits as a way into thinking about violence allows us to consider the connections and feedback loops between Northern and Southern practices, giving a more internationalised account that is better attuned to the operation of power in contexts of armed violence. The concept of circuits illuminates the ways that places usually separated out as zones of war and zones of peace are deeply connected: violence "over there" in Gaza or Ukraine is also made in Israel, the West, and Russia.

An empirical focus on the arms trade also highlights one of the weaker aspects of feminist political mobilising. Given the international disparities in arms production and the economic costs of military production, weapons control has to focus on domestic military production and its contribution to militarisation as much as it does on international transfers. That requires a demand of demilitarisation and for conversion away from military production towards socially useful production. Yet there has been a relative disappearance of historical feminist commitments to disarmament. In part, this represents a pragmatic choice by campaigners, but it also "exposes the lack of compatibility between the ontologies of feminist peace and the state system" (Tickner and True 2018: 229). Feminist accounts of gender-based violence (GBV) suggest that all violence (direct and structural) facilitated by the circulation of weapons is gendered, and that therefore all weapons transfers have the potential for GBV: this is indicative of the scale of the challenge facing antimilitarist accounts of weapons control (see Kirby and Shepherd 2024; Stavrianakis 2020).

This brief tour of feminist theorising shows the ways it has helped us reconceptualise war and violence. Today, war is being explicitly valorised in Ukraine and Gaza, state resources are being increasingly oriented towards it, and legitimating claims about its contribution to economic and political life are gaining momentum. The concept of the war economy helps us navigate this. The concept has two broad meanings or uses: the economy *in* war e.g. "all economic activities carried out in wartime" (Goodhand 2004:157; Pugh and Cooper with Goodhand 2004); and the use of war, military spending, and rearmament as an economic strategy – the idea of the "permanent war economy" and military Keynesianism, that is, that the economy can produce both "guns and butter" (Melman 1985; 'see chapter 1, this volume'). The contemporary moment has elements of both, as wars in Ukraine, Sudan, Ethiopia, and elsewhere, and genocide in Palestine, are supported by the steering of the global economy towards war, including via arms production.

While gender is hardly ever mentioned in either celebratory or critical accounts of the war economy, the concept has been adopted by a handful of feminists (Kostovicova et al. 2020; Peterson 2013). They have identified and highlighted those processes and connections that are hidden from view and normalised via their invisibility, via a focus on informalisation (Peterson 2013) and the "criminal and illegal activities of a war economy" (Kostovicova et al. 2020:254). While they query the distinction between local and global dynamics, and between formal and informal actors, in practice such analysis focuses on local actors that are "part of criminalized politico-military structures connected to the global economy." Yet the transnational web of state actors, banking and financial institutions, and arms companies and their intermediaries – the "shadow world" of the arms trade (Feinstein et al. 2012) – are often not criminalised; indeed, they are often at the echelons of state and corporate power.

Notorious individuals such as Viktor Bout, nicknamed the 'merchant of death' for his role in supplying weapons to conflicts in contravention of UN arms embargoes, are more likely to garner international condemnation than a company like Lockheed Martin or BAE Systems, both of which supply weapons to states such as Saudi Arabia and Israel for use in the wars in/on Yemen and Palestine, and are also known to facilitate corrupt payments to agents in arms-buying countries (Stavrianakis 2024). The arms trade therefore exemplifies both strands of the war economy: the informal, criminal practices, and also the formal, state-sanctioned practices and the "fusion of capitalist accumulation with state militarization" led and dominated by the United States (Acheson 2022:147). If we remember that legality is a political construct, then power comes back into view. The arms trade is a central site of the internationalised operation of power and a good way in to seeing the connections between political economy, global (in)securities, and global (dis)order.

## Gendered circuits of the war economy: the arms trade

Arms production and trade have an ambivalent relationship to the neoliberal global economy. Despite the claims made in favour of military Keynesianism, military spending does not stimulate growth or investment (Dunne and Smith 2020), the market is marked by monopsony and oligopoly, and, as Ng neatly summarises it, "the defense sector attracts capital because of cost-plus contracts with guaranteed profits and cash flow, generous tax breaks, and a non-competitive business environment that is free of transparency" (Ng 2024). The arms trade is disproportionately susceptible to corruption, accounting for 40% of global corruption (Feinstein et al. 2011; Roeber 2005).

The arms industry is state-owned in Russia and China, which are both major arms producers and exporters, but in even where the arms industry is privately owned, such as in the United States, the United Kingdom, and much of Europe, research and development costs are paid in large part by the state, and the market is a monopsony and monopoly market (see e.g. Peltier 2021). Costs are socialised – that is, paid for by taxpayers – and the profits are privatised. Profits increasingly make their way to asset and investment managers (Rogaly 2023; Marshall 2023a, 2023b). Between 2020 and 2022, financial institutions – banks, insurance companies, investment, sovereign wealth and pension funds, and public institutions – poured at least $1 trillion into the defence industry (GABV 2024:5).

The combination of militarisation and the neoliberalisation of the wider economy reduces the public sector's ability to provide for social security (Elveren and Moghadam 2022:430). While the connections between big finance and arms capital are not new, militarisation and financialisation are parallel processes (True and Hozić 2020:1200) that are accelerating and deepening to generate a "convergence of the financial sector, the tech sector, and the military industrial complex." In this convergence, global finance is "reshap[ing] the US war economy to match [the] business model" of venture capital, itself subsidised by the state (Marshall 2023a).

Simultaneously, the actual labour of producing weapons follows some of the same racialised and gendered patterns familiar from the wider global economy. Raytheon missile parts, for example, are made "in the same Mexican border towns that figure centrally in our discussions of low migrant labor," where workers face racialised and gendered harms (Marshall 2023b). These patterns indicated circuits that are global but also asymmetrical and hierarchical, making the arms trade a key site for understanding the operation of the global war economy. In engendering new sources of economic growth and debt and serving as a point of contact between so-called "peace worlds" and "war zones," the arms trade facilitates militarisation and financialisation, as well as physical violence and resistance to it, drawing out "the connections between war and peace and how violence and harm are exacerbated through the global economy" (True and Hozić 2020: 1194).

One line of argument goes that if the arms trade were to be more fully neoliberalised, there would be a lot more money for other sectors, as subsidies and excessive state support would be eliminated. Yet while feminist analysis of and demands for social welfare continue, attention to the political economy of militarism has not received the same attention. The Women, Peace and Security (WPS) agenda has grown in prominence over the past two decades and gained traction on specific issue areas, yet the "highly masculinized and militarized authoritarian 'security state'" not only endures but "is complemented by neoliberal political economic state transformations" (Elias 2015:407). As Kirby and Shepherd argue, the "anti-militarist case against the global arms economy" has been displaced in WPS work. Violence against women and girls has been articulated as a security problem, "but not at the expense of established parameters of military expenditure and reasons of state" (Kirby and Shepherd 2024:192, 196).

The "systemic coincidence of states, militarism, and the arms industry" (Kirby and Shepherd 2024:199) has created an unevenly internationalising global war economy. Internationalisation of the arms industry is most pronounced in North America and Europe and much less so in Russia and China, mirroring geopolitical ties and antagonisms. That is, arms companies headquartered in North America and western Europe have a larger number of foreign entities – often within the global North but including in countries of the global South – compared to Russian and Chinese-headquartered companies (Béraud-Sudreau et al. 2020). And state power is itself transnationalised where, for example, US Foreign Military Financing provides 16% of Israel's military budget and Israel has been allowed to spend US tax dollars to pay for the development of its own weaponry as well as purchases of US arms (Yousif and Stohl 2023). Meanwhile, growing "South-South circuits of exchange" are increasing the trade in weaponry between countries of the global South in ways that are not purely derivative of North–South relations (Dahi 2023).

The wars in Ukraine and Gaza are bringing the dynamics of war economies to light. Russia's invasion of Ukraine has increased its exclusion from the global capitalist economy and yet the war has stimulated economic growth (Foucart 2024) and "increasingly structural militarisation" (Ribakova 2024). War costs are spread across and hidden in the wider budget (Grozovski 2023), indicating the militarisation of the entire economy, with its associated gendered harms. In Ukraine, IFI-mandated austerity has interacted with wartime militarisation to reinforce and intensify gendered economic inequalities (Mathers 2020:1251; O'Sullivan 2020:8). Ukrainian feminists have faced the challenge of the accusation of the "untimeliness" of demanding gender equality during a war (Khromeychuk 2018:52).

Increasing military spending while downgrading social spending in Ukraine is typical in war economies (O'Sullivan 2020:7). Both the Russian and Ukrainian militaries are systemically and historically corrupt (Outhwaite 2023; Cranny-Evans and Ivshina 2022; Mathers 2020). The Ukrainian government has rolled back anti-corruption measures to speed up weapons procurement for the war (Mitiuk 2024). Corruption is deeply gendered, in what Mathers calls the "feminization of survival on a grand scale" (Mathers 2020:1242): while social spending falls and women bear the burden, the wealthiest and most powerful men are shielded. And yet Ukrainian feminists were among those making early demands for weapons, in the name of survival and self-defence (Tysmbalyuk and Zamuruieva 2022). As Cynthia Enloe reminds us, "militarism is not an all-or-nothing proposition": Ukrainian feminists help us understand that "fighting a war of self-defense is not the same as supporting a war of aggression, or autocratic perpetuation, or neo-colonial intervention" (Enloe 2024:291), while domestic violence increases as a result of militarisation (Tsymbalyuk et al. 2022).

In 2023, Ukraine became the world's fourth-largest arms importer, with at least 30 states supplying weapons (SIPRI 2024b); arms industry order books are at record levels (Pfeifer and Sugiura 2023). As well as providing a boon for the arms industry, the war in Ukraine has also contributed to the positive legitimation of ideas around war economies: militarily supporting Ukraine's self-defence is being mobilised as one of the key step changes in western re-militarisation and investment in – and crucially, legitimation of – war economies. A key indicator of this is the way environmental, social, and governance (ESG) agendas – typically one of the few means to try and rein in political and economic support for the arms industry – are now being mustered in support of investment in the industry and increasingly militarised foreign policies. Arms manufacturers claim that they make a positive contribution to ESG goals and asset managers are increasing their investments in them (Braw 2024), providing arms companies with the opportunity to "exit the ESG doghouse" (Jucca 2023). Investing in arms is increasingly justified by claims that it primarily produces defensive, as opposed to offensive, weapons, and that democracy relies on military back-up (Jucca 2023).

The inclusion of arms companies in ESG funds has also raised concerns in relation to Israel's genocidal assault on Gaza (Sax 2024). ESG funds continue to invest in big US- and UK-based companies like Lockheed Martin and BAE Systems and Israeli firms such as Elbit (Azizuddin 2024). The Israeli arms industry is a significant player in the international arms trade, with weapons that it advertises as battle-tested on Palestinians (Dana 2020; Halper 2015; Loewenstein 2023; Musleh 2018); it operates with low levels of transparency and has minimal civilian oversight (Hever 2018:31).

The Israeli economy is systematically dependent on military and high-tech industry and on US support. Israel is the largest cumulative recipient of US military aid since 1945, the largest portion of which comes in the form of Foreign Military Financing (FMF) – grants of US taxpayer dollars to allow recipients to buy US military equipment (Yousif and Stohl 2023). US FMF accounts for virtually all of Israel's procurement budget (Freilich 2017). High-tech industry is a key pillar of the Israeli economy and is fostered to a significant degree by military incubators and interests (Dana 2024; Musleh 2018). The war economy is a permanent feature of Israel's political economy and "fuels the infrastructure of occupation, enables territorial expansion, facilitates the erasure of Palestinian presence, generates massive revenues, and supports Israel's geopolitical ambitions" (Dana 2024).

The growth of the Israeli arms industry has been one significant historic factor in the proletarianisation of Palestinians, particularly women, beyond the systemic immiseration of the Palestinian population through dispossession (Samed 1976). More generally, Israel's war economy has facilitated the "de-development" of Palestine, indicating "the *purposeful* deconstruction" (Kadri 2014:3) and "systematic dismantling" of the economy (Roy 2024:38). Such "econocide," understood as "the wholesale destruction of an economy and its constituent parts" (Roy 2024:39), features deeply gendered processes (Ihmoud 2024; Mikdashi 2014) of political, economic, and social strangulation and Palestinians' expulsion and dispossession from their land (Dana 2024).

The experiences of Ukraine and Gaza indicate the urgency of the task of analysing war economies and the circuits that facilitate the continuum of violence. While much analysis of the arms trade focuses on the use of weapons in direct physical violence, this is prefaced by the socio-economic preparation for war and ecological "beforemaths" of extraction (Griffiths and Rubaii 2024) and followed by the aftermaths. Having explored the gendered politics of the war economy and the transnational dynamics of the arms industry and militarism, let us turn to look at a key dimension of the preparation for war: the labour dimensions of military production, with a focus on the United States and the United Kingdom as two of the world's largest arms producers.

## Gender, race, and class in militarised labour relations

Feminists have explained how "situating factory or domestic workers within broader sets of socially reproductive relations" makes visible the gendered costs and harms of low-paid, labour-intensive work (Elias and Rai 2015:428). When we consider arms production, we need an additional feminist question: what happens if we centre and make visible the gendered, racialised, and classed dynamics not only of the work itself, but of the effects of what is being made, i.e., weapons? That is, what forms of violence and inequality do women working *in* arms production face, and what violence and inequality do they *perpetuate* by doing that work – harms, violence, and inequalities being experienced in Gaza, Ukraine, and elsewhere?

Existing scholarly literature and policy work mostly focus on the former, with a focus on women's empowerment to work in the arms industry, access to formal and better-paid work, and the impact on gender relations. The historical literature focuses on women's participation in the military industry during the First and Second World Wars, particularly in western states. Focusing on women implicitly racialised as White, this literature explores the interplay between class and gender in the United Kingdom (Fara 2023, Wightman 1999; Woollacott 1994, 1996) and elsewhere in the Anglophone empire and Commonwealth (e.g. Dickson 2015; Harris 2021; Wood 2019). During the Cold War, Wainwright's 1983 study explored how most women in arms production were in "clerical, unskilled or semi-skilled manufacturing work," predominantly in electronics, "with all its 'fine,' delicate circuitry," where they formed "a ghetto of wirers, winders and circuit assemblers" (Wainwright 1983:137). Financial constraints meant that "For the women who wire or repair the weapons … financial independence is not enough for them to help prevent war" (Wainwright 1983:140).

In more recent scholarship, Riley observes the decline of scholarly attention to women's participation in military industry (Riley 2010:206). As Cynthia Enloe puts it, "We chart fighter planes as if it only matters who pilots them, not also who designed and assembled them" (Enloe 2015:437). Recent feminist scholarship has explored arms trading as a site of the threefold conflation of "masculinity with legitimacy with political power" (Carver and Lyddon 2022:59), examined the sexualised as well as gendered and racialised politics of the arms fair (Edwards 2024) and the active role that arms companies play in the construction of neoliberal feminist subjects through their social media presence (Jester 2023). Overall, while feminists have studied the "embodied material production" that help us understand "the circulation of violent relations and logics that make war possible" (Tidy 2019:221), there remains an absence of contemporary work focused directly on the gendered and racialised labour politics of the manufacture of weapons.

Riley (2010) describes women arms workers as "the actual practice of militarized femininity" – women who "make weapons for a living while claiming that what they do does not contribute to war." Her interview findings echo the observations made in previous decades by Hugh Gusterson (1996) and Carol Cohn (1987) in their ethnographic studies of weapons design and production. Common themes in these long-standing justifications include that military production is fragmented, meaning that no individual worker thinks they are the ones producing actual weapons; workers drawing distinctions between defensive and offensive weapons, legitimising the work that they do; and the centrality of economic considerations for taking on arms work (also Wainwright 1983).

These themes continue to resonate in the contemporary moment, from the Raytheon head of government relations telling a journalist, "I can tell you I certainly didn't kill anybody" in Yemen (Merat 2020), to the Northrop Grumman worker taking "comfort" from the fact his building does not make weapons for Israel, even if other buildings at the site do (Barnes 2024). A sense of western benevolence pervades workers' experience: "I wanted to defend… It was never about killing." Yet this is sometimes accompanied by a dose of casual racism: "If the Arabs want to kill one another, that's their business. We just sell the weapons; we don't pull the trigger" in Yemen (Merat 2020). A recent survey of US and UK arms industry workers indicated three broad categories of views among workers: pride and support for the defence sector as necessary for security combined with the security of well-paid jobs; perceived harm caused by the industry and associated guilt; and the profit motive and power of arms companies combined with attachment to jobs in a high technology sector (Bell et al. 2024).

The intersections of gender, class, and race are situated in the political and economic context of regional inequalities in the British and US economies. British arms manufacturing jobs are most concentrated in the northwest and southwest of England; arms employment is 93% White and almost 80% male, compared to 82% and 70% in wider manufacturing, respectively (Make UK 2021:9), with older men better represented and paid (JEDHub 2024). Median salaries are £10,000 better than for other manufacturing jobs nationally, with men better represented in the higher salary brackets: nearly 90% of engineering, manufacturing and production roles are performed by men (JEDHub 2024). Arms companies also engage in significant apprentice and trainee employment. In Glenrothes, Scotland, Raytheon is the only substantial electronics firm left in the town. Food banks have proliferated, and one in three children live in poverty. Raytheon is the "golden goose": "it's decent work … And there's not much of that around here anymore" (Merat 2020).

The geography of US arms contract spending shows it to be concentrated in states that border Mexico (California, Arizona, Texas) and Florida, and cluster around the nation's capital, such as Virginia, New York, and Pennsylvania (OLDCC 2023; see also Pemberton 2023). Wages are generally higher in arms manufacturing, as it is traditionally male-dominated. Yet in the United States, the absence of any affirmative action or childcare provision requirements for arms contractors makes it harder for single parents to access these higher wages (Barnes 2023a). And gendered stratification within arms production persists: "While men hold the majority of the prestigious and high paying jobs in defense corporations, these industries could not exist without women's labor" (Riley 2004:22), and the military is a pipeline into the industry, meaning a higher representation of male workers.

The US' and world's largest arms company, Lockheed Martin, operates out of 335 locations, mostly in the United States, and over half its workforce is comprised of engineers, scientists, and IT professionals. 23% of Lockheed Martin staff are women and 25% are people of colour: these categories are counted separately so the crossover between them is unclear. But while women make up 25% of executives, the proportion of executives of colour drops to 17% (Lockheed Martin 2023). Lockheed Martin is typical of the gender dynamics of employment in the largest arms companies. Women account for only around one-quarter of the workforce of the top five US defence contractors, compared to 46.8% of the US labour force in general (Barnes 2023a). Yet there are more female CEOs in the arms industry than in other industries: four of the world's five largest arms companies are headed by women (Stevenson 2024).

The class dynamics of arms employment are inseparable from race and gender dynamics. In the United States, arms companies are increasingly moving from union-friendly to unfriendly ones known as "right to work" states, which are themselves typically states in which these employment laws grew out of the legacy of slavery and "conservative states' alarm over seeing Black and white workers come together in the union movement" (Barnes 2023b). In one such state, former South Carolina governor Nikki Haley explicitly mobilised feminist tropes when boasting that she "wears high heels in order to kick organized labor out of South Carolina" (in Barnes 2023b). Across the country in New Mexico, Los Alamos County – home to the Los Alamos National Laboratory – is 71% White and near the top of the list of US per capita income with the best schools in the state, while at the other end of the canyon, Rio Arriba County is 90% Hispanic or sovereign nation pueblo and sits near the bottom of the list with a reputation as the heroin overdose capital of the United States. As Miriam Pemberton puts it, "The trip from the bottom to the top of the canyon … traces one of the most extreme wealth divides in America" (Pemberton 2023:121).

In the face of this empirical evidence, a liberal framing of women's equality in arms production sublimates the connection between militarism and sexual and gendered violence. The UK non-profit organisation Women in Defence uses examples of the change that happens when women reach 20–30% of workers in an industry. They say that when a "critical mass" of women is employed in a sector, challenges to sexism generate momentum: from the US military's sexual assault protocol to the #MeToo movement to the White House press corps. They mobilise these examples to make the case for improving women's representation in the defence sector and draw an explicitly militarised metaphor of critical mass and nuclear explosions to claim that "Accumulate enough, set it off and there is no other outcome than boom!" (Women in Defence 2023). It's as if there have not been decades of feminist theorising about the connections between sexual violence, patriarchy and war preparation (e.g. Cockburn 2013; Moon 1997; Wright 2015).

With the wars in Ukraine and Gaza, arms companies across North America and Europe are hiring faster than at any time since the end of the Cold War, even compared to the time of the wars in Iraq and Afghanistan (Pfeifer et al. 2024). Alongside war as a driver of recruitment, it is also prompted by competition from other sectors such as tech and consultancy. One effect of this is the intensification of the arms industry's relationships with universities, which are themselves one element of the wider and historical implication of educational establishments in martial politics (Howell 2018). Arms companies frame the causes of the gender pay gap in terms of the difficulties in recruiting women for STEM jobs (BAE Systems 2023). Yet a preliminary survey of UK-based STEM students suggests that they would prefer to do civilian over military work where possible (Demilitarise Education 2024). Student encampments in support of Palestinian liberation and demands for divestment from the arms industry, fossil fuels, and Israeli occupation of Palestinian land often explicitly tie the question of Palestinian liberation to the marketisation of higher education (BRISMES 2024; Giroux 2024; Jameela 2024), indicating that universities are a site of politico-economic struggle.

Organised labour also plays an ambivalent role in relation to arms production. Trade unions have historically supported high levels of military spending (Pemberton 2023:34) and their leadership and organisational positions are generally in favour of increased military spending, increased coordination with employers and the state, and the protection of jobs in the arms sector. In the United Kingdom, the General and Municipal Workers' Union (GMB) called in 2023 for the extension of the exemption of defence procurement from international competition and for procurement to be used as a mechanism to support UK jobs and for more investment in the arms industry, noting its alarm at suggestions that arms workers may be retrained to work in other sectors (GMB 2023:208–209). Nonetheless, GMB opposed the UK government's decision to continue arming Israel (GMB 2024) and in September 2024 the Trades Union Congress, made up of 48 member unions, called on the UK government to end all arms exports to Israel (Middle East Monitor 2024). Yet in response to rank-and-file organising against the war on Gaza, the general secretary of the Unite union, Sharon Graham, explicitly prioritised the protection and advancement of members' interests at work and promised to combat "groups that look to build networks inside trade unions to undermine the defence industry" (Labour CND 2024). Workers in the United States have also found that union protections often only extend to issues directly about working conditions, with limited legal protections for political speech. The promotion of diversity – from "rainbow capitalism" initiatives and celebration of single mothers who advance their careers – does not extend to political dissent (Barnes 2024).

Nonetheless, the war on Gaza has also rejuvenated unions' rank-and-file members (Ziadah and Fox-Hodess 2023; New Socialist 2023), who are responding to the Palestinian trade union call for an end to military cooperation with Israel (Workers in Palestine 2023). There has been a significant up-tick in protest and direct against military production and circulation with Israel, aimed not only at arms production sites (Workers for a Free Palestine 2024) but also at nodal points in the circulation of weapons, such as dockworker solidarity activism (Fox-Hodess 2022), at universities that conduct military research (Kain and Sharif 2024), and within the state bureaucracies that authorise arms exports (Brown 2024). While the arms sector is one where "the dominant culture is pro-partnership with management, pro-militarism, and pro-nuclear weapons," the war on Gaza has also benefited from and contributed to the growth of women's and younger people's activism within unions (Cimo 2024).

The difference in political orientation between some of the rank and file and their union leadership speaks to a contestation over the economic, political, and social role of trade unions. Labour organising in the arms sector is hard for anti-militarists, but workers and activists are potential allies, with opportunities to collaborate to reorient the economy, convince people that they can change local and national economies to be more just (Radicals in Conversation 2024). The confluence of militarism and climate crisis has prompted a growing debate about the necessity and urgency of a just transition (Rogaly 2024; Bell et al. 2024). Arms manufacturing workers are highly trained and skilled, so the debate about a transition away from military manufacturing has to include a "just transition" for these workers: "Most of them are not going to become teachers" (arms worker, quoted in Pemberton 2023:34). And historically, two of the preconditions for organising for conversion are specifically gendered, in that they have been more likely to be absent among women: "political and industrial confidence which comes from strong shop floor and company wide trade union organisation," and "the familiarity and confidence with the design and production process which comes from being highly skilled" in the skills that are valued in the profession (Wainwright 1983:141). Yet conversion plans can overcome "the false dilemma of jobs versus disarmament" (Wainwright 1983:143; see Garrett-Peltier 2017; Rogaly 2024).

## Conclusion

Writing in 2015, Jacqui True sketched out some of the opportunities for feminist political economy to generate new areas of research and insight into international security issues. Examples included the increases in defence budgets while foreign aid budgets are slashed, and the trade-offs between military and social spending (True 2015:423). Feminist research is flourishing in relation to the gendered politics of militarism, armed struggle, sexual violence, the WPS agenda, and other topics, yet there is still a need for more empirically grounded, theoretically informed research into the intersections of political economy and (in)security in the arms trade. The arms trade is a key source of diverse gendered insecurities and a key contributor to the three layers of structural violence found in household economies, the global economy, and militarised war economies (True 2012:20).

Feminist political economy is "less wedded to the state as an object of analysis" even as war economies have typically been "perceived as a state-driven top-down project, which subordinates economic activity – especially in manufacturing and research and development – to military needs" (Hozić and True, this volume). This chapter has sought to demonstrate both the centrality of the state to arms production and the ways in which it is gendered as well as racialised and classed. Yet feminist analysis must indeed also transcend the state because of "the structural invisibility of the sphere of social reproduction" and "the constantly shifting public/private divide within particular states" (Hozić 2021:176). As such, the connections between arms production and wider social harms need to be central to the analysis through the global circuits that simultaneously link geographically distant sites in chains of violence while allowing the disavowal of the link through that very distance. Feminist political economy and security studies need to tackle arms production and the war economies of militarised capitalism to better understand the diversity of gendered harms across space and time.

## References

Acheson R (2022) *Abolishing State Violence. A World Beyond Bombs, Borders, and Cages*, Haymarket Books, Chicago.

Azizuddin K (11 June 2024) *ESG funds maintain exposure to Israeli arms manufacturer Elbit Systems*, Responsible Investor. https://www.responsible-investor.com/esg-funds-maintain-exposure-to-israeli-arms-manufacturer-elbit-systems/

BAE Systems (2023) *BAE Systems 2023 Annual Report*, https://annualreport.baesystems.com/2023

Barnes T (6 April 2023a) *Flush with Federal Funds, Defense Contractors Employ Few Women*, Inkstick Media. https://inkstickmedia.com/flush-with-federal-funds-defense-contractors-employ-few-women/

Barnes T (19 July 2023b) *Top Defense Contractors Favor Relcations, Expansions in Anti-Union States*, Inkstick Media. https://inkstickmedia.com/top-defense-contractors-favor-relocations-expansions-in-anti-union-states/

Barnes T (7 June 2024) *Workers at Defense Contractors Navigate Dissent over Gaza War,* Inskstick Media. https://inkstickmedia.com/workers-at-defense-contractors-navigate-dissent-over-gaza-war/

Bell K, Price V, McLoughlin K, Pemberton M (2024) 'Converting the United States and United Kingdom defence sector to civilian production: The views of defence workers', *Peace and Change,* 49:101–123.

Béraud-Sudreau L, Marksteiner A, Lopes da Silva D, Tian N, Kuimova A, Wezeman PD, Wezeman ST (7 December 2020) *Mapping the International Presence of the World's Largest Arms Companies,* SIPRI Insights on Peace and Security.

Braw E (22 Feburary 2024) *How Do-Gooders Are Deflating the Defense Industry,* Foreign Policy. https://foreignpolicy.com/2024/02/22/defense-weapons-manufacturers-esg-investment/

BRISMES (7 May 2024) *BRISMES Stands in Solidarity with Student Encampments.* https://www.brismes.ac.uk/news/brismes-stands-in-solidarity-with-student-encampments

Brown F (4 April 2024) *Civil Servants Request to Stop Work Over Arms Sales to Israel,* Sky News. https://news.sky.com/story/civil-servants-threaten-to-stop-work-over-arms-sales-to-israel-13107895

Carver T, Lyddon L (2022) *Masculinities, Gender and International Relations*, Bristol University Press, Bristol.

Cimo E (2024) *Building Palestine Solidarity in An Arms Factory, Labor Notes.*

Clark LC (2022) 'Delivering life, delivering death: Reaper drones, hysteria and maternity', *Security Dialogue*, 53(1):75–92.

Cockburn C (2004) 'The Continuum of Violence: A Gender Perspective on War and Peace', in Giles W and Hyndman J (eds) *Sites of Violence, Gender and Conflict Zones*, University of California Press, Berkeley, pp. 24–44.

Cockburn C (2010) 'Gender relations as causal in militarization and war', *International Feminist Journal of Politics*, 12(2):139–157.

Cockburn C (2013) 'War and security, women and gender: An overview of the issues', *Gender & Development*, 21(3):433–452.

Cockburn C, Enloe C (2012) 'Militarism, patriarchy and peace movements', *International Feminist Journal of Politics*, 14(4):550–7.

Cohn C (1987) 'Sex and death in the rational World of Defence intellectuals', *Signs, Journal of Women in Culture and Society,* 12(4):687–718.

Cooper N, Pugh M with Goodhand J (2004) *War Economies in a Regional Context: The Challenges of Transformation*, Lynne Rienner Publishers, Boulder.

Cranny-Evans S, Ivshina O (12 May 2022) *Corruption in the Russian Armed Forces,* Royal United Services Institute. https://rusi.org/explore-our-research/publications/commentary/corruption-russian-armed-forces

CRS (2023) https://crsreports.congress.gov/product/pdf/RL/RL33222

Dahi O (2023) *South-South Trade in Arms: New Frameworks Needed?* PRISME Initiative. https://prismeinitiative.org/app/uploads/2023/11/dahi-south-south-trade-in-arms.pdf

Dana T (2020) 'A cruel innovation: Israeli experiments on Gaza's great march of return', *Sociology of Islam,* 8(2):175–198.

Dana T (2024) *Merchants of Death: Israel's Permanent War Economy*, Security in Context. https://www.securityincontext.org/posts/merchants-of-death-israels-permanent-war-economy

Davies S, Pettersson T, Engström G, Öberg M (2024) 'Organized violence 1989–2023, and the prevalence of organized crime groups', *Journal of Peace Research,* 61(4):673–693.

Davies S, Pettersson T, Öberg M (2023) 'Organized violence 1989–2022, and the return of conflict between states', *Journal of Peace Research*, 60(4):691–708.

Demilitarise Education (2024) *Arms Industry Student Opportunities: A Survey of University STEM Students*. https://ugc.production.linktr.ee/a1b9f378-7ca7-4179-99c8-fc842ca30ada_Arms-Industry-Student-Opportunities-A-Survey-of-University-STEM-Students.pdf
Dickson B (2015) *Bomb Girls. Trading Aprons for Ammo*, Dundurn, Toronto.
Dunne PJ, Smith R (2020) 'Military expenditure, investment and growth', *Defence and Peace Economics*, 31(6):601–614.
Edwards N (8 March 2024) *Sex, Power and Play at Europe's Largest Arms Fair*, The Disorder of Things. *https://thedisorderofthings.com/2024/03/08/sex-power-play-at-europes-largest-arms-fair/*
Elias J (2015) 'Introduction: Feminist security studies and feminist political economy: Crossing divides and rebuilding bridges', *Politics & Gender*, 11:406–438.
Elias J, Rai S (2015) 'The everyday gendered political economy of violence', *Politics & Gender,* 11(2):424–429.
Elveren AY, Moghadam VM (2022) 'Militarization and gender inequality: Exploring the impact', *Journal of Women, Politics & Policy*, 43(4):427–445.
Enloe C (2015) 'Closing reflection: Militiamen get paid; women borrowers get beaten', *Politics & Gender*, 11(2):435–438.
Enloe C (2024) 'Women and war: Gender and militarism in wartime Ukraine. An interview with Cynthia Enloe', *Journal of International Affairs*, 75(2):285–291.
Fara P (2023) 'Chemical 'canaries': Munitions workers in the First World War', *History of Science*, 61(4):546–560.
Farr V, Myrttinen H, Schnabel A (eds.) (2009) *Sexed Pistols: The Gendered Impacts of Small Arms and Light Weapons*, United Nations University Press, Tokyo.
Feinstein A, Holden P, Pace P (2011) 'Corruption and the Arms Trade: Sins of Commission', *SIPRI Yearbook 2011: Armaments, Disarmament and International Security.* https://www.sipri.org/sites/default/files/SIPRIYB1101.pdf
Feinstein A, Holden P, Pace B (2012) *The Shadow World: Inside the Global Arms Trade*, Penguin, London.
Foucart R (22 February 2024) *Russia's economy is Now Completely Driven by the War in Ukraine – It Cannot Afford to Lose, But Neither Can It Afford to Win*, The Conversation. https://theconversation.com/russias-economy-is-now-completely-driven-by-the-war-in-ukraine-it-cannot-afford-to-lose-but-nor-can-it-afford-to-win-221333
Fox-Hodess K (2022) 'Global Solidarity on the Docks', *New Labor Forum*, 31(1):50–58.
Freilich C (7 February 2017) *Israel's dependence on the United States is existential,* Belfer Center. https://www.belfercenter.org/publication/israels-dependence-united-states-existential
Frey B (2017) 'The Gender Implications of Small Arms and Light Weapons in Conflict Situations', in Ní Aoláin F, Cahn NR, Haynes DF and Valji N (eds) *The Oxford Handbook of Gender and Conflict,* Oxford University Press, Oxford.
GABV (Global Alliance for Banking on Values) (2024) *Finance for War. Finance for Peace. How Values-Based Banks Foster Peace in a World of Increasing Conflict.* https://www.gabv.org/wp-content/uploads/2024/02/Finance-for-War.-Finance-for-Peace.pdf
Garrett-Peltier H (24 May 2017) *Job Opportunity Cost of War*, Watson Institute Costs of War Project. https://watson.brown.edu/costsofwar/costs/economic
Giroux H (9 May 2024) *Campus Protests are Fighting Militarism and Corporatization at Home and Abroad*, truthout. https://truthout.org/articles/campus-protests-are-fighting-militarism-and-corporatization-at-home-and-abroad/
GMB (2023) *GMB National Policy Guide.* https://www.gmb.org.uk/assets/gmb-national-policy-guide-23.pdf

GMB (2024) *CEC statement on Israel and Palestine*. https://www.gmb.org.uk/assets/media/downloads/2970/cec-statement-on-israel-and-palestine-congress-2024-final.pdf

Goodhand J (2004) 'From war economy to peace economy? Reconstruction and state-building in Afghanistan', *Journal of International Affairs,* 58(1):155–174.

Gray H (2016) 'Domestic abuse and the public/private divide in the British military', *Gender, Place and Culture: A Journal of Feminist Geography*, 23(6):912–25.

Griffiths M, Rubaii K (2024) Late modern war and the *geos:* The ecological 'beforemaths' of advanced military technologies', *Security Dialogue,* 56(1):38–57, doi:10.1177/096701062412656

Grozovski B (7 September 2023) *Russia's Unprecedented War Budget Explained,* Wilson Center. https://www.wilsoncenter.org/blog-post/russias-unprecedented-war-budget-explained

Gusterson H (1996) *Nuclear Rites. A Weapons Laboratory at the end of the Cold War,* University of California Press, Berkeley.

Halper J (2015) *War Against the People: Israel, the Palestinians and Global Pacification,* Pluto Press, London.

Harris R (2021) 'Women's wartime work at Hendon small arms ammunition factory, 1939–45', *Journal of the Historical Society of South Australia*, 49:15–26.

Hever S (2018) *The Privatization of Israeli Security,* Pluto Press, London.

Hozić A (2021) 'Follow the bodies. Global capitalism, global war, global crisis and feminist IPE', *International Relations*, 35(1):173–177.

Howell A (2018) 'Forget 'militarization': Race, disability and the 'martial politics' of the police and of the university', *International Feminist Journal of Politics*, 20(2):117–136.

IDMC (Internal Displacement Monitoring Center) (2024) *Global Report on International Displacement,* IDMC, Geneva.

Ihmoud S (3 April 2024) *The Cunning of Gender Violence in Israel's War on Palestinian Women*, Jadaliyya. https://www.jadaliyya.com/Details/45884

Jackman A, Brickell K (2022) "Everyday droning': Towards a feminist geopolitics of the drone-home', *Progress in Human Geography*, 46(1):156–178.

Jameela M (6 June 2024) *University of Sheffield Threatens to Remove Palestine Encampment As Students Dig In,* Now Then. https://nowthenmagazine.com/articles/university-of-sheffield-threatens-to-remove-palestine-encampment-as-students-dig-in

JEDHuB (Joint Economic Data Hub) (2024) *2024 Annual Economic Report. Capturing and Quantifying the Contribution of the Defence Sector to the UK Economy.* https://jedhub.org/docs/2024/20242904_JEDHub_Annual_Economic_Report_2024_v1.0.pdf

Jester N (2023) 'Making martial politics palatable: Constructing neoliberal feminist subjects in arms manufacturers' social media feeds', *International Feminist Journal of Politics,* 25(2):310–333.

Jucca L (20 February 2023) *Ukraine Yet to Make Defence a Safe Investor Haven*, Reuters. https://www.reuters.com/breakingviews/ukraine-yet-make-defence-safe-investor-haven-2023-02-20/

Kadri A (2014) *Arab Development Denied: Dynamics of Accumulation by Wars of Encroachment,* Anthem Press, New York.

Kain I, Sharif B (17 May 2024) *How UC Researchers Began Saying No To Military Work,* Labor Notes. https://labornotes.org/blogs/2024/05/how-uc-researchers-began-saying-no-military-work

Khromeychuk O (2018) 'From the Maidan to the Donbas: The Limitations on Choice for Women in Ukraine', in Attwood L, Schimpfössl E and Yusupova M (eds) *Gender and Choice after Socialism,* Palgrave Macmillan, London.

Kirby P and Shepherd LJ (2024) *Governing the Feminist Peace: Vitality and failure in the Women, Peace and Security Agenda,* Columbia University Press, New York.

Kostovicova D, Bojicic-Dzelilovic V, Henry M (2020) 'Drawing on the continuum: A war and post-war political economy of gender-based violence in Bosnia and Herzegovina', *International Feminist Journal of Politics*, 22(2):250–272.

Labour CND (31 March 2024) *Labour CND Statement: Why Unite the Union is Wrong to Attack Groups Picketing Weapons Manufacturing Companies.* https://www.labourcnd.org.uk/2024/03/labour-cnd-statement-why-unite-the-union-is-wrong-to-attack-groups-picketing-weapons-manufacturing-companies/

Lockheed Martin (2023) *Lockheed Martin Corporation 2023 Annual Report.* https://www.lockheedmartin.com/content/dam/lockheed-martin/eo/documents/annual-reports/lockheed-martin-annual-report-2023.pdf

Loewenstein A (2023) *The Palestine Laboratory: How Israel Exports the Technology of Occupation Around the World*, Verso, London.

Marshall S (7 December 2023a) *The Military Industrial Venture Capital Complex*, Security in Context. https://www.securityincontext.com/posts/the-military-industrial-venture-capital-complex

Marshall S (May 2023b) *Theorizing the Intersection of Financialization and Militarism*, Security in Context. https://www.securityincontext.com/posts/theorizing-the-intersection-of-financialization-and-militarism

Mathers, JG (2020) "Women, war and austerity: IFIs and the construction of gendered economic insecurities in Ukraine," *Review of International Political Economy*, 27(6): 1235–1256.

Melman S (1985) *The Permanent War Economy: American Capitalism in Decline*, Simon & Schuster, New York.

Merat A (3 March 2020) *Making a Killing: Inside the Scottish Town Built on the Arms Trade*, Prospect. https://www.prospectmagazine.co.uk/essays/39896/making-a-killing-inside-the-scottish-town-built-on-the-arms-trade

Middle East Monitor (11 September 2024) *TUC Motion for End to All Arms Sales to Israel Welcomed by Pro-Palestine Group.* https://www.middleeastmonitor.com/20240911-tuc-motion-for-end-to-all-arms-sales-to-israel-welcomed-by-pro-palestine-group/

Mikdashi M (23 July 2014) *Can Palestinian Men be Victims?*, Jadaliyya. https://www.jadaliyya.com/Details/30991

Mitiuk D (28 February 2024) *Ukraine Charges Key Figure in Arms Trade with Corruption*, New York Times. https://www.nytimes.com/2024/02/28/world/europe/ukraine-weapons-politician-charged-corruption.html

Moon KHS (1997) *Sex Among Allies: Military Prostitution in US-Korea Relations,* Columbia University Press, New York.

Munira K (2023) 'War, from the South', *Public Culture* 35(1):113–134.

Musleh AH (2018) 'Designing in real-time: An introduction to weapons design in the Settler-Colonial Present of Palestine', *Design and Culture*, 10(1):33–54.

Mutimer D (2006) 'A serious threat to peace, reconciliation, safety, security: An effective reading of the United Nations Programme of Action', *Contemporary Security Policy, 27*(1):29–44.

New Socialist (27 October 2023) *Trade unionists for Palestine.* https://newsocialist.org.uk/transmissions/trade-unionists-for-palestine/

Ng J (2024) 'Book review. Six stops on the national security tour: Rethinking warfare economies', *Peace & Change,* 49:182–184.

OLDCC (Office of Local Defense Community Cooperation) (2023) *Defense Spending by State. Fiscal Year 2022*, U.S. Department of Defense. https://oldcc.gov/defense-spending-state-fiscal-year-2022

O'Sullivan M (2020) 'The forgotten lives: Connecting gender, security, and everyday livelihoods in Ukraine's Conflict', *Politics and Gender,* 16(3):6–10.

Outhwaite R (2 August 2023) *A Corrosion of Corruption: The Parlous State of the Russian Military*, Action on Armed Violence. https://aoav.org.uk/2023/the-corrosion-of-corruption-the-state-of-the-russian-military/

Peltier H (December 2021) Arms, Tanks, and Munitions: The Relationship between Profits and Monopoly Conditions, Security in Context, *Working Paper No. 1, Security in Context.*

Pemberton M (2022) *Six Stops on the National Security Tour: Rethinking Warfare Economies,* Routledge, London.

Peterson VS (2013) 'Gendering Insecurities, Informalization, and 'War Economies'', in Tripp AM, Ferree MM and Ewig C (eds) *Gender, Violence, and Human Security. Critical Feminist Perspectives*, NYU Press, New York.

Pfeifer S, Sugiura E (27 December 2023) *Global Defence Orders Surge as Geopolitical Tensions Mount*, Financial Times. https://www.ft.com/content/001d2e1c-8e59-444b-a07b-9a62be620431

Pfeifer S et al. (16 June 2024) *Global Defence Groups Hiring at Fastest Rate in Decades Amid Record Orders*, Financial Times.

Radicals in Conversation (28 May 2024) *Labour Movement Solidarity with Palestine*, Podcast episode 94.

Ribakova E (2 May 2024) *Russia's New Economy May End Up Prolonging Its War*, Financial Times. https://www.ft.com/content/3fd6b61b-f9f4-47dc-9369-27909868a0b6

Riley R (2004) Hidden Soldiers: Women with Jobs in the Defense Industry Must Keep the Nature of Their Work Secret, from Friends, Family, and Even Themselves', *Women's Review of Books,* 21(12):22–23.

Riley R (2010) 'Hidden Soldiers. Working for the 'National Defense'', in Hohn M and Moon S (eds), *Over There: Living with the U. S. Military Empire from World War Two to the Present,* Duke University Press.

Roeber J (27 August 2005) *Hard-Wired for Corruption*, Prospect. https://www.prospect-magazine.co.uk/essays/56912/hard-wired-for-corruption

Rogaly K (July 2023) *The Asset Manager Arsenal: Who Owns the UK Arms Industry?* Common Wealth.

Rogaly K (October 2024) *A Lucas Plan for the Twenty First Century: From Asset Manager Arsenal to Green Industrial Strategy*, Common Wealth, London.

Roy S (2024) 'Econocide in Gaza', in Stern-Weiner J (ed) *Deluge. Gaza and Israel from Crisis to Cataclysm,* OR Books, New York, pp. 37–55.

Samed A (1976) *The Proletarianization of Palestinian Women in Israel*, MERIP Reports, 50:10–26.

Sax S (16 February 2024) *They're Supposed to be Socially Conscious Investors. Why Are They Funding the War on Gaza?,* The Nation. https://www.thenation.com/article/economy/esg-funds-gaza-weapons-manufacturers/

SIPRI (April 2025a) *Trends in World Military Expenditure, 2024*, SIPRI Fact Sheet.

SIPRI (March 2025b) *Trends in International Arms Transfers, 2023*, SIPRI Fact Sheet.

Sjoberg L and Via S (2010) (eds) *Gender, War and Militarism: Feminist Perspectives*, Praeger, Santa Barbara, CA.

Stavrianakis A (2019) 'Controlling weapons circulation in a postcolonial militarised world', *Review of International Studies,* 45(1):57–76.

Stavrianakis A (2020) 'Towards a postcolonial, anti-racist, anti-militarist feminist mode of weapons control', in Basu S, Kirby P and Shepherd LJ (eds) *New Directions in Women Peace and Security,* University of Bristol Press, pp. 153–168.

Stavrianakis A (2024) 'The global arms trade and its control', in Rossi N and Riemann M (eds) *Security Studies. An Applied Introduction,* Sage, London, pp. 175–193.

Stevenson J (2024) *Female Leaders Take Flight.* https://www.kornferry.com/insights/this-week-in-leadership/women-leaders-aerospace

Tickner JA, True J (2018) 'A century of international relations feminism: From World War I women's peace pragmatism to the Women, Peace and Security Agenda', *International Studies Quarterly,* 62(2):221–465.

Tidy J (2019) 'War craft: The embodied politics of making war', *Security Dialogue, 50*(3):220–238.

True J (2012) *The Political Economy of Violence Against Women,* Oxford University Press, Oxford.

True J (2015) 'A tale of two feminisms in international relations? Feminist political economy and the women, peace and security agenda', *Politics & Gender*, 11(2):419–424.

True J and Hozić A (2020) 'Don't mention the war! International Financial Institutions and the gendered circuits of violence in post-conflict', *Review of International Political Economy*, 27(6):1193–1213.

Tysmbalyuk D, Zamuruieva I (16 March 2022) *Why We as Feminists Must Lobby for Air Defence for Ukraine,* Open Democracy. https://www.opendemocracy.net/en/odr/ukraine-russia-war-feminists-we-must-lobby-for-air-defence/

Tsymbalyuk D, Zamuruieva I, Tonya & Masha from ReSew sewing cooperative, Iakovlenko K, Khvyl A, Kostyshyna I (1 April 2022) *We Talked to Fellow Feminists from Ukraine and Military Aid, Here's What They Told Us*, Blok. https://blokmagazine.com/we-talked-to-fellow-feminists-from-ukraine-about-military-aid-heres-what-they-told-us/

Wainwright H (1983) 'The Women Who Wire Up the Weapons. Workers in Armaments Factories', in Thompson D (ed) *Over Our Dead Bodies. Women Against the Bomb,* Virago, London, pp. 136–145.

Wibben A (2020) 'Everyday security, feminism, and the continuum of violence', *Journal of Global Security Studies*, 5(1):115–121.

Wightman C (1999) *More than Munitions: Women, Work and the Engineering Industries, 1900–1950,* Longman, London.

Wilcox L (2017) 'Drones, swarms and becoming-insect: Feminist utopias and posthuman politics', *Feminist Review*, 116(1):25–45.

Women in Defence (n.d.) *Women in Defence Charter.* https://www.womenindefenceuk.com/charter

Women in Defence (2023) *Changing the Face of Defence.* https://www.womenindefenceuk.com/

Wood K (2019) 'Pioneer girls and flappers: Australia's early female ammunition workers', *Labour History,* 117:23–46.

Woollacott A (1994) *On Her Their Lives Depend: Munitions Workers in the Great War*, University of California Press, Berkeley.

Woollacott A (1996) 'Women munitions makers, war and citizenship', *Peace Review*, 8(3):373–378.

Workers for a Free Palestine (2024) *What Do We Do?*. https://workersforafreepalestine.com/index.php/what-do-we-do/

Workers in Palestine (2023) *An Urgent Call From Palestinian Trade Unions: End All Complicity, Stop Arming Israel*. https://www.workersinpalestine.org/the-calls-languages/english

Wright H (2015) 'Ending sexual violence and the war system or militarizing feminism?', *International Feminist Journal of Politics*, 17(3):503–507.

Yadav P, Horn DM (2021) 'Continuums of Violence', in Väyrynen T, Parashar S, Féron É and Confortini CC (eds) *Routledge Handbook of Feminist Peace Research*, pp. 2–11.

Yousif E, Stohl R (13 October 2023) *In Shadow of War, a Snapshot of US Military Assistance to Israel*, Stimson Center. https://www.stimson.org/2023/in-shadow-of-war-a-snapshot-of-u-s-military-assistance-to-israel/

Ziadah R, Fox-Hodess K (13 December 2023) *Unionists Around the World Block Weapons Bound for Israel*, Labor Notes. https://labornotes.org/2023/12/unionists-around-world-block-weapons-bound-israel

# 3

# THE FEMINIST POLITICAL ECONOMY OF MILITARISATION IN MEXICO

*Daniela Philipson Garcia*

## Introduction

This chapter examines the effects of militarisation and war economy policies on gender-based violence in Mexico's so-called "war on drugs" from a feminist political economy approach. For this purpose, I define militarisation as "the process whereby [public safety] increasingly draws from, and patterns itself around, the tenets of militarism and the military model" (Kraska 2007). Militarisation differs from "war economy" in that the latter refers to the subordination of economic affairs to war purposes. While both terms are not interchangeable, they often go hand in hand, with war economies providing the material means to sustain processes of militarisation. In the Mexican case, the use of the military for public safety purposes has translated into budgetary and economic policies that privilege the military over other key social spending and investment areas, such as healthcare, science and technology and environmental protection (Intersecta 2023; México Evalúa 2023). It is henceforth critical to underscore that militarisation in Mexico is underpinned by war economy policies that transfer capital to and empower military agencies.

In Mexico, law enforcement and public life, in general, are rapidly becoming militarised under the pretence of the war on drugs (Ramalho et al. 2020; Robledo Hoecker and Verdes-Montenegro 2023). The resulting escalation of human rights violations, homicides, and disappearances in the context of increasing militarisation has led scholars to label Mexico's security crisis as a "criminal war" (Lessing 2015; Zepeda Gil 2022). Unlike traditional wars, Mexico's criminal war does not follow a logic of competitive state-building between state and non-state actors (Kalyvas 2006). Indeed, framing Mexico's conflict as being fought between two opposing groups (i.e. state actors versus armed non-state actors) fails to grasp the complexities of the criminal war (Pereda 2022).

DOI: 10.4324/9781003571667-4

In Mexico, warring parties are rarely constrained by delimited boundaries. Opposing factions often involve the collusion between state and non-state actors, with civilians experiencing the brunt of the violence. According to Lessing (2015), the key distinction between traditional and criminal wars is that the latter obey a logic of constraint under which state and non-state actors seek, not to replace the state, but to shape policy outcomes. Thus, criminal wars are characterised by the active participation of state actors, who strategically shape the terms of the conflict and cooperate with criminal and non-criminal organisations alike (Zepeda Gil 2022; Trejo and Ley 2020). In the study of illicit international political economy, pundits agree that the state "defines the boundaries of illegal market activities" by criminalising certain economic sectors, such as the drug trade (Andreas 2011).

The consequences of militarisation are detrimental to gender-based violence and other human rights violations. Statistical evidence shows a causal relationship between militarisation and increased human rights violations, inter-cartel wars, and state-criminal confrontations (Flores-Macías and Zarkin 2024; Trejo and Ley 2020). According to the Uppsala Conflict Dataset, the number of deaths caused by armed force between warring parties (i.e. battle-related deaths) in Mexico increased 90-fold from 204 in 2005 to 18,850 in 2021 (DPCP 2023). Further data shows that militarisation has led to an increase in homicides of women (Intersecta 2020). Although Mexico's so-called war on drugs is not classified as an armed conflict, the relationship between militarisation and gender-based violence in Mexico is closely aligned with the literature on conflict-related sexual and violence against women, which describes gendered violence as a deliberate warfare strategy and a form of political violence driven by societal discrimination (Farr 2009; Davies and True 2015).

Feminist international relations scholarship explains how militarism justifies military priorities and reshapes cultural, economic and political affairs to the extent that it transforms societies and the collective psyche of their citizens (Enloe 2016). Militarism reinforces the notions that men are protectors and women are victims in need of their protection, that hierarchies are natural in a society, that enemies are ubiquitous, that physical force is a legitimate and suitable means to resolve conflict and that soldiers deserve special praise. The central notion of militarised masculinities upholds men's role as the protectors of women and communities. It follows from this emphasis on men as soldiers that female agency is diminished and undermined through military solutions to conflict (Eichler 2014; Cockburn 2013).

Under war economies, the gendered implications of militarisation are magnified with public resources and services redirected away from marginalised populations to serve the military and defence purposes. Feminist political economy analysis of gender-based violence argues that material gender inequalities between women and men are the root cause of structural violence against women (True 2012). In societies where gender roles and inequality limit women's access to employment, equal wages, services (such as childcare, education, and healthcare), and decision-making power, women are increasingly vulnerable to gender-based violence and have less chance to bargain and advocate for themselves both within the household and the political/public sphere. War economies deepen structural violence against women and marginalised communities by diverting resources away from "public welfare to the military apparatus" (Hedstrom 2022:62). Moreover, as access and quality to public goods and services decline, social reproduction and communal care work are disproportionately shouldered by women. As a result, women tend to provide the invisible resources necessary to uphold war economies and militarisation – emotional, material, and symbolic (Hedstrom 2022).

Drawing on feminist scholarship, this chapter explores the compounded impact of militarisation and war economy policies on Mexico's criminal war. I examine how these phenomena dismantle social infrastructure via gendered circuits of violence and capital, making disadvantaged populations – such as women and Indigenous communities – disproportionately vulnerable to structural violence. This chapter is structured as follows. First, I review feminist political economy and political science perspectives on militarisation and Mexico's criminal war. Second, I situate militarisation and war economy measures within the framework of gendered circuits of violence and capital. Third, I untangle the mechanisms through which militarisation and war economy policies dismantle social infrastructure by depleting public goods – natural resources and public infrastructure – and eroding public services – access to public safety and justice. Lastly, it analyses the effects of gendered circuits of violence and capital on environmental defenders and *buscadoras*. To conclude, I argue that the gendered circuits of violence and capital at work in Mexico's criminal war are replicated globally across liminal sites of militarisation that similarly elude categories of armed conflict and civil war. Thus, Mexico's case study is particularly suitable for unpacking gendered circuits of violence and capital in the context of increased militarisation at a global scale.

## Militarisation from a feminist political economy perspective

Gender is not an accidental consequence of neoliberalism but a deliberate construct that fuels and perpetuates globalisation and capitalism. Feminist political economy analysis explains the nature and prevalence of gender-based violence as inherent to the neoliberal machine and current economic order. In her book, *The Political Economy of Violence Against Women*, Jacqui True argues that feminist political economy "attends to the local and global contexts in which violence against women occurs" (True 2012:7). Thus, gender is used to justify, reaffirm, and entrench hierarchical power dynamics and structural violence. Moreover, gender is strategically instrumentalised by global markets to devalue women's formal and informal work, exploiting women for "cheap labour." In the process, gender is not only (re) affirmed through paid and unpaid work but also (re)produced (Weeks 2011:11). Moreover, social reproduction is rendered invisible, and its unequal distribution is used to perpetuate a sexual division of labour. Hence, gender coding defines what is and isn't considered economically productive (Peterson 2010).

As with global economic processes, militarisation (re)affirms and (re)produces gender. It constitutes the process by which those offering "protection" – masculinised bodies – gain control over productive and reproductive resources over feminised bodies, thus reordering the material basis and gendered inequalities upon which gender-based violence thrives (True 2012:121). In Mexico, the framing of public safety as a masculine and military issue has had economic, political and gendered implications (Arana Aguilar and Phillipson Garcia 2025). Militarisation has resulted in the military taking prominence regarding public spending and the administration of public goods and services in line with austerity measures. Hence, militarisation is deeply entrenched within neoliberalism and should be studied in tandem.

Moreover, militarisation is also anchored in global and asymmetrical relationships. In Mexico, militarisation cannot be understood without considering Mexico-US bilateral relations. One of the key drivers of militarisation in Mexico has been the diplomatic pressure from the United States. Financed by bilateral policies, such as the Iniciativa Mérida, which injected millions of dollars into the Mexican arms trade and security apparatus, militarisation has coincided with improved international credit rankings and macroeconomic stability (Paley 2020:38). According to Paley (2020), since 2006, the United Stated and Mexico have spent $80 billion in security, revealing the deep ties between both countries and the high degree of US interventionism (Paley 2020:41). Likewise, Valencia situated the emergence of Mexico's narco-state, and the ensuing criminal war, in the signing of the North American Free Trade Agreement, which diminished the Mexican middle class and opened avenues to participate in illicit economies (Valencia 2016:47). Moreover, Mexico's criminal war yields billions in revenue for US firearm manufacturing companies and in transnational illicit financial flows (García Reyes 2021).

Feminist political economy offers additional theoretical avenues for capturing multiple overlapping dimensions of violence from a feminist standpoint. Specifically, Peterson (2008, 2016) describes how militarisation, conflict, and gender shape informal (war) economies within and beyond state regulation. Peterson (2008) identifies three distinct (war) economies: coping, combat, and criminal informal economies. In Peterson's words, the coping informal economy "is the most obviously feminised" as it facilitates the social reproduction of families and households via informal means that are more easily accessible to women. True and Hozić (2020) use the term "gendered circuits of violence" to explore the continuities of different forms of violence across temporalities and geographies. In the Mexican context, gendered circuits of violence and capital are particularly useful to understand how violence is embodied and carried across liminal spaces; spaces that are neither classified as armed conflicts nor at peace, just like Mexico's criminal war.

Some scholars have addressed gender, albeit in the context of "new wars," not criminal wars. Peterson (2008, 2016) and Chinkin and Kaldor (2013) have addressed this gap in the literature, recognising how armed conflicts reshape gender stereotypes. Applebaum and Mawby (2018) sought to apply Chinkin and Kaldor's "new wars" and gender framework to the rise of extreme violence and, specifically, gender-based violence in El Salvador. However, their analysis focused on conflict driven by relatively smaller decentralised gangs that differ from Mexico's larger, more centralised criminal groups and drug cartels. Moreover, the implications of Kaldor and Chinkin's argument – that gender stereotypes constructed in a criminal war are specific and different from those constructed in other wars – remain unexplored. Likewise, Peterson's argument regarding how gender relations are renegotiated in the context of a (criminal) war economy is not addressed by the existing scholarship.

## The war economy and militarisation as gendered circuits of violence and capital

War economy measures and militarisation go hand in hand. Since 2018, the Mexican armed forces have been allocated exponentially more resources. By contrast, social infrastructure and services have been dismantled due to budget cuts under so-called "republican austerity" measures. In this section, I link the gendered circuits of violence and capital to the funding and creation of Mexico's National Guard and the development of the Mayan Train in the Yucatán Peninsula. I end this section by analysing the government's federal spending and how it reproduces gendered circuits of violence and capital.

In 2018, then-President Andrés Manuel López Obrador backtracked on his *abrazos no balazos* ('hugs not bullets') campaign promise. This change involved ejecting the military from civilian tasks after failed attempts to "win the war on drugs." Instead, López Obrador dismantled the existing Federal Police and created a new security body, the National Guard. By law, the National Guard was meant to be a civilian-led body under the Citizen Security and Protection Ministry's jurisdiction. Nonetheless, according to a study by the Mexican Senate, approximately eight out of every ten National Guard members are trained to be soldiers or marines (Instituto Belisario Domínguez 2023). The same study highlighted that four out of ten National Guard officials lack a police training certificate. A separate study shows that around 60% of National Guard officials are hired and paid by the Defence Ministry (Mexicanos Contra la Corrupción y la Impunidad 2022). Moreover, all regional National Guard coordinators were members of the armed forces (Ortega and Torres 2023).

Despite being composed of mostly military personnel, the National Guard is assigned to carry out traditionally civilian duties, such as immigration enforcement, customs clearance, intelligence collection, and aiding public safety institutions. Since the National Guard's creation, physical and gendered violence has increased across the country. The National Guard is increasingly deployed with a presence in all 32 states (Storr 2023). However, its deployment has not led to any reductions in crime. To the contrary, in Guanajuato and Michoacán, the homicide rate increased by 26% and 12%, respectively, after 6,000 National Guard elements were deployed to both states between 2019 and 2022 (Jasso González and Baltazar Landeros 2023). According to government statistics, the military alone killed more than 5,000 people between 2007 and 2021. Human rights complaints against the military and the National Guard during the same period have also skyrocketed (Human Rights Watch 2023).

Nonetheless, since 2018, militarisation has intensified, exacerbating structural violence and prioritising defence spending over social provisioning. Moreover, militarisation has shifted from being an undercover measure to a national war economy effort. Only three years after creating the National Guard, López Obrador successfully pushed for a reform to shift its jurisdiction from the Citizen Security and Protection Ministry to the Defence Ministry, formalising its militarisation *de jure*.[1] Shortly after, the military's personnel increased by 17%, while the National Guard's decreased by 12% between 2019 and 2022. Likewise, the armed forces budget increased by 50%, while the National Guard's budget decreased by 28% (Ortega and Torres 2023). According to Storr (2023), "the National Guard has operated as a vehicle to consolidate the military's permanent participation in public safety tasks."

At the same time as the National Guard was created and consequently militarised, the military was assigned increasingly expansive roles. The military's newly allocated tasks spread across a wide range of areas, including reforestation, tourism, academic partnerships, food quality control, communications, and transportation and the management and supervision of critical infrastructure developments (Intersecta 2024). The so-called Mayan Train, a signature project of López Obrador's administration aimed to bring economic growth to Mexico's most underdeveloped region, symbolises an important tipping point in the country's growing militarisation. The train consists of a $30 billion railway, spanning approximately 1,500 kilometres around the Yucatán Peninsula, and the train's construction, operation, and management have been assigned to the military by López Obrador. To build the train, the military decimated a good portion of the Mexican jungle and forcibly displaced several Mayan communities. Moreover, despite the country's severe water crisis, the military built the train atop an ancient system of underground freshwater caverns known as *cenotes* (De Miguel et al. 2024).

In addition to building and managing the Mayan Train, a study by Intersecta found that the Mexican government has transferred 291 tasks and resources to the military since 2006. To do so, the government pushed forward two constitutional reforms, 12 legislative federal reforms, 19 presidential accords and decrees, and 258 private contracts (Intersecta 2024). Despite being labelled a country "at peace," the Mexican military is now in control of key resources and services that are integral to public provisioning for citizens, especially traditionally marginalised populations. Along with policies to empower the military, López Obrador slashed government spending as part of his republican austerity agenda. Indeed, security has often served as a justification to significantly cut back government spending, dismantling the remaining vestiges of social infrastructure and deepening structural inequalities and violence (Valencia 2016:48).

War economy measures, disguised as austerity policies, selectively reduce social spending while increasing the military's budget (Pérez Pacheco 2023). Specifically, Pérez Pacheco (2021) found that the Defence Ministry's budget increased at the expense of public health, human rights, and interior affairs. For example, more resources are spent on bonuses for military personnel relative to public daycare facilities (Intersecta 2023). An analysis of Mexico's 2024 federal budget by Fundar found that spending to advance gender equality and reduce violence against women and girls decreased since the beginning of the current administration in 2019. The report also found that the Public Health System is under-resourced and urged Congress to increase spending on maternal health, reproductive health and sexual rights (Fundar 2023). At the same time, the armed forces' budget increased by 38% between 2017 and 2021 (Intersecta 2023). Moreover, while fiscal austerity fosters trust among private investors, it is particularly detrimental to women and Indigenous communities because it widens structural gender inequalities (Clavellina Miller 2023).

In 2019, governmental financial support to civil society was cut in full, causing all publicly funded shelters for survivors of domestic violence to shut down (Intersecta 2023).[2] In 2022, while Mexico was still suffering the lingering impacts of the COVID-19 pandemic, cuts were made in education and care services. The Public Education Secretariat eliminated all after-school programmes and the provision of meals for students (Donaji Núñez 2022). Due to the disproportionate exposure of women to domestic violence and the uneven distribution of unpaid housework and care work between genders, these economic measures had negative disproportionate effects on women. As a result, these measures reduced alternatives to cohabitation with domestic abusers and removed after-school care programmes for carers, who are primarily women.

Overall, these policy changes – the creation of the National Guard, the reallocation of resources, and the increased role of the armed forces – have signalled the prioritisation of military relations over civilian ones, opening the valves of gendered circuits of violence and capital.

## Vacuums of public goods and services

In this section, I explore the presence of gendered circuits of violence and the war economy's effects on essential public goods (land, water, and infrastructure) and public services (public safety and access to justice). I argue that these circuits are manifested in the depletion of natural resources, the militarisation of critical infrastructure in Mexico's Yucatán Peninsula, and the erosion of public services, including access to public safety and justice across the country.

The lack of access and poor quality of public goods and services expand and magnify physical and structural violence by disproportionately affecting those who rely more on social provisioning by the state due to historical economic, social, and political exclusion. Moreover, an increased military presence has eroded and undermined community life by instilling terror among the population and disarticulating the core foundations of community organising – trust, autonomy, and land (Paley 2020:24). According to Paley (2020), militarisation has been instrumentalised as a tactic to suppress and neutralise social movements to facilitate neoliberal extractivism and expropriation to the benefit of transnational interests. Thus, Paley (2020) concludes that militarisation has been critical for advancing neoliberal policies. Zavala (2022:9) arrives at the same conclusion as Paley that the real purpose of the so-called war on drugs is the depopulation of territories rich in natural resources, ready to be exploited by American and international corporations.

Indeed, it is unsurprising to see war economy measures rolled out alongside militarisation. Both measures advance the neoliberal framework promoted by International Financial Institutions (IFIs) and maximise the interests of private investors. IFIs distribute harm and comfort via debt servicing, microfinance programmes, extractive resource economics, taxation, budgeting, and austerity in the state sector in both war and peace contexts (True and Hozić 2020). Yet it is essential to underscore that both the outcomes and frameworks used to roll out these measures are gendered in that they (re)affirm and (re)produce gender categories via economic and militarisation processes.

### *Depletion of natural resources and militarisation of public infrastructure*

The militarisation of the tourism industry, including the Mayan Train, in the Yucatán Peninsula has deepened the water crisis and dispossession of land, disproportionately harming women and Indigenous communities who depend on communal crops and water sources for their livelihoods and cultural identity. The insufficient access to and dispossession of water and land in the Yucatán Peninsula due to increasing militarised tourism is an acute manifestation of gendered circuits of violence and capital. The lack of water has especially impacted women and their ability to carry out everyday tasks, such as cooking, cleaning, and childrearing (Philipson Garcia 2023).

The expropriation of land is also gendered. Women rarely have rights to communal lands and are doubly dispossessed when land rights are stripped from them. Not only is the land, and the potential it holds in future crops, taken away from them, but they often receive little or no payment for disowning it. The profits, if any, are given to those with the rights to the land – primarily men. The military, alongside private actors and armed groups, often forcibly vacate communal lands to develop militarised infrastructure projects (Gasparello 2021). In turn, structural violence and organised crime grow exponentially due to insufficient public services, lacking social infrastructure and the labour exploitation orchestrated by the military and transnational corporations (Gasparello 2021:185).

The Mexico-US border and other export processing zones (Salzinger 1997; Biemann 1999; True 2012) have often been explored as globalised, liminal sites of gendered circuits of violence and capital. Increasingly militarised tourist destinations display similar dynamics where extreme structural violence and socioeconomic, gendered, and racialised inequalities coexist. In Cancún, Playa del Carmen, and Tulum, precarious working conditions, ubiquitous illicit financial flows, transient populations, and poor local infrastructure have created the perfect conditions for the armed forces, transnational businesses, and criminal organisations to exploit and pillage the labour and resources of the local communities.

### *Erosion of public services – access to public safety and justice*

War economy policies have eroded critical public services, particularly access to public safety and justice. By replacing civilian security forces with military personnel trained in national defence and impoverishing the civilian justice apparatus, everyday public safety and access to justice have been under-resourced and dismantled. Because of their military nature and training, the National Guard and military are particularly inept at dealing with civilians to resolve sexual and domestic violence crimes. Valencia (2016) writes that Mexico's government security bodies are not interested in curbing structural violence. Rather, they seek to constrain and wield it in their self-interest (Valencia 2016:48). As a result, access to justice for victims-survivors of violence is evaded. In this sense, militarisation and the war economy have created a power vacuum for the state and impunity crisis, forcing citizens to seek justice by their own means and devices.

In Mexico, approximately 92% of crimes go unpunished (Kloppe-Santamaria 2024). Concerning homicidal violence, only one in ten homicides are solved and less than half of femicides are investigated and sentenced (Impunidad Cero 2022). In many cases, citizens decide to take justice into their own hands. Forms of extra-legal justice vary widely, from lynching (Kloppe-Santamaría 2020) to communal mechanisms, such as public tribunals (Rodríguez Everaert 2022). In other cases, citizens opt to collaborate with authorities and pursue legal avenues while taking on the investigative burden themselves. One notable example is that of the *buscadoras*. *Buscadoras* are women searching for family members who have likely been disappeared by criminal groups and/or state actors (Kitroeff and Bergman 2023). In their search, they often form collectives to raise funds, educate themselves in forensics and criminal law, and provide support and care for one another.

The degree to which *buscadoras* and their families have replaced state authorities in seeking and providing justice is carefully documented by Paley (2020). In her book, Paley recounts events from her fieldwork in Coahuila where she conducted research with *buscadoras* and their families. Paley narrates how on one occasion she witnessed how Oscar and Silvia, the parents of a missing young woman named

Fanny, searched an alleged mass grave, while soldiers and state authorities looked on without moving a finger:

> Oscar tied a rope around his chest and descended into the hole. Around him, I counted 18 soldiers and state authorities in uniform, wearing firearms tied to their chest, to their wastes and in their hands. All the [soldiers and state authorities] were on duty, getting paid, while they looked onto Oscar as he lowered himself further into the darkness.
>
> *(Paley 2020:11, author's translation)*

This appalling event is emblematic of the military's negligence in addressing Mexico's so-called criminal war. Instead of state authorities, parents, mothers, sisters, daughters, and relatives search for the disappeared. However, the burden tends to fall disproportionately on women, who have been traditionally responsible for social reproductive labour. As a result, searching for the disappeared has taken on new gendered dimensions of care and social reproduction.

In the next section, I explore how the *buscadoras* are at the front lines of Mexico's so-called criminal war and its coping economy. While searching, they not only take on the responsibility of *searching*, but their care workload doubles, and they are simultaneously exposed to extreme forms of gender-based violence. I end by briefly recounting the gendered circuits of violence and capital in the care labour and high-risk activism conducted by environmental defenders.

## Gendered circuits of violence and capital in environmental defenders and *Buscadoras*

War economies subordinate women and Indigenous communities to forms of precarious employment and non-remunerated social reproductive work such as searching for disappeared family members and seeking justice by any means available. Here, gendered and racialised circuits of violence and capital manifest via multiple avenues, chiefly via the unequal allocation of public resources and services and the asymmetrical division of social reproductive work.

War economies and neoliberal policies (such as austerity) serve the interests of transnational enterprises at the expense of local communities and social movements (Paley 2020). Both processes operate together to dismantle and disarticulate any vestiges of resistance to the advancement of transnational capital. It is in this context that (forced) disappearances are operationalised as a brutal tactic to weaken social ties, sow confusion regarding accountability and avenues for justice and depoliticise extreme violence (Paley 2020:82–84).

However, it is essential to note how disappearance as a repression tactic manifests as a gendered circuit of violence and capital by indirectly targeting women's societal roles and social reproductive labour. Contrary to Valencia's (2016:30) claim that "life no longer matters and is only valued for its commercial potential," in the margins of capitalism within which social reproduction is made possible, several feminists and women, as well as Indigenous communities and human rights defenders, shoulder the labour necessary to maintain the minimal conditions for life and community to exist (Fraser 2022). In late-stage capitalism, all forms of expropriation and exploitation are underpinned by wage-free social reproduction; political agreements, actors, and institutions; racial and colonial relations; and the (finite) availability of natural resources. Yet, advanced capitalism depletes these conditions by placing them outside the economic realm and rendering them "unproductive" (Fraser 2023).

### *The depletion of social reproduction in Buscadoras and Indigenous women*

Searching for the disappeared is a dangerous job, and *buscadoras* often face significant risks and threats. Despite taking on these monumental burdens, they face intimate-partner violence and domestic abuse from their families for neglecting their household chores while searching for their loved ones (Zulver 2024). The state also often re-victimises *buscadoras* by ignoring them or trapping them in bureaucratic legal labyrinths without providing answers, accountability or justice. In some extreme cases, they have been killed or disappeared themselves when becoming too visible and uncomfortable both for criminal organisations and government authorities (Associated Press Mexico 2024).

In many cases, *buscadoras* are grandmothers whose lives and relationships with their grandchildren are upended by the disappearance of a relative, forcing them to re-establish themselves as the primary caretakers while they take on the burden to search for their missing loved ones. *Buscadoras* sometimes describe this form of caretaking as a "labour of love," characterising their search as a form of social reproductive labour (Zulver 2024). Notably, this pressure falls predominantly on women who are expected to care for others, particularly minors. Hence, the challenges facing *buscadoras* are especially gendered in nature.

The *buscadoras'* tireless search and labour show that war economy measures layer multiple burdens on women, inside and outside the home. Such burdens are compounded by the state's inability (or unwillingness) to impart justice, under-resourced social infrastructure and entrenched gender stereotypes that force women to assume their household's and community's social reproduction. Consequently, women experience multiple, overlapping burdens (i.e. social reproductive labour) and various forms of violence, including intimate-partner violence, institutional violence, femicide, and forced disappearance.

Recalling Paley's (2020) and Zavala's (2022) theory regarding the aims of forced disappearance as a strategy to dismantle community resilience and organising, women are specifically targeted and cast into constrained gender roles to weaken communities' social ties. When they are diverted away from fulfilling their expected roles by capital and gender circuits of violence, their families and communities are consequently weakened, with women experiencing the brunt of violence and stigma.

### *Criminalisation of environmental defenders*

In response to overlapping forms of systemic dispossession, community leaders in the Yucatán Peninsula have stepped onto the frontlines to defend their land and resources. Indigenous women have played a vital role in carrying out communal care work as a specific form of social reproductive labour. Communal care work is defined as the set of tasks required to sustain the life of humans, animals, and physical and symbolic communal goods. These tasks may be carried out by individuals or collectives without pay and extend beyond the private domain (ONU Mujeres et al. 2022:13). Communal care work is traditionally done by women without pay and with little recognition. Moreover, the disproportionate burden of care work, including communal care, on women is a key factor behind the feminisation of poverty. Thus, more and better access to quality public goods and services, as well as the redistribution of care work across gender lines, is indispensable to ensure gender equality and eradicate gender-based violence (ONU Mujeres et al. 2022:21–23).

Access to land, water, and a healthy environment is a human right (Amnesty International 2023). Yet being an environmental defender in Mexico is especially perilous. In 2021, Mexico was the country with the highest number of environmental defenders killed (Global Witness 2022). A report by the Mexican Chapter of Amnesty International highlighted three case studies of environmental defenders who were criminalised for peacefully protesting the dispossession of their land and water sources.

One case highlights the criminalisation of two Indigenous environmental defenders, César Hernández Feliciano and José Luis Gutiérrez Hernández, who protested the construction of National Guard barracks in their home state of Chiapas. César and José Luis were imprisoned for "rioting" during a peaceful demonstration that was brutally repressed by municipal authorities and members of the National Guard. The report concludes that environmental defenders face increased risk and threats, which are augmented by the unrestrained expansion of militarisation and private interests (Amnesty International 2023). Threats against women defenders are further charged with gendered violence, disproportionately emphasising sexual violence. As a result, militarisation and neoliberal policies hinder public protest and participation in public life, impoverishing democratic values.

## Conclusion

Women and Indigenous communities experience differentiated forms of violence across a continuum of violence. In this chapter, I have explored the multiple capital and gender circuits of violence flooded by the compounded effects of militarisation and neoliberal economic policies (i.e. 'republican austerity'). The amassing of military spending at the expense of social infrastructure disadvantages women and marginalised communities by cutting back on the availability and quality of public goods and services on which underserved populations depend the most. Moreover, critical resources, such as land and water, are further exploited by the combined forces of militarisation and neoliberalism.

Women and Indigenous communities are criminalised and face increasing risks and threats when defending their way of life, which is symbolically and materially sustained by their land and natural resources. Essential public services (i.e. public safety and access to justice) are also eroded, normalising extra-legal and independent avenues to seek justice. However, they face significant challenges and violence in doing so. Lastly, Mexico shows how a highly militarised and neoliberal environment fosters gendered divisions of labour and violence.

To date, only academics in partnership with think tanks, NGOs and journalists – Kloppe-Santamaria and Zulver (2023), Intersecta (2020), and MUCD (2021) – have produced research on the effects of militarisation on homicides of women. Although homicides of women and femicides require urgent attention and solutions, they only represent the less prevalent and most extreme forms of gender-based violence within the violence continuum.

Identifying and studying the effects of militarisation and war economies on more prevalent forms of gender-based violence at the community and household levels is necessary to address the more prevalent experiences and structural foundations of gender-based violence. Moreover, this type of research is required to inform policy solutions to prevent everyday forms of gender-based violence, such as women not being allowed to work or leave their homes without permission from their partners or being catcalled, from escalating to more severe, lethal forms of gender-based violence.

## Notes

1 The Supreme Court has since declared the move unconstitutional. However, the federal government has so far ignored the Supreme Court sentence and maintained the National Guard within the Ministry of Defense's jurisdiction. In mid-2024, President López Obrador introduced new legislation to reform the constitution, allowing the National Guard to be assigned to the Defence Ministry's jurisdiction.

2 This decision was ultimately reversed due to protests from civil society.

## References


Andreas P (2011) 'Illicit International Political Economy: The clandestine side of globalization', *Review of International Political Economy,* 11(3):641–652. doi:10.1080/0969229042000252936

Amnesty International Mexico (13 September 2023) *Mexico: Tierra y ¿Libertad? Criminalización de Personas Defensoras de Tierra, Territorio y Medio Ambiente*. https://www.amnesty.org/es/documents/amr41/7076/2023/es/

Applebaum A and Mawby B (2018) 'Women and "New Wars" in El Salvador', *Stability: International Journal of Security and Development*, 7(1). doi:10.5334/sta.641

Arana Aguilar D and Philipson Garcia D (2025) 'Las Masculinidades Militarizadas en los Instrumentos de Política en Seguridad Pública en México', *CONfines*, 21(40).

Associated Press (2024) *Mexican Activist Who Searched for Disappeared Brother Now Missing after Attack*, The Guardian, accessed 3 January 2025. https://www.theguardian.com/world/2024/jan/17/mexico-activist-abducted-attack-missing-people-desaparecidos-lorenza-cano

Biemann U (1999) *Performing the Border*, MACBA Collection, accessed 3 January 2025. https://www.macba.cat/en/obra/r1826-performing-the-border/

Chinkin C and Kaldor M (2013) 'Gender and New Wars', *Journal of International Affairs*, 67(1):167–187. https://www.jstor.org/stable/24461677

Clavellina Miller (2023) *Austeridad, debilidad institucional y presupuesto: Comparativo 2018 vs 2024*, CIEP, accessed 3 January. https://ciep.mx/austeridad-debilidad-institucional-y-presupuesto-comparativo-2018-vs-2024/

Cockburn C (2013) 'War and Security, Women and Gender: An Overview of the Issues', *Gender & Development*, 21(3):433–452. doi:10.1080/13552074.2013.846632

Davies, SE and True J (2015) 'Reframing Conflict-Related Sexual and Gender-Based Violence: Bringing Gender Analysis Back In', *Security Dialogue* 46(6): 495–512. doi.org/10.1177/0967010615601389.

De Miguel T, Janetsky M and Abd R (2024) *An Underwater Paradise Under Threat*, Associated Press, accessed 6 January 2025. https://apnews.com/projects/mexico-tren-maya-climate-yucatan//

Donaji Núñez A (3 August 2022) *Con hechos, queda más claro el despojo*, Animal Politic, accessed 7 January 2025. https://animalpolitico.com/analisis/invitades/con-hechos-queda-mas-claro-el-despojo

DPCP (Department of Peace and Conflict Research) (2023) *Uppsala Conflict Data Program*, Uppsala Universitet, accessed 8 October 2024. https://ucdp.uu.se/

Enloe C (2016) *Globalization and Militarism: Feminists Make the Link, Second Edition*, Rowman & Littlefield Publishers.

Flores-Macías G and Zarkin J (2024) 'The Consequences of Militarised Policing for Human Rights: Evidence from Mexico', *Comparative Political Studies*, 57(3):387–418. doi:10.1177/00104140231168362

Fraser N (2022) *Cannibal Capitalism: How our System is Devouring Democracy, Care and the Planet – and What We Can Do About It*, Verso.

Fundar (2023) *Sin recursos no hay derechos. Análisis del Paquete Económico 2024*, accessed 3 January 2025. https://fundar.org.mx/publicaciones/sin-recursos-no-hay-derechos-analisis-del-paquete-economico-2024/

García Reyes K (2021) *Morir es un alivio*, Planeta, México.

Gasparello G (2021) 'Turismo, economias ilegales y violencias en Quintana Roo: Evidencias, tendencias y riesgos del megaproyecto Tren Maya", Giovanna Gasparello y Violeta Núñez (coordinadGsaoras), *Pueblos y territorios frente al Tren Maya. Escenarios sociales, económicos y culturales*, México, Bajo Tierra, pp. 149–210, http://bajotierraediciones.com/wp-content/uploads/2022/04/tren-maya-ener...

Global Witness (2022) *A Decade of Defiance*. https://www.globalwitness.org/en/campaigns/environmental-activists/decade-defiance/

Human Rights Watch (2023) *Mexico: Events of 2022*, *Share this via Facebook*, accessed 7 January 2025. https://www.hrw.org/world-report/2023/country-chapters/mexico

Instituto Belisario Domínguez (2023) *Elementos para la evaluación de la Guardia Nacional*, México, accessed 7 January 2025. https://bibliodigitalibd.senado.gob.mx/handle/123456789/6132

Intersecta (2020) *Las Dos Guerras*, Mexico. https://www.intersecta.org/posts/las-dos-guerras, accessed 4 October 2025.

Intersecta (2023) *Dinero para reducir la violencia hay, pero ¿en qué lo invierte el Estado?*, México, accessed 8 October 2024. https://assets-global.website-files.com/64c019456bb62d07dc3af2b9/65035d5f4828e4f7219bd620_xjmnRkQpj8dYPOWdG2v5J-sePNg7YbKDuIoZWSlXDBg.pdf

Intersecta (2024) México Unido Contra la Delincuencia and Programa de Política de Drogas, *Inventario Nacional de lo Militarizado, actualización*, accessed 7 January 2025. https://www.intersecta.org/posts/inventario-nacional-de-lo-militarizado-actualizacion

Jasso González C and Baltazar Landeros E (2023) '¿El despliegue de la Guardia Nacional reduce la violencia homicida?', *Nexos*, accessed 7 January 2025. https://seguridad.nexos.com.mx/el-despliegue-de-la-guardia-nacional-reduce-la-violencia-homicida/

Kalyvas SN (2015) 'How Civil Wars Help Explain Organized Crime—and How They Do Not', *The Journal of Conflict Resolution*, 59(8):1517–1540, accessed 7 October 2024. https://www.jstor.org/stable/24546352

Kitroeff N and Bergman R (2 September 2023) *Why Did a Drug Gang Kill 43 Students? Text Messages Hold Clues*, The New York Times, accessed 7 October 2024. https://www.nytimes.com/2023/09/02/world/americas/mexico-iguala-students-kidnapping.html

Kloppe-Santamaría, Gema. 2020. *In the Vortex of Violence: Lynching, Extralegal Justice, and the State in Post-Revolutionary Mexico*. Violence in Latin American History 7. University of California Press.

Kloppe-Santamaria G (2024) 'Violence Against Women Is at the Center of Mexico's Security Crisis', *Americas Quarterly*, accessed 17 April 2024. https://americasquarterly.org/article/violence-against-women-is-at-the-center-of-mexicos-security-crisis/

Kloppe-Santamaria G and Zulver J (2023) *Beyond Collateral Damage: Femicides, Disappearances, and New Trends in Gender-Based Violence in Mexico*, Wilson Center, accessed 3 January 2025. https://www.wilsoncenter.org/article/beyond-collateral-damage-femicides-disappearances-and-new-trends-gender-based-violence

Kraska PB (2007) 'Militarisation and Policing--Its Relevance to 21st Century Police', *Policing*, 1(4):501–513. doi:10.1093/police/pam065

Mexicanos Contra la Corrupción y la Impunidad (2022). https://contralacorrupcion.mx, accessed 4 October 2025.

México Evalúa (2023) 'Inversión 2024: recorte y militarización', *Números de Erario*, accessed 8 April 2025. https://numerosdeerario.mexicoevalua.org/2023/11/09/inversion-2024-recorte-y-militarizacion/

ONU Mujeres et al. (2022) *Los cuidados comunitarios en América Latina y el Caribe: Una aproximación a los cuidados en los territorios*, accessed 7 January 2025. https://lac.unwomen.org/es/digital-library/publications/2022/11/los-cuidados-comunitarios-en-america-latina-y-el-caribe

Ortega AE and Torres MF (15 April 2023) *El fraude del carácter civil de la Guardia Nacional*, Nexos, accessed 7 January 2025. https://eljuegodelacorte.nexos.com.mx/el-fraude-del-caracter-civil-de-la-guardia-nacional/

Pérez Pacheco FA (2021) *Guardia Nacional: origen, composición y presupuesto*, CIEP, accessed 3 January 2025. https://ciep.mx/guardia-nacional-origen-composicion-y-presupuesto/

Paley DM (2020) *Guerra Neoliberal. Desaparición y búsqueda en el norte de México*, Libertad bajo palabra.

Peterson VS (2008) '"New Wars" and Gendered Economies', *Feminist Review*, 88(1):7–20. doi: 10.1057/palgrave.fr.9400377

Peterson VS (2010) 'Global Householding amid Global Crises', *Politics & Gender*, 6(2):271–281. doi:10.1017/S1743923X10000073

Peterson VS (2016) 'Gendering Insecurities, Informalization and "War Economies"', in Harcourt W (ed) *The Palgrave Handbook of Gender and Development: Critical Engagements in Feminist Theory and Practice*, Palgrave Macmillan UK (pp. 441–462). doi: 10.1007/978-1-137-38273-3_30

Philipson Garcia D (2023) *Security for whom? New Report on Feminist Perspectives on Militarism & Climate*, Women's Environmental and Development Organization and the Centre for Feminist Foreign Policy, accessed 7 January 2025. https://wedo.org/security-for-whom-new-report-on-feminist-perspectives-on-militarism-climate/

Ramalho JA, Diamint R and Sánchez L (2020) *La militarisación de la seguridad y el regreso de los militares a la política en América Latina*, Friederich Ebert Stiftung México, accessed 8 October 2024. https://library.fes.de/pdf-files/bueros/la-seguridad/16106.pdf

Robledo Hoecker and Verdes-Montenegro (2023) Militarización, militarismo y democracia: ¿nuevas tendencias en América Latina?, Fundación Carolina.

Rodríguez Everaert AS (19 October 2022) *El Tribunal de las Mujeres en Oaxaca*, accessed 7 January 2025. https://www.nexos.com.mx/?p=66497

Salzinger L (1997) 'From High Heels to Swathed Bodies: Gendered Meanings under Production in Mexico's Export-Processing Industry', *Feminist Studies*, 23(3). https://www.jstor.org/stable/3178386.

Storr S (18 April 2023) *¿Qué es la Guardia Nacional (en 2023)?* Seguridad Vía Civil, accessed 7 January 2025. https://seguridadviacivil.ibero.mx/2023/04/18/que-es-la-guardia-nacional-en-2023/

Trejo G and Ley S (2020) *Votes, Drugs, and Violence: The Political Logic of Criminal Wars in Mexico*, 1st ed., Cambridge University Press. doi:10.1017/9781108894807.

True J (2012) *The Political Economy of Violence against Women*. Oxford University Press. doi:10.1093/acprof:oso/9780199755929.001.0001

True J and Hozić AA (2020) 'Don't Mention the War! International Financial Institutions and the Gendered Circuits of Violence in Post-Conflict', *Review of International Political Economy*, 27(6):1193–1213. doi:10.1080/09692290.2020.1732443

Valencia S (2016) *Capitalismo Gore. Control económico, violencia y narcopoder*, EDICIONES CULTURALES PAIDOS SA DE CV. https://construcciondeidentidades.wordpress.com/wp-content/uploads/2016/11/sayak-valencia-capitalismo-gore.pdf

Weeks K (2011) *The Problem with Work Feminism, Marxism, Antiwork Politics, and Postwork Imaginaries*, Duke University Press.

Zavala O (2022) *Drug Cartels Do Not Exist. Narcotrafficking in US and Mexican Culture*, Vanderbilt University Press. https://www.vanderbiltuniversitypress.com/9780826504661/drug-cartels-do-not-exist/

Zulver JM (2024) 'Complex Gendered Agency in Mexico: How Women Negotiate Hierarchies of Fear to Search for the Disappeared', *European Journal of Politics and Gender*, 7(2): 239–255. Doi.10.1332/251510821X16746579646888

# 4

# ECONOMIC WARFARE, WAR ECONOMY, AND GENDERED CIRCUITS OF VIOLENCE IN IRAN

*Asma Abdi*

On 13 April 2024, Iran launched over 300 drones and missiles against Israel in response to Israel's unlawful[1] air strike on Iran's embassy compound in Damascus, leaving 13 Iranians killed in the embassy (BBC 2024). Being the first direct conflict between Iran and Israel in nearly half a century of political hostility, this came to represent a moment of significant military escalation in the region. The hashtag #worldwar3 began trending on social media, and multiple media outlets speculated about the possibility of "a full-blown regional war" in the Middle East (The Economist 2024). On the same day, Iranian authorities initiated a new urban operation named the "Light ray Plan" [*Tarh-e-Noor* in Farsi], targeting women who choose not to wear hijab in the streets and other public spaces (Parent 2024). This operation reintroduced the notorious morality police (*Gasht-e-Ershad* in Farsi), tasked with enforcing women's dress codes in public spaces, to the streets of Tehran and other major cities. This move came after an almost 18-month retreat from the practice, following intense popular pressure from the nationwide uprising in September 2022, which was ignited by the tragic death of *Jina-Mahsa Amini* while in the custody of the morality police.

The synchronicity between the two attacks by the Iranian state – one on the territory of the enemy and the other on women's bodies – was not a mere coincidence. Indeed, feminist scholars in International Relations (IR) and International Political Economy (IPE) have consistently underscored how various forms of gendered violence underpin and are perpetuated by the politics of war and peace (Enloe 2014; True 2012; Tickner 1992, amongst others). This attack on women, as this chapter later shows, was merely a gendered display of war in its most visible and choreographed form – one which cannot be understood in isolation from the broader gendered and racialised "circuits of violence" (True and Hozić 2020, p. 1194), that have defined the decades-long geopolitical tensions between Iran, the United

DOI: 10.4324/9781003571667-5

States, and its regional allies. The incident of military escalation and Iran's attack on Israel also was not an isolated or ahistorical event, as they were mostly depicted by Western media and polity.[2] If we understand war as "a display of structural violence at its extremity" (Peterson 2016:441), then this attack on Iran's sovereignty was only the latest incident – manifested perhaps in its most extreme and visible form – in a chain of decades-long, structurally unequal incidences of violence and conflict between Iran and the United States.

The decades-long hostility between Iran and the United States had intensified since the early 2010s, following the imposition of what Obama Administration has dubbed "the most crippling sanctions" (ABC News 2012) ever imposed on any country. The term "crippling,"[3] with its hyper-masculinist, racist, and ableist connotations, aptly describes the sanctions' effects as they have triggered severe geopolitical, political, and economic crises. Regionally, they have deepened a (geo) political impasse, fuelled Iran's growing militarisation and involvement in regional wars, and contributed to the broader militarisation of, and tensions, in the Middle East (Moghadam 2024). Economically, sanctions have "crippled" the lives and livelihoods of many Iranians, while efforts by successive governments to address the "problem" of sanctions through diplomacy have consistently failed.

This failure is partly due to the broader political crises within the country, where certain political factions – particularly hardliners – have increasingly viewed war and escalating tensions as solutions to these overlapping crises (especially the state's deep-seated crisis of legitimacy). This failure also reflects the wider crisis of the so-called "liberal" international world order, where, in a betrayal of liberal/multilateral principles, the Trump administration unilaterally withdrew from the Joint Comprehensive Plan of Action (JCPOA) – or what was widely known as Iran's "nuclear deal." Following the conclusion of the deal in 2015, sanctions on Iran were eased, but despite Iran's compliance with the terms of agreement, they were reimposed and tightened after the Trump administration's unilateral withdrawal in 2018, and the imposition of its "Maximum Pressure" policies (Landler 2018). This backdrop of sanctions, along with the socio-economic and geopolitical crises they exacerbate, is crucial for understanding the emergence of a war economy in Iran over the last decade. The concept of the war economy in the Middle East (mostly used in the context of Syria) has often been understood as the economy that develops in the context of war, narrowly defined as military conflict (Bojicic-Dzelilovic and Turkmani 2018). Similarly, in the context of Iran, the term has typically been used to describe the country's economy during its war with Iraq in the 1980s (Mather 2009). However, in this chapter, I define the war economy in Iran differently. I discuss it as the emergence of war as a solution to multiple crises and the subordination of the economy – including reproductive economies and livelihoods– to war and militarisation. I also use the concept of war in a broader sense to also encompass technologies of warfare/peace beyond military conflict, such as economic sanctions.

This chapter examines the relationships between economic warfare, war economy, and "gendered circuits of violence," in the context of Iran under the intensified regime of sanctions since the early 2010s. I use the concept of "gendered circuits of violence," drawing on Hozić and True's theorisation (2020, 1194), to capture the continuities of violence across various "types" – e.g., structural, physical, sexual, political, and discursive – and "temporalities" (e.g., everyday, normalised violence of the war economy, the outbreak of war and military escalations). The chapter traces these continuities across multiple scales, from the global politics of sanctions imposition to the everyday gendered regimes of labour and survival in Iran. On a macro/global scale, the next section of the chapter focuses on the structural forms of racialised violence in the politics of sanctions imposition. The section in particular highlights the racialised violence inherent in the liberal conceptualisation of sanctions as "peaceful." The normalisation of sanctions as "peace," I argue, has historically served to obscure the violence of sanctions by legitimising them as lawful tools of coercion "wielded [with impunity] by the most powerful, the US and its allies in Western Europe and beyond, against [often] the poor and weak in the poorest countries of the Global South" (Davis and Ness 2022:3). The chapter then moves to the next section, which traces the continuities of gendered and racialised violence at a meso-level. An ever-tightening regime of sanctions, crises, and growing threats of war, as I argue in this section, has led to the formation of a state-led war economy, with austerity and militarisation emerging as its key pillars.

The normalisation of various forms of gendered violence (e.g., the reinforced violent imposition of hijab and the policing of women's bodies) is a significant dimension of this war economy. As contributions in this book and existing feminist work on the war economy (Peterson 2008, 2016) underscore, war economies rely on specific gendered identities, reproductive regimes, and labour divisions. As detailed in the last section of the chapter, the war economy in Iran has entailed a progressively authoritarian and patriarchal reorganisation of reproductive economies through a wide range of interventions in matters of marriage, (social) reproduction, and women's work. As the feminist political economy conceptualisation of gendered violence (True 2012) highlights, structural forms of gendered inequality are connected to and enhance the exposure to everyday experiences of physical and sexual violence. In the case of Iran too, these structural forms of gendered and racialised violence have increasingly exposed women to physical and sexual forms of violence on an everyday level. Methodologically, the chapter provides a feminist IPE analysis of the gendered shifts in policies and discourses of the Iranian state over the last decade through a review of the literature, speeches, decrees, newspaper articles, government official websites, and policy documents. Additionally, it draws on insights gained through a six-month period of (online) fieldwork in Iran (March 2021 to September 2021), which involved 25 semi-structured interviews with middle-class urban women. Although this chapter does not directly engage with the interview material, the insights from the fieldwork inform the analysis of the shifting gendered regimes of labour and survival in Iran.[4]

The chapter makes two interconnected contributions to the literature on war economy. First, it expands the conceptualisation of war to include sanctions – as underexplored economic tools of warfare. The reconceptualisation of sanctions as war complicates existing debates on the interconnections between geopolitics (war) and capitalism (economy) by not only exposing the "internal" relationality of war, capitalism, and crisis, as argued by Bieler and Morton (2018:6) but also demonstrating, on the one hand, capitalism's reliance on hidden or invisible forms of war (or "peace"), and, on the other, how advancements in capitalism have necessitated and enabled new technologies of peace/war. Second, the chapter contributes to feminist IPE debates on the war economy through a geographical expansion to an authoritarian Middle Eastern context. The case of Iran, as a country involved in an "inter-state" rather than "intra-state" conflict, provides a more nuanced analysis of the state's role in shaping gendered divisions of labour and reproductive regimes essential to the reproduction of the war economy.

## Sanctions as war and racialised violence

> Apply this economic, **peaceful,** silent, deadly remedy and there will be no need for force. It is a terrible remedy. It does not cost a life outside the nation boycotted, but it brings a pressure upon the nation which, in my judgment, no modern nation could resist.
>
> *(Woodrow Wilson et al., Address in 1919, quoted in Mulder 2022:1–2, emphasis added)*

The exclusion of economic/financial sanctions, from the legal definition of war – which is narrowly defined as military conflict – has arguably led to their increased normalisation, depoliticisation, and invisibility of violence. A feminist politicisation of our understanding of sanctions should thus encompass not only efforts to highlight the gendered consequences of sanctions but also how existing racialised hierarchies of "the international" have facilitated their normalisation and legitimisation. To this end, this section draws on the small yet growing body of critical literature on sanctions (Nanopoulos 2019; Mulder 2022; Davis and Ness 2022) to contextualise sanctions, and their conceptualisation as "peace," in relation to broader global structures of racialised violence, (neo)colonial histories and (neo) liberal capitalist exploitations.

Mainstream historiography of sanctions, perhaps not surprisingly as it is the general trend of Western-centric historiography in mainstream IR (Geeta and Nair 2013), has usually been narrated in trans-historical and Eurocentric terms. This historiography frequently connects the association of sanctions with "peace" – or their use as a standalone tool without accompanying military conflict – to the "idealist" and anti-war climate of the post-World War I era, particularly to the oft-cited speech of Woodrow Wilson quoted above. Working against such trans-historical approaches, Nanopoulos (2019) argues that the conditions for decoupling of sanctions from war, and its emergence as "peace," became necessitated by the political conditions of the time and enabled by the advancements in capitalism. Indeed, the "idealist" and "anti-war" rhetoric of the post-World War I era necessitated the emergence of more sanitised forms of violence, while the transition to "the monopoly phase of capitalism and the division of the world amongst the main capitalist powers… created the conditions for the outlawing of war and the emergence of sanctions as tools to dissuade aggression" (Nanopoulos 2019:215). Economic sanctions, therefore, emerged not as a "peaceful" alternative to military conflict but as equally powerful tools of control, order building, disciplining, and policing of the capitalist and colonialist world order, with the advantage that their (violent) effects were less visible for the public to see. "Peace" in this liberal capitalist world order, therefore, is not in opposition to war, but rather as another technology of "police" and domination (Nanopoulos 2019).

The necessity for this disaggregation has become even greater in the post-Cold-War era, when the fall of the Soviet Union and the end of the Cold War, as Warde (2007) explains, ushered in a "new paradigm of sanitized high-tech warfare" (Warde 2007:32), demanding fewer physical casualties, enhanced public visibility, ethical engagement, and cost-effectiveness. This explains the concurrent trends of exponential growth in the popularity of sanctions since the 1990s (Peksen 2019), as well as the emergence of ideas such as "smart" or "targeted" sanctions in this era, which have arguably served to further sanitise – and normalise – the application of sanctions as legitimate tools of violence and coercion. Conventional wisdom in IR understands "the shift from comprehensive sanctions imposed against states to sanctions imposed against named individuals, entities, or groups" (Nanopoulos 2019:1) – as motivated by the large-scale humanitarian effects of sanctions in the 1990s. Hence, as detailed by Nanopoulos (2019), these processes of "smartization" or "individualization" of sanctions, are often read as a global endeavour to make sanctions more "targeted," "precise," and hence "peaceful." Nonetheless, these processes became necessitated by the political conditions of the time and possible due to certain advancements in global capitalism. In particular, "the globalisation of a finance-led system of accumulation," the demise of welfare states, new modes of regulation of finance outside national boundaries, and "the neoliberal reorganisation of American hegemony" enabled the financial sanctioning of individuals and entities, instead of states (Nanopoulos 2019:232; Warde 2007:32). Politically, these processes served to maintain and reproduce the perception of sanctions as "peaceful" – a concept which was in jeopardy, as the humanitarian effects of sanctions in the 1990s, especially those imposed on Iraq, drew significant public attention.[5]

Claims about the "targeted-ness" of sanctions have arguably played a pivotal role for the United States in garnering international support for implementing one of the most severe sanctions regimes on Iran, just a decade after the Iraq experience, which had led to widespread global scepticism about US sanctions policies. This is evident, for example, in the following excerpt from "The Art of Sanctions" by Nephew (2018:149) the former Deputy Coordinator for Sanctions Policy in the Obama State Department, and a self-proclaimed 'major architect' of the Iran sanctions policy during the 2000s–2010s: while reflecting on the obstacles of global consensus-building about imposing sanctions on Iran following Iraq's experience, Nephew argues, "this more targeted approach would be sellable to an international audience as well as translatable to an Iranian audience" (Nephew 2018:149). Nonetheless, as also noted by Moret (2015), and as I would further detail in the remainder of this chapter, economic sanctions on Iran have remained "targeted" only in technical terms. Sanctions on Iran have targeted a vast array of individuals, entities, banks, and various sectors of the economy, including the oil sector[6] in ways which "they can be considered de facto comprehensive sanctions, widely associated in the past with negative humanitarian consequences" (Moret 2015:120).

Although my discussion below will specifically focus on the intensification of the sanctions regime on Iran since the early 2010s, it is crucial to note that Iran's initial encounter with sanctions is linked to its history of (semi)colonial relations with the British. The first imposition of sanctions on Iran dates to the 1950s, when the country sought to nationalise its oil industry, then under British control, in "defiance of the Euro-American world order" (Osanloo 2023:256). This effort was initially met with the UK's blockade of oil exports in 1951, which led to subsequent crises and labour unrest (Harris 2017:58). Two years later, it culminated in the infamous 1953 CIA-led coup against Mossadegh, Iran's first democratically elected prime minister, and the restoration of Iran's dictator with US support. In persuading the new US Eisenhower administration to support the blockade and coup, a British cable at the time stated: [t]he security of the free world is dependent on large quantities of oil from Middle Eastern sources. If the attitude in Iran spreads to Saudi Arabia or Iraq, the whole structure may break down...." (Cited in Harris 2017:58)

This brief history situates the sanctions on Iran within its (semi)colonial past, defined by racialised violence, resource extraction, and the theft of its natural wealth – dynamics that have historically shaped the "international" relations between the West and the rest (Chowdhry and Ling 2010; Geeta and Nair 2013). The various physical, sexual, and structural types of gendered violence (re)produced by sanctions on Iran, and the war economy they have created, should be understood in their intersections with such global continuums of racialised violence, which have underpinned the liberal normalisation of sanctions as "peace" and defined the past and present histories of sanctions imposition on Iran.

## Sanctions and war economy in Iran

Iran has endured multiple waves of US-led sanctions since the 1970 revolution, which ended the symbiotic relationship between the United States and the US-backed dictator of Iran, Mohammad Reza Shah Pahlavi ( Al Jazeera 2012; Fayazmanesh 2003). These sanctions were notably intensified in the early 2010s, culminating in 2012, when the EU, as one of the most major trade partners of Iran (Batmanghelidj 2020), joined the United States in implementing oil embargoes against the country. Furthermore, previous measures were expanded to encompass financial sanctions that disconnected Iranian banks from the SWIFT electronic banking system, alongside secondary sanctions targeting individuals and entities involved in trade with Iran (Moghadam 2024; Salehi-Isfahani 2023; Al Jazeera 2012).

As indicated by a growing body of literature on the economic impacts of sanctions on Iran (Salehi-Isfahani 2020, 2023; Laudati and Pesaran 2023; Zahirinejad 2019; Fardoust 2020; Mazarei 2020), the tightening of the sanctions regime on Iran has been successful in creating a full-blown "economic crisis." Perhaps one of the most dramatic macroeconomic impacts of sanctions has been the nearly fourfold decline in Iran's GDP, which has fallen from \$644.04 billion in 2012 to \$239.74 billion in 2020 (World Bank Data). Although the economy briefly rebounded for two years after the conclusion of the Joint Comprehensive Plan of Action (JCPOA) in 2015, it suffered a sharper decline after the Trump administration's withdrawal from the deal in 2018 and its subsequent campaign of "maximum pressure" on Iran. Economic growth fell from 13% in 2016 to –7.6% in 2019 (Salehi-Isfahani 2020). Sanctions have particularly impacted oil exports, leading to a reduced foreign exchange supply and significant inflationary spikes (Salehi-Isfahani 2020). For instance, following the US withdrawal from the JCPOA, Iran's inflation rate nearly quadrupled from 9.6% in 2017 to over 40% in 2018 (Fardoust 2020). Additionally, Iran's currency value has depreciated by approximately 300% each time sanctions were tightened, first under the Obama Administration in 2012 and then under the Trump administration in 2018 (Salehi-Isfahani 2020). The effects of sanctions have been exacerbated by the COVID-19 pandemic, particularly as the Iranian state was unable to access an estimated \$100 billion in frozen assets (Batmanghelidj 2021), hampering the purchase of essential medicines. According to the World Bank's 2023 Poverty and Equity Brief, poverty and inequality in Iran have continually risen over the past decade due to "the severe economic recession and tightening of sanctions" (World Bank 2023). Iran now faces an unprecedented surge in poverty rates, sharp inflation hikes, a rapidly devaluing currency, increased migration, and a shrinking middle class (Fardoust 2020; Mazarei 2020; Salehi-Isfahani 2020, 2023; Zahirinejad 2019). As manifested in multiple nationwide riots and uprisings, which now occur as frequently as once a year, citizens have increasingly lost their trust in the viability of their political and social institutions, and the state has increasingly lost its legitimacy, due to its reduced capacities and increased lack of inability to address these multiple crises. The 2019 Human Rights Watch report, already before the outbreak of COVID-19, warned about a humanitarian crisis, as the "Maximum Pressures" policies of the Trump administration "have drastically constrained the ability of the country to finance humanitarian imports, including medicines" (Human Rights Watch 2019).

Examining shifts in the Iranian state's expenditures, it seems that these multiple crises, combined with the ever-increasing proximity of war, have increasingly pushed the Iranian state towards adaptation of a war economy, or what the state has frequently referred to as the "resistance economy" (Batmanghelidj 2020), with austerity and militarisation as its key tenets. The intensification of sanctions on Iran has intensified tensions in the Middle East (Moghadam 2024) between US regional allies and adversaries. Although the economic pressures of multilateral sanctions (Harris 2020; Dizaji and Farzanegan 2021) have prevented an increase in military spending, it has remained relatively high, constituting 17% of government expenditure in 2022 – a figure significantly higher than the share of military expenditure in any pre-2012 era (since the end of Iran–Iraq war in 1990) (World Bank Data[7]). Iran's military spending still remains much lower than that of regional counterparts such as Israel, Saudi Arabia, Oman, and Jordan (Moghadam 2024), yet its regional military engagement has significantly intensified over the last decade. Since 2011, the Iranian state has actively aimed to expand its influence in the Middle East by supplying military equipment to its "axis of resistance" in Iraq, Syria, Lebanon, and Yemen (Soltaninejad 2019; Steinberg 2021), and through direct involvement of its armed forces in some of the regional conflicts. In 2015, for example, the Islamic Revolutionary Guards Corps (IRGC) fought alongside Iraq and Russia to support Syria against ISIS (Moghadam 2024).

As further detailed in the next section, e, this shift towards militarisation has "reinforced militarised masculinities and bolstered the patriarchal political forces in Iran" (Moghadam 2024:1199). Various gendered structures of inequality and violence have been entrenched and intensified. For instance, the control and policing of the obligatory hijab – enforced through police violence against women – and the imposition of idealised Islamic forms of womanhood on all women as symbols of the nation (Yuval-Davis 1997) have visibly escalated. Iran's involvement in various regional wars including in Syria has repeatedly been framed as a defence of both "Iranian women" and "Shi'ism" (*harim-va-haram* in Farsi) (Tasnim News 2024b). The use of militaristic language to describe Iranian women's responsibilities to observe the law of the obligatory hijab has become ubiquitous in Iranian officials' vernacular. For example, *Tasnim News* quotes Qasem Soleimani, the Iranian major general and commander of the Quds Force fighting in Syria, as likening women's adherence to wearing the hijab inside Iran to fighting in the war abroad (Tasnim News 2024a). Similarly, the Islamic Republic News Agency *(IRNA)* has published a martyr's will in which the writer addresses Iranian women, stating, "the enemy is more scared of the blackness of your hijab than the redness of my blood" (IRNA 2014).

These quotations bring into view the continuums/continuities of violence across multiple *territories* from battle zones in Syria where (male) Iranian soldiers are fighting, to the streets/public spaces of Iran where women are expected to defend the nation and fight the war by adhering to state-defined Islamic/Shia womanhood. This reinforced emphasis on the obligatory hijab and the policing of women's bodies, in the context of Iran's intensified militarisation and regional wars, also serves as a warning sign of the normalisation of inequality and oppression into war preparedness. This entrenchment of structural gendered inequality has translated into heightened exposure to physical and sexual violence in public spaces. Over the past decade,

Iranian women have faced increasing levels of policing in public spaces, with the killing of *Jina-Mahsa Amini* in the custody of the morality police in September 2022 serving as a stark example of this state-sanctioned gendered violence.

Sanctions, war, and their proximity have frequently been employed in the state's rhetoric and discourse to justify and promote specific economic policies. Over the past decade, this has included the repeated invocation of what the Iranian state terms a "resistance economy." In 2014, the decree issued by the Supreme Leader on the "resistance economy" outlined various economic policy objectives for pushing back against the "imposed economic war on the Iranian nation" (as stated in the decree's preamble).[7] Despite the ideologically charged rhetoric of "resistance" to the West and sanctions, the decree is merely the Supreme Leader's re-endorsement of liberalisation policies, (and the values of *efficiency*, *competitiveness*, and *entrepreneurship*), but one conditioned by the specificities of sanctions and escalating tensions with the West. Strategies such as diversifying production and exports, as well as forging new trade relationships with China, India, and neighbouring nations such as Iraq and Afghanistan to replace the EU (formerly one of Iran's largest trade partners before sanctions), exemplify this approach (Batmanghelidj 2020). This subordination of economic policy to the exigencies of war and sanctions, along with the use of war threats to justify economic policies, forms a key characteristic of Iran's resistance/war economy. The adoption of highly controversial austerity measures, including budget cuts and reductions in social spending (except in health) (Harris 2020), has been a significant aspect of Iran's resistance or war economy. The past decade has consistently seen budget cuts and the withdrawal of subsidies on housing, education, food, and fuel (Laudati and Pesaran 2021; Amirahmadi 2015; Fathollah-Nejad 2017). Some of these cuts and subsidy withdrawals have been highly contentious and have sparked nationwide political unrest. For instance, the withdrawal of petrol subsidies in November 2019 led to a sudden 200% increase in gasoline prices overnight, resulting in one of the largest nationwide protests in the country since the 1979 revolution.

A detailed discussion of Iran's welfare programmes, and its specificities, is beyond the scope of this paper (Harris 2017). Yet it is imperative to mention that promising equality and providing welfare to the poor and the rural became a significant part of post-revolutionary Iranian state's popular claim-making. The immediate post-revolutionary Iran, therefore, experienced an expansion of welfare and infrastructure in rural areas – in particular, in the health and education sectors (Harris 2017). The post-revolutionary welfare state has often been seen as a crucial factor in improving women's education, health, and reproductive rights (Halper 2010; Sameh 2012; Harris 2017). For example, a 2018 IMF report highlights the "tremendous strides" of post-revolutionary Iran in "eliminating gender gaps in education and health indicators" noting thatfor about a decade now, there has been virtually no gap between male and female enrolment in primary and secondary education [while] the gender gap in tertiary education enrolment is small... . (IMF 2018:16; also see Halper 2010)

The expansion of healthcare clinics to rural areas, described as the "most transformative welfare measure" (Harris 2017:118) of the post-revolutionary state, has been instrumental in implementing the family planning programmes of the 1990s. These programmes led to a dramatic and rapid decline in childbearing, from 5.6 births per woman in 1985 to 2.0 in 2000 (Roudi-Fahimi 2002). These improvements in education, health, and reproduction have implicated political processes in Iran, as they have produced a politically mobilised and highly educated female citizenry, which has become one of the most major political forces challenging the Iranian state and advocating for democracy and gender equality in recent decades (Sameh 2012). In the long term, therefore, these austerity measures will have implications not only for women's everyday lives but also for women's movements and the wider political movements in Iran.

## War economy, reproductive regimes, and gendered circuits of violence and Labour

The restructuring of the state's apparatuses around a war economy agenda, characterised by militarisation and austerity, has occurred in profoundly gendered ways. In addition to what discussed in the previous section, these processes have involved a (re)structuring of reproductive economies across a patriarchal gendered division of labour. As a result, matters of social reproduction, such as marriage, women's reproductive and productive roles, as well as reproduction have increasingly emerged as sites of the state's politics in specific ways. Perhaps not entirely irrelevant to the dominant exceptionalist/Orientalist views in Middle Eastern studies (Baumann and Roccu 2023), these gendered shifts have often been understood and explained in terms of Islamic *ideologies*, and *local* structures of oppression (e.g., see Barlow 2018). Consequently, the analysis of these gendered shifts, including state-women relations, has largely remained disconnected from the wider structural violence (e.g., the violence of sanctions imposition, the multiple sanctions-induced crises, and the state's shift towards militarisation and austerity) described thus far (except for Moghadam 2024). Nonetheless, as widely discussed by feminist scholars in IR and IPE, both militarisation (Eichler 2014; Enloe 2014; Pettman 1996) and crises (Hozić and True 2016; Griffin 2015; Elias 2016) are deeply gendered processes. Crises, most particularly, increase the need for the unpaid socially reproductive labour of women in the household where women are expected to fill the gaps with their unpaid socially reproductive labour. As such, governance responses to crises are also highly gendered (Griffin 2015; Roberts and Elias 2018), being often "informed by assumptions around gender" (Whitworth 2000:96). Crises hence can give rise to female caregiver and male breadwinner discourses of crisis (Griffin 2015; Abdi 2025) perpetuating the private/public sexual divisions of labour.

The few existing feminist IPE work on war economy (Peterson 2008, 2016), including the contributions of this volume, have also highlighted the reliance of war economies on specific gendered identities, reproductive regimes, and labour divisions. For example, Peterson (2008:14) distinguishes between various dimensions of war economies, including "coping" and "combat" economies, and highlights the gendered dimensions of each. She identifies "coping" economies, which "facilitate individual survival and the social reproduction of families and households" (Peterson 2008:15), as among the most feminised economies of wartime due to the patriarchal sexual division of labour that associates women primarily with social reproduction (on social reproduction in conflict and post-conflict settings also, see Rai et al. (2019)). The "combat economy," described as "the most apparently masculinised" dimension of war economy (Peterson 2008:15), also unleashes various forms of gendered violence against women, as militarisation reinforces militarised masculinities and "identity politics" (Peterson 2008:16). This leads to increased pressure on women – often seen as symbols of the nation and culture (Yuval-Davis 1997) – to "conform to rigid (masculinist/patriarchal) expectations regarding their appearance and behaviour" (Peterson 2008:16). The Iranian state's heightened enforcement of women's dress codes and the obligatory hijab in public spaces, as discussed in the previous section, exemplifies a key form of gendered violence motivated by the "combat" dimension of Iran's war economy.

The "coping" gendered dimensions of war economy described by Peterson (2008) are also present in the case of Iran. Peterson's (2008) argument, nonetheless, focuses on the analysis of "new wars," which are predominantly "intra- rather than inter-national" (2008:13) forms of conflict. Therefore, her argument does not involve an analysis of the role of the state in (re)shaping these gendered regimes of labour and survival/coping. As I have argued elsewhere (2025), the Iranian state has played an active role in (re)shaping the gendered regimes of labour and survival/coping in Iran. Specifically, the last decade has witnessed a notable reinforcement of patriarchal male breadwinner and female caregiver ideologies in state policies and rhetoric.[8] This may not constitute an *ideological* shift, given the long-standing codification of a patriarchal gender contract by the post-revolutionary Iranian state (Afshar 1997; Moghadam 2003). Indeed, the post-revolutionary state has codified such patriarchal gendered division of labour in its constitution where in its preamble enshrines motherhood as women's "crucial duty" (Afshar 1997). Nonetheless, on a *policy* level, the last decade has witnessed the emergence of some policies and measures which signify the greater commitment of the state to such a patriarchal gendered order.

This reinforced emphasis on such patriarchal gendered order is in particular evident in the Supreme Leader's 2014 decree "on population,"[9] and the 2016 decree "on family."[10] The decree "on population" has particularly called to "promote the dynamics, growth, and youthfulness of the population by an increase in fertility which should be above the replacement threshold" (First article, Supreme Leader's decree on population). As part of this pro-natalist strategy, women's reproductive bodies and rights have increasingly emerged as sites of state politics and violence (Ladier-Fouladi 2021:907). Most notably, the policy shift has controversially rolled back the family planning programme implemented during the 1990s. This programme provided free access to contraception, reproductive education in schools, encouragement of birth spacing of three to four years, discouragement of adolescent pregnancy, and promotion of family sizes of two children or fewer. The 2016 decree "on family,"[11] on the other hand, focuses on the gendered dimensions of families and households, reiterating the importance of promoting "an Iranian-Islamic model of the family that supports the dignity of traditional gender roles, including motherhood, housekeeping, and the economic and paternal roles of men" (Article 12; translated by the author). This state-led restructuring of reproductive economies has played a key role in the formation of a feminisation of survival and coping in the country (Abdi 2025), as it has increasingly pushed women to the households where they are expected to fill the gaps with their unpaid socially reproductive labour (Abdi 2025). These shifts could also be understood as the subordination of reproductive economies to the aims of war and geopolitical conflict. For instance, the Iranian state's pro-natalist strategy, which includes aggressive interventions in women's reproductive rights, has been largely pursued as a mechanism for "asserting Iran's demographic and geopolitical significance within the region" (Ladier-Fouladi 2021:2).

This heightened emphasis on a patriarchal model of family and the shift to a national pro-natalist strategy has been coupled with a wide range of violent interventions in areas as diverse as employment, marriage, family, education, and reproduction. This includes, among other measures, pro-early marriage rhetoric and specific policies designed to "facilitate marriage for the youth" (read men) in response to what the Iranian state has repeatedly framed as a "marriage crisis." For example, Article 2 of the Supreme Leader's decree "on population" insists on the necessity of lowering the age of marriage through policies that remove the "obstacles" to marriage. This removal of "obstacles" to marriage has, however, often come at the expense of women's rights to education and formal employment, which have repetitively been blamed for allegedly "high" marriage ages. A particularly notable and controversial policy to "facilitate" marriage has been the exponential 25-fold increase in marriage loans within a short span of four years (from 2016 to 2019),[12] during the period in which austerity measures and reductions in social provisioning in other areas have been implemented. This significant rise in marriage loans in the context of increased poverty has promoted certain types of gendered and sexual violence. For example, many women's rights activists have argued that, in the absence of sufficient legal protections against child marriage and amidst rising poverty, these loans could exacerbate violence against young girls, particularly in rural areas where parents may marry off their daughters to access the marriage mortgage.[13] Indeed, these pro-marriage policies have already led to an increase in child marriages. For example, Mohammad Mehdi Tondguyan, an Iranian official in the Ministry of Youth and Sport, warned in 2018 that "following an increase in the amount of marriage loans, child marriage has increased four-fold in some areas of the country."[14] As such, this entrenchment of structural violence and gendered inequality has facilitated various everyday forms of gendered violence.

## Conclusion

From the global politics of sanctions imposition on Iran to the everyday gendered circuits of coping and survival, this chapter traces the continuums of gendered and racialised violence in Iran across multiple types, temporalities, and territories. The intensification of the sanctions regime on Iran, as the chapter shows, has led to the emergence of overlapping economic and geopolitical crises. In this context, the shift towards war and militarisation – evident in the country's increasing involvement in regional conflicts and rising military expenditures – has become the Iranian state's primary solution to these multifaceted crises. In this context, the threat and proximity of war have been repeatedly mobilised in state discourses, not only as a means of addressing its legitimacy crisis but also to justify and implement otherwise controversial neoliberal policies, such as austerity and budget cuts. For example, under the framework of its so-called "resistance economy," the Iranian state has pursued privatisation and extensive budget cuts. This shift to the resistance/war economy has occurred in deeply gendered ways. Austerity measures and economic crises, in turn, have facilitated various discursive, structural, physical, sexual, and economic forms of gendered violence. Women are increasingly associated in state discourses and rhetoric as mothers and wives, leading to the emergence of policies that aim to confine women to these roles. The discursive violence of associating women with socially reproductive labour, combined with economic violence of restricting women's access to education and formal employment, has heightened their vulnerability to physical and sexual violence. For instance, child marriage and early pregnancy have been on the rise, while exposure to domestic and sexualised violence has increased as women become increasingly dependent on male breadwinners.

The chapter examines these gendered interventions as part of the state's broader effort to subordinate social reproduction to the war economy. On the one hand, pushing women back into the household is seen as a necessity to facilitate the "coping" of households, communities, and the state itself, all of which have become increasingly reliant on the unpaid reproductive labour of women for survival. On the other hand, these policies reinforce state-defined ideologies and identities. For example, policies emphasising women's return to the household and the enforcement of the obligatory hijab on women, as symbols of the nation, facilitate the reproduction of state-defined Islamic identities within the "combat" and "militarisation" dimensions of the war economy. This subordination of reproduction and women's bodies – both in their materiality and symbolic representation – to the war economy has entrenched gendered structures of inequality. These inequalities have translated into immediate and everyday experiences of physical and sexual violence for women. The chapter also bridges the temporal and spatial dimensions of these forms of gendered violence, linking Iran's (semi)colonial history of sanctions imposition, to the contemporary emergence of the war economy, and the normalisation of gendered violence as part of it.

## Notes

1 According to UN Human Rights Office of the High Commissioner (OHCHR), Israel's attack on Iran was against international law as "Israel does not appear to have been exercising self-defence on 1 April because it presented no evidence that Iran was directly committing an 'armed attack' on Israel or sending non-state armed groups to attack it". OHCHR's report of the military attack can be found online here: https://www.ohchr.org/en/press-releases/2024/04/israel-and-iran-must-de-escalate-conflict-protect-human-rights-warn-un.

2 An example of such an ahistorical view of the incident was the then UK Prime Minister Rishi Sunak's condemnation of Iran "in the strongest terms" for its "reckless" attack against Israel. His statement omitted any mention of the wider structural issues, including Israel's illegal attack on Iran's embassy, which contributed to the conflict. Rishi Sunak's full condemnation statement can be found online here: https://www.gov.uk/government/news/pm-statement-on-iranian-regimes-reckless-attack-against-israel

3 For a decolonial affective analysis of sanctions as "crippled-ness" and (colonial) "injury," see Tafakori (2023).

4 For a more detailed version of this argument, see Abdi (2025).

5 Sanctions on Iraq were frequently characterised as a "genocidal tool" (Simons, 2015), tools of "mass deconstruction" (Mueller and Mueller 1999), or "deadly" (Arnove and Abunimah 2003).

6 A timeline of sanctions on Iran including the full list of sanctioned entities, individuals, banks, and sectors since 2005 is available at: https://iranprimer.usip.org/resource/timeline-us-sanctions

7 The 2014 Decree may be accessed in Farsi from Khamenei's official website: https://farsi.khamenei.ir/news-content?id=25370. A loose English translation of the text may be found in Khajepour's (2014) article.

8 For example, the Supreme Leader's official website in Farsi now has a section on "women, family and lifestyle", https://farsi.khamenei.ir/tag-content?id=19693 and https://farsi.khamenei.ir/speech-family. Additionally, platforms on Instagram and Twitter such as @khameneireyhane [joined Twitter in Oct. 2015] https://twitter.com/khameneireyhane (last accessed May 2023) regularly publish the supreme leader's decrees and views on questions of "women and family".

9 The decree "on population" can be accessed in Farsi on Khamenei's official website https://farsi.khamenei.ir/news-content?id=26440 (last accessed May 2023).

10 The decree "on family" can be accessed in Farsi on Khamenei's official website https://farsi.khamenei.ir/news-content?id=34254 (last accessed May 2023).

11 The decree "on family" can be accessed in Farsi on Khamenei's official website https://farsi.khamenei.ir/news-content?id=34254 (last accessed May 2023).

12 The surge in marriage loans and concerns over an increase in child marriage was, for example, reported in the Iranian Student News Agency (ISNA), ازدواج افزایش ۴ برابری کودک همسری در برخی نقاط کشور بدنبال افزایش وام: [Four-time increase in child marriage rates in some areas in Iran following an increase in marriage loans] accessible in Farsi at http://bit.ly/2MQMHVb (last accessed May 2023).

13 Further discussions on the impact of these loans may be found in the following reports by ISNA: کودک ایرانی به قلم طیبه سیاوشی حقوق گمشده‌ی [the Lost Rights of Iranian Children (2019), by Tayebeh Siyavashi] available in Farsi at http://bit.ly/2NXeNyI (last accessed May 2023); کودکان تناقضات قانونی بین پرداخت «وام ازدواج» و «ازدواج»:[Legal contradictions between "Marriage Loan" and "Child Marriage"(2019)], available in Farsi at http://bit.ly/30fGQM5 (last accessed May 2023); عیین محدودیت سنی برای «وام ازدواج» در قانون بودجه: [Limiting the age of marriage for marriage loans (2019)], available in Farsi at http://bit.ly/3sK1HDA (last accessed May 2023).

14 This interview is quoted in the following news report in the Iranian Student News Agency (ISNA), برابری کودک همسری در برخی نقاط کشور بدنبال افزایش وام ازدواج افزایش ۴: accessed May 2023).

## References


ABC News (2012) *Vice Presidential Debate Transcript*, ABC News. https://abcnews.go.com/Politics/OTUS/vice-presidential-debate-transcript-danvilel-ky-oct-11/story?id=17457175

Abdi A (2025) 'A Feminist International Political Economy of Sanctions: Crises and the Shifting Gendered Regimes of Labour and Survival in Iran', *International Feminist Journal of Politics, 27*(1), *81–104. https://doi.org/10.1080/14616742.2025.2454462*

Afshar H (1997) 'Women and Work in Iran', *Political Studies, 45*(4):755–767. https://doi.org/10.1111/1467-9248.00110

Al Jazeera (2012) *Timeline: Sanctions on Iran*, Al Jazeera. https://www.aljazeera.com/economy/2012/10/17/timeline-sanctions-on-iran

Amirahmadi, H. (2015, February 14). *Rouhani's New Budget Offers Pain Without Hope*. American Iranian Council. http://www.us-iran.org/news/2015/2/14/iranian-budget-2015

Arnove A and Abunimah A (eds) (2003) *Iraq Under Siege: The Deadly Impact of Sanctions and War* (Updated ed.) Pluto.

Batmanghelidj E (2020) *Resistance Is Simple, Resilience Is Complex: Sanctions and the Composition of Iranian Trade*, Rethinking Iran @ Johns Hopkins SAIS. https://europe.jhu.edu/DOCUMENTS/ResistanceFile.pdf

Batmanghelidj, E. (2021, November 1). *Explainer: Iran's Frozen Assets | The Iran Primer*. https://iranprimer.usip.org/blog/2021/nov/01/explainer-iran%E2%80%99s-frozen-assets

Barlow, R. (2018). 'The Women's Movement and State Responses to Contentious Campaigns in Iran'. In D. Conduit & S. Akbarzadeh (Eds.), *New opposition in the Middle East,* Palgrave Macmillan:15–40.

Baumann, H., & Roccu, R. (2023). 'International political economy and the state in the Middle East'. *Globalizations*, 1–13. https://doi.org/10.1080/14747731.2023.2223951

BBC News (14 April 2024) *Why Have Israel and Iran Attacked Each Other?* BBC News, accessed 15 January 2025. https://www.bbc.com/news/world-middle-east-68811276

Bieler A and Morton AD (2018) *Global Capitalism, Global War, Global Crisis*, Cambridge University Press.

Bojicic-Dzelilovic V and Turkmani R (2018) 'War Economy, Governance and Security in Syria's Opposition-Controlled Areas', *Stability: International Journal of Security and Development*, *7*(1):1–17.

Chowdhry G and Ling LHM (2010) 'Race(ing) International Relations: A Critical Overview of Postcolonial Feminism in International Relations', in Chowdhry G and Ling LHM (eds) *Oxford Research Encyclopedia of International Studies*, Oxford University Press, doi:10.1093/acrefore/9780190846626.013.413

Davis, S.H. and Ness, I. (eds) (2022) Sanctions As War: Anti-Imperialist Perspectives on American Geo-Economic Strategy, Leiden; Boston: Brill *Studies in Critical Social Sciences*.

Dizaji, S. F., & Farzanegan, M. R. (2021). 'Do Sanctions Constrain Military Spending of Iran?', *Defence and Peace Economics, 32*(2), 125–150. https://doi.org/10.1080/10242694.2019.1622059

Eichler M (2014) 'Militarized Masculinities in International Relations', *The Brown Journal of World Affairs*, *21*(1):81–93.

Elias J (2016) 'Whose Crisis? Whose Recovery? Lessons Learned (and Not) from the Asian crisis', in Hozić AA and True J (eds) *Scandalous Economics*, Oxford University Press:109–125, doi:10.1093/acprof:oso/9780190204235.003.0007

Enloe C (2014) *Bananas, Beaches and Bases: Making Feminist Sense of International Politics*, 2nd ed., Completely Revised and Updated, University of California Press.

Fardoust S (2020) *Macroeconomic Impacts of US Sanctions (2017–2019) on Iran*, Rethinking Iran @ Johns Hopkins SAIS. https://www.rethinkingiran.com/iran-sanctions-reports/fardoust

Fathollah-Nejad, A. (2017). *Rouhani's Neoliberal Doctrine has Failed Iran.* Middle East Institute. https://www.mei.edu/publications/rouhanis-neoliberal-doctrine-has-failed-iran

Fayazmanesh S (2003) 'The Politics of the U.S. Economic Sanctions Against Iran', *Review of Radical Political Economics*, *35*(3):221–240. doi:10.1177/0486613403254535

Geeta C and Nair S (eds) (2013) *Power, Postcolonialism and International Relations,* Routledge, doi:10.4324/9781315017181

Griffin P (2015) 'Crisis, Austerity and Gendered Governance: A Feminist Perspective', *Feminist Review*, *109*(1):49–72. doi:10.1057/fr.2014.44

Halper, L. (2010). 'Law and Iranian women's activism'. In Z. R. Kassam (Ed.), *Women and Islam* (1st edition), Praeger: 3–18.

Harris, K. (2017). *A social revolution: Politics and the welfare state in Iran*. University of California Press.

Harris, K. (2020). '*Iran's Government Expenditure Priorities and Social Policy Burdens During Sanctions'*. Rethinking Iran @ Johns Hopkins SAIS. https://static1.squarespace.com/static/5f0f5b1018e89f351b8b3ef8/t/607edcc8aa744840a99b8b9c/1618926793201/IranUnderSanctions_Harris_v2.pdf

Hozić AA and True J (eds) (2016) *Scandalous Economics: Gender and the Politics of Financial Crises* (Illustrated ed.), Oxford University Press.

Human Rights Watch (2019) Iran: Sanctions Threatening Health, *Human Rights Watch*, https://www.hrw.org/news/2019/10/29/iran-sanctions-threatening-health.

International Monetary Fund (IMF) (2018) 'Islamic Republic of Iran: Selected Issues'. Washington, D.C.: International Monetary Fund. https://www.imf.org/en/Publications/CR/Issues/2018/03/29/Islamic-Republic-of-Iran-Selected-Issues-45768

IRNA (Islamic Republic News Agency) (22 June 2014) *A Martyr's Will: 'My Sister, the Blackness of Your Hijab Is More Effective Than The Redness Of My Blood' [In farsi].* خبرگزاری جمهوری; ایرنا اصلی صفحه| اسلامی |, IRNA News Agency. https://www.irna.ir/news/81238342/خواهر حجاب-شما-کوبنده-تراز-خون-سرخ-من-استوم-صیت-شهید-

Ladier-Fouladi M (2021) 'The Islamic Republic of Iran's New Population Policy and Recent Changes in Fertility', *Iranian Studies*, *54*(5–6):907–930, doi:10.1080/00210862.2021.1884970

Landler M (8 May 2018) *Trump Abandons Iran Nuclear Deal He Long Scorned*, The New York Times. https://www.nytimes.com/2018/05/08/world/middleeast/trump-iran-nuclear-deal.html

Laudati D and Pesaran MH (2023) 'Identifying the Effects of Sanctions on the Iranian Economy Using Newspaper Coverage', *Journal of Applied Econometrics*, *38*(3):271–294, doi:10.1002/jae.2947

Mather Y (2009) 'The Latest Economic Crisis in Iran and the Continued Threat of War', *Critique*, *37*(1):67–79.

Mazarei A (2020) *Inflation Targeting in the Time of Sanctions and Pandemic*, Rethinking Iran @ Johns Hopkins SAIS. https://www.rethinkingiran.com/iran-sanctions-reports/mazarei

Moghadam VM (2003) *Modernizing Women: Gender and Social Change in the Middle East*, 2nd ed., L. Rienner.

Moghadam VM (2024) 'The gendered politics of Iran-U.S. relations: Sanctions, the JCPOA and women's security', *Third World Quarterly*, *45*(7):1199–1218. doi:10.1080/01436597.2024.2314005

Moret ES (2015) 'Humanitarian Impacts of Economic Sanctions on Iran and Syria', *European Security*, *24*(1):120–140. doi:10.1080/09662839.2014.893427

Mueller J and Mueller K (1999) 'Sanctions of Mass Destruction', *Foreign Affairs*, *78*(3):43. doi:10.2307/20049279

Mulder, N. (2022). *The Economic Weapon: The Rise of Sanctions as a Tool of Modern War*. Yale University Press.

Nanopoulos, E. (2019). *The juridification of individual sanctions and the politics of EU law*. Hart.Nephew R (2018) *The Art of Sanctions: A View from the Field*, Columbia University Press.

Osanloo A (2023) Entangled Lives: Enduring Under Sanctions. *Humanity: An International Journal of Human Rights, Humanitarianism, and Development*, *14*(2):262–279, doi:10.1353/hum.2023.a917000

Parent D (24 April 2024) *Iranian Women Violently Dragged from Streets by Police Amid Hijab Crackdown*, The Guardian. https://www.theguardian.com/global-development/2024/apr/24/iranian-women-violently-dragged-from-streets-by-police-amid-hijab-crackdown

Peksen D (2019) 'When Do Imposed Economic Sanctions Work? A Critical Review of the Sanctions Effectiveness Literature', *Defence and Peace Economics*, *30*(6):635–647. doi: 10.1080/10242694.2019.1625250

Peterson, V. S. (2008). '"New Wars" and Gendered Economies'. *Feminist Review, 88*(1), 7–20. https://doi.org/10.1057/palgrave.fr.9400377

Peterson, V. S. (2016). 'Gendering Insecurities, Informalization and "War Economies"'. In W. Harcourt (Ed.), *The Palgrave Handbook of Gender and Development*. Palgrave Macmillan UK: 441–462. https://doi.org/10.1007/978-1-137-38273-3_30

Pettman JJ (1996) *Worlding Women: A Feminist International Politics*, Routledge. doi: 10.4324/9780203991442

Rai S, True J and Tanyag M (2019) 'From Depletion to Regeneration: Addressing Structural and Physical Violence in Post-Conflict Economies', *Social Politics: International Studies in Gender, State & Society*, *26*(4):561–585. doi:10.1093/sp/jxz034

Roberts A and Elias J (2018) 'Financial Crises in Historical Perspective', in Elias J and Roberts A (eds) *Handbook on the International Political Economy of Gender*, Edward Elgar Publishing. doi:10.4337/9781783478842.00028

Roudi-Fahimi, F. (2002). '*Iran's family planning program: Responding to a nation's needs*'. MENA Policy Brief. https://www.prb.org/wp-content/uploads/2016/09/IransFamPlanProg_Eng.pdf

Sameh, C. Z. (2012). '*Signatures, rights, networks: Iranian feminism in the transnational sphere*'. PhD dissertation, Rutgers University. https://rucore.libraries.rutgers.edu/rutgers-lib/37471/

Salehi-Isfahani, D. (2020) '*How sanctions and the pandemic affect Iran's economy*', Qatar University Institutional Repository, http://qspace.qu.edu.qa/handle/10576/15883

Salehi-Isfahani D (2023) 'The impact of sanctions on household welfare and employment in Iran', *Middle East Development Journal*, *15*(2):189–221. doi:10.1080/17938120.2023.2248697

Simons G (2015) *Imposing Economic Sanctions: Legal Remedy Or Genocidal Tool?*, Pluto Press. doi:10.2307/j.ctt18fsbnn

Soltaninejad, M. (2019). 'Coalition-Building in Iran's Foreign Policy: Understanding the "Axis of Resistance"'. *Journal of Balkan and Near Eastern Studies, 21*(6), 716–731. https://doi.org/10.1080/19448953.2018.1506295

Steinberg, G. (2021). *'The "axis of resistance": Iran's expansion in the Middle East is hitting a wall'* (Vol. 6/2021). Stiftung Wissenschaft und Politik -SWP- Deutsches Institut für Internationale Politik und Sicherheit. https://doi.org/10.18449/2021RP06

Tafakori S (2023) 'The Intimate Public as a Decolonial Lens: "Cripping" Affect, Nationalism and Imperial Violence', *Review of International Studies*, *49*(4):694–720.

Tasnim News (22 August 2024a) *Qasem Suleimani's advice to women on how to defend Shi'ism in Syria*, Tasnim. https://www.tasnimnews.com/fa/news/1403/06/13/3134741/%D8%AA%D9%88%D8%B5%DB%8C%D9%87-%D8%AD%D8%A7%D8%AC-%D9%82%D8%A7%D8%B3%D9%85-%D8%A8%D9%87-%D8%AF%D8%AE%D8%AA%D8%B1%D8%A7%D9%86%DB%8C-%DA%A9%D9%87-%D9%85%DB%8C-%D8%AE%D9%88%D8%A7%D8%B3%D8%AA%D9%86%D8%AF-%D9%85%D8%AF%D8%A7%D9%81%D8%B9-%D8%AD%D8%B1%D9%85-%D8%B4%D9%88%D9%86%D8%AF

Tasnim News (21 November 2024b) *The Soldiers in Syria Are Defenders of Both Women and Shia Religion [In Farsi].* خبرگزاری تسنیم | Tasnim. //www.tasnimnews.com/fa/news/1403/09/27/3220840/سربازان-مدافعان-حرم-و-حریم-هستند

The Economist (14 April 2024) *Iran and Israel's Shadow War Explodes into the Open*, The Economist. https://www.economist.com/middle-east-and-africa/2024/04/14/iran-and-israels-shadow-war-explodes-into-the-open

Tickner JA (1992) *Gender in International Relations: Feminist Perspectives on Achieving Global Security*, Columbia University Press.

True J (2012) *The Political Economy of Violence Against Women*, Oxford University Press. doi:10.1093/acprof:oso/9780199755929.001.0001

True J and Hozić AA (2020) 'Don't Mention the War! International Financial Institutions and the Gendered Circuits of Violence in Post-Conflict', *Review of International Political Economy*, *27*(6):1193–1213. doi:10.1080/09692290.2020.1732443

Warde I (2007) *The Price of Fear: Al-Qaeda and the Truth Behind the Financial War on Terror*, Tauris.

Whitworth, S. (2000). Theory and exclusion: Gender, masculinity, and international political economy. In R. Stubbs & G. R. D. Underhill (Eds.), *Political economy and the changing global order* (2nd ed). Oxford University Press.Yuval-Davis N (1997) *Gender & Nation*, Sage Publications.

Zahirinejad M (2019) 'The Economic Effects of Sanctions and the Iranian Middle Class', in Gärtner, H., & Shahmoradi, M. (Eds.). *Iran in the International System: Between Great Powers and Great Ideas (1st ed.)*, Routledge:108–129.

# PART II

# Gendered Circuits (II)

## Temporalities

# 5

# THE MATERIAL BASIS OF GENDER-BASED VIOLENCE AND ITS CIRCUITS

## A political economy perspective on post-war Bosnia and Herzegovina

*Vesna Bojicic-Dzelilovic, Denisa Kostovicova and Marsha Henry*

When the killer livestreamed on Instagram the abuse and murder of his ex-wife in the small town of Gradačac in northeastern Bosnia and Herzegovina in the summer of 2023, the violence and the manner of its execution made femicide brutally visible in this post-conflict country and globally.[1] Although a contested term, femicide refers to the murder of a woman because she is a woman (Dawson and Mobayed Vega 2023: 5–6). A phenomenon of femicide involves a complex reality surrounding the act of murder, which may include abuse that preceded the murder not being taken seriously by police when reporting abuse, or delays in investigating abuse (Hefti 2022: 2). All of these applied in the case of this Bosnian victim who perished at the hands of a former partner with a police record. Bosnians took to the streets demanding the end to violence against women. However, since this shocking killing, condemned by the Spokesperson for the Secretary-General of the United Nations Stéphane Dujarric (AP 2023), the country recorded new murders that took place out of the public eye and received limited media attention. The United Nations in Bosnia and Herzegovina (2024) have been "alarmed by the frequency of these horrific crimes and the worsening situation of gender-based violence." According to Ingrid Macdonald, the United Nations Resident Coordinator in Bosnia and Herzegovina, 60 women were killed by their current or former partners in the country from 2018 to 2024 (*Sarajevo Times* 2024). Moreover, the number of women victims of men's violence in Bosnia and Herzegovina has been rising amidst inaction (SEESAC 2023a: 7), primarily in the legal sphere. Femicide is not included as a separate criminal offence either in the Bosnian state's penal code or in the penal codes of Bosnia's two entities (Konstantinović Vilić and Petrušić 2022). Yet, for the judicial system to send "a clear message that femicide is unacceptable, it has to be named as such" (Đukanović 2020: 11).[2]

DOI: 10.4324/9781003571667-7

As many other countries, Bosnia and Herzegovina is witnessing a vigorous debate over the persistence of violence against women – an issue that remains prominent in the country's post-conflict recovery. We explore the complex, overlapping, and mutually reinforcing gendered circuits of violence – where the legacies of war intersect with the realities of peacebuilding, and local political, economic, and social conditions are inseparable from global forces. Our research highlights the diverse forms and underlying causes of gender-based violence, with economic factors emerging as the most prominent. This frequently noted insight from conversations with women across Bosnia and Herzegovina has motivated us to examine the material basis of gender-based violence in societies recovering from militarised conflict – such as the 1992–1995 war in Bosnia and Herzegovina. Historically, studies on militarised conflicts have underemphasised the crucial role of material processes in enabling, driving, and sustaining armed violence. There has been a surprising lack of attention to how armed conflicts reshape resource control and distribution, often normalising violence as a means of acquiring economic assets.

Violence, especially in conflicts where identity plays a central role, is strategically directed at specific social groups and targets locations rich in resources. Acts of killing, physical harm inflicted on human bodies for asset seizure, ethnic cleansing, dispossession of livelihoods, and sexual violence – including rape – all constitute economic predation tactics used both to finance combat and for personal financial gain (Le Sage 1998; Laudati and Mertens 2019). In the context of violence against women, this dynamic is captured by the "rape-resource" narrative on the armed conflict in the Eastern Democratic Republic of Congo (DRC), where sexual violence is framed as a "tool for accessing mineral wealth" (Laudati and Mertens 2019: 59). These practices are a part of the political economy of resource control and redistribution, where violence functions as a factor of production, distribution, and competition, which themselves are profoundly gendered (Cockayne 2010).

While these violent practices are intrinsic to militarised conflict, their persistence beyond wartime is exacerbated by the ongoing resilience of wartime actors, vested interests, and political agendas. As such, they impact governance in the long run. Post-war economic governance that is aligned with a globalised peacebuilding agenda aims to establish competitive liberal markets. However, this transition has often resulted in diminished and inequitable economies that underpin women's precarious economic status, while making them vulnerable to multiple other harms. Our analysis seeks to contribute to structural explanations of post-conflict gender-based violence against women that foreground the continuum of gender-based violence across war and peace (Cockburn 2004; Cockburn 2014). The political economy perspective we adopt critically examines distinctions and overlaps– both theoretical and practical – between war and post-war economic conditions, between local and global dynamics and between formal and informal actors in post-conflict societies. Understanding their intersections is essential to understanding the making and the remaking of the material basis that sustains circuits of gender-based violence.

Ultimately, the material basis of gender-based violence emerges as a cumulative consequence of intertwined local and global political and socio-economic dynamics along the war-to-peace trajectory. This process manifests in the form of unequal and fragile economic systems that reinforce women's economic poverty and material insecurity. The endurance of such inequities is not incidental but rather the result of purposeful actions by main protagonists in war economies that insert themselves in the governance structures of post-war societies. As war-affected countries reintegrate into global markets in the course of peacebuilding, these actors remain posed to maintain and protect inequalities in access to resources and opportunities, which in turn rekindles other types of violence constituting its gendered circuits.

Our methodology involves a qualitative multi-method analysis of multiple sources of data on gender-based violence in Bosnia, while heeding requirements for ethical research practice (Boesten and Henry 2018). We draw on field notes and observations from workshops and informal interviews with practitioners from Bosnia specialising in support for victims of gender-based violence held in the United Kingdom and in Bosnia in 2017. They also informed the follow-up research that included semi-structured interviews with human rights activists and analysts in Bosnia in 2018. Systematic analysis of local newspapers, laws, and reports issued by governmental bodies, international organisations as well as international and local civil society organisations was used to triangulate observational and interview data.

## Material processes of war and continuities of gender-based violence

Continuities of violence by type, space and temporalities have been variably theorised in the feminist scholarship interested in gender-based violence and in this volume on war economy as gendered circuits. Kelly's (1987, 1988) ground-breaking study theorised the continuity of violence in relation to sexual violence, drawing attention to wider systems and structures that undergird such phenomena in conflict-affected societies. Kelly (1987, 1988) uses the continuum of violence to contextualise women's experiences across a range of behaviours, incidents and experiences, embedding them in structural rather than purely individual or emotional explanations. Krause (2015) proposes that the complexities of gender relations in conflict-affected societies demonstrate an array of vulnerabilities in relation to the continuation of the exercise of gendered forms of power. Violence persists because of three factors: gendered power structures, ineffective or insufficient law enforcement, and traumatic events (Krause 2015: 16). Jacqui True (2012) argues that the political and economic structures of capitalism make women more vulnerable to various forms of violence than is generally recognised. She suggests that where, which, and how violence occurs against women cannot be understood independently of economic policies of the state, the gendered division of labour and the gender-specific dimensions of war (True 2010). This line of argument is extended by Alsaba and Kapilashrami (2016: 12) who demonstrate how location (in all its aspects) relates to forms of violence that women experience during a conflict and in its aftermath.

These approaches to the continuities of gender-based violence recognise the need to consider structural dimensions in the wider political context of victims' lives to understand how violence occurs at multiple (macro-, meso- and micro-) levels. They demonstrate that an explanation incorporating structural dimensions is crucial for understanding both the incidence and varied forms of gender-based violence in post-conflict contexts, as well as resistance against patriarchy and the potential for social transformation. The political economy perspective in these accounts provides a compelling analysis of the *types* and *spaces* where gender-based violence occurs. However, a significant gap remains in theorising its persistence, highlighting the need to examine political economy across war and peace as the structural condition shaping post-conflict environments. Viewed through this lens, the political economy perspective not only explains how women experience harm but also reveals how structural, direct, and cultural/symbolic violence intersect to create systemic vulnerability, alienation, and suffering – along with their material underpinnings (Galtung 1990). Foregrounding interconnectedness in structural conditions across local and global scales provides insights into factors conducive to emergence and entrenchment of circuits of violence against women during transition from war to peace.

## A political economy of war and its aftermath

From a political economy perspective, war functions as a system of power, profit, and protection (Keen 2008; Cramer 2006), serving as a form of social order that exacerbates material inequalities. Therefore, understanding war-induced economic changes and how they shape post-war economic governance is essential to analysing the material foundations of continuing violence against women.

Warfare inherently involves economic activities conducted through illegal, coercive, and extractive means, deeply impacting local societies. Resource mobilisation occurs within a context of severe disruption to economic, institutional, and security structures, often compounded by limited access to external funding – including support from friendly foreign states, which is influenced by great power contestation. While not unique to any one era, this self-financing model has been particularly pronounced in post-Cold War conflicts, which coincided with a peak of contemporary era of globalisation. Indeed, their inner workings at the nexus of identity politics, armed violence, and criminality were often described as akin to "shadow globalisation" (Jung 2002).

Criminal enterprises such as sex trafficking frequently serve as self-financing mechanisms for certain armed groups, operating alongside other violent forms of resource extraction – such as the expropriation of food supplies – that disproportionately affect women (Laudati and Mertens 2019). The transnationalisation of warfare has enabled politico-military elites to leverage their connections to the global marketplace, including criminal connections, to compete and collude in violence as a means of securing rapid financial gains. This process has significantly weakened the state's ability to monopolise violence, effectively manage resource extraction, and provide for the public in ways that ensure equity and socially just outcomes as attributes of positive peace (Heupel 2006; Wennmann 2011).

In armed conflict environments, local economies – integrated into both legal and illicit global resource flows – blur the distinction between local and global, as well as between formal and informal economic activities and their actors. Through violent resource reallocation, societies are reordered, and in the aftermath of war, neoliberal globalisation becomes central to their functioning, at the same time as it generates new incentives in governance that prioritise pursuit of private interests through public institutions. This governance model fosters extreme forms of structural inequity and unequal distribution of power. The ascendance of a new class of (male) rent-seeking war entrepreneurs is paralleled by large segments of the population struggling to meet their basic needs (Staniland 2013). Among the most vulnerable are women – many of whom have experienced wartime sexual violence, displacement, and the loss of both livelihood and male breadwinner security (O'Reilly 2012; Kondylis 2010).

Neoliberal economic policies, practices, and norms within the context of institutional dysfunction of post-war environments reinforce harmful conditions for women by shaping domestic authorities' policy choices. Wartime actors, including perpetrators of rape and other war crimes, are frequently integrated into post-war structures of authority, securing immunity and impunity. Such consolidation of power ensures that structural inequality, with its gendered dimensions, becomes embedded in post-war governance (O'Reilly 2018). The resulting governance practices privilege men and women of certain identities – primarily those connected to wartime elites engaged in predatory economic activities. Consequently, peacebuilding morphs into "war by other means," in other words negative peace as local authorities selectively implement externally mandated economic reforms to serve particular actors and interests (Goodhand 2004). Resources intended for reconstruction are frequently redirected away from investments in socio-economic infrastructure that could mitigate gender-specific vulnerabilities and, instead, flow into private hands (Kurtenbach and Rettberg 2018). Rather than being a mere consequence of inadequate implementation of a liberal peace model under international oversight, widespread poverty, exclusion, and marginalisation emerge as defining features of a particular type of evolving neoliberal capitalism in post-conflict regions. This system – shaped by global economic dynamics – ultimately reinforces the material foundations for continued gender-based violence long after the war's end.

Traditional feminist political economy has not always thoroughly examined the connections between war and peace, or between formal and informal actors and institutions, in explaining gender-based violence in post-conflict settings.

Specifically, it has not fully addressed conceptually the blurring of distinctions among political, military, economic, and criminal elites in contemporary wars, nor the implications of this fusion for post-war economic governance (Bojicic-Dzelilovic et al. 2022; Le Sage 1998; Goodhand 2004). Therefore, we argue that the interconnectedness of local and global dynamics, alongside the deepening of social, political, and economic inequalities within emergent neoliberal capitalism – rooted in wartime capital accumulation – deserves further scrutiny in understanding continuities of violence and its gendered circuits. While scholars have explored neoliberal, transitional, and conflict dynamics to analyse gender-based violence (Đurić Kuzmanović and Pajvančić-Cizelj 2018), the challenge lies in moving beyond treating these processes as parallel or sequential. Instead, it is necessary to investigate how they co-constitute the material basis of gender-based violence both during war and in its aftermath.

Extensive feminist political economy research demonstrates that post-war economic recovery under neoliberal transition often reproduces conditions of poverty – such as joblessness – and limits access to social welfare for both women and men. Within this framework, women's already marginalised socio-economic position heightens their vulnerability to male dominance and violence. What requires further attention is how the socio-economic and governance structures characteristic of this neoliberal capitalist model, which is pursued in the context of weak state institutions, and which integrates conflict-affected societies into global governance systems, reinforce patriarchal ideologies and gender hierarchies.

Post-conflict gender-based violence should be understood as occurring at the intersection of these processes, as formal and informal, local and global forces

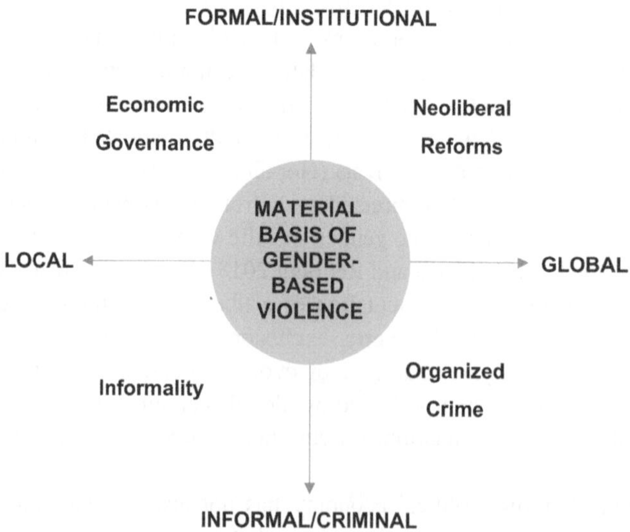


FIGURE 5.1 War and Post-War Political Economy and the Continuum of Violence.

simultaneously shape structural conditions that perpetuate violence at the local level (see Figure 5.1). Our empirical analysis underscores the interconnectedness of these dynamics, which is essential to understanding the material basis sustaining gender-based violence in all its forms within post-war contexts.

While not intending to be prescriptive, we use the quadrant to capture the interconnectedness of the war and post-war political economy in our conceptual framing and to analyse the material basis of gender-based violence.

## Gender-based violence in Bosnia's war and peace

Although Bosnia and Herzegovina has been at peace for some 30 years, the country – and much of the Western Balkans – remains marked by a latent threat of armed violence, sustained by proponents of ethno-national politics and an economic order shaped by illicit wartime wealth accumulation that benefits them. This linkage between ethno-nationalism and an inequitable economy (Bojicic-Dzelilovic 2013) has created a system that reproduces violence in multiple forms: from direct physical harm to invisible systemic oppression and cultural and symbolic forms of violence.

Ample evidence attests to this ongoing cycle of violence, which continues to disrupt the everyday lives of local people and communities. It is reflected in the statistics on rising crime rates – including armed robberies, murders, and kidnappings – and in the persistent discrimination and marginalisation of certain social groups and regions. One stark example is the segregation of schoolchildren along ethnic lines under the "two schools under one roof" policy in Bosnia, as well as their tacit segregation in other social spaces. Additionally, cultural dominance manifests through public assertions of identity, such as displays of ethnic nationalism during football matches. Within this volatile landscape, gender-based violence – including femicide, its most extreme form – has continued to rise unchecked, reflecting a troubling continuity with the violence women suffered during the war.

Sexual violence, including rape, against women and men was a prominent feature of the Bosnian war. In the case of women, it occurred on a mass scale (Clark 2017). It was integral to the conduct of war strategically. But it was also a type of opportunistic behaviour in the context of the break-down of law and order and was used widely as a tool of resource appropriation (Hansen 2000). While there are difficulties involved in establishing precise figures (Lazarević and Tadić 2018: 7; Babović et al. 2013), research points to a steady increase of certain forms of gender-based violence in Bosnia since the war's end. It has culminated in a "femicide epidemic" (Fena 2017). New patterns of victimisation have emerged. Victims of violence are increasingly younger including school-age girls, and violence inflicted by small arms, such as "Kalashnikov" rifles, is rising (*Žurnal* 2009; Isović 2012; UNDP/SSEESAC 2007: 3). The proliferation of these weapons is a direct consequence of armed conflict. Many soldiers brought weapons and other explosive devices home after demobilisation. Large quantities of illicit weapons that circulate in the country and are available on the black market also contribute to the regional instability (Kržalić 2011: 8). An estimated 750,000 unregistered firearms from the 1992 to 1995 war have remained in Bosnia and Herzegovina (Rose 2016). There has been some progress in efforts to collect and destroy illicit weapons and ammunition (SEESAC 2023b), but these have yet to make a palpable difference.

Violence against women in post-war Bosnia must be understood within the broader context of social stigma – a form of symbolic violence that, as Galtung (1990: 291) explains, "can be used to justify or legitimize direct or structural violence." The persistence of patriarchal norms, reignited by ethno-national politics during the war, is evident in practices such as disowning women who decide to leave abusive partners (Bljesak 2017). Women are frequently blamed for the violence inflicted upon them (CEDAW 2005), leading many to remain silent about their abuse (Denda Borjan 2016). As in many cases of intimate partner violence, women often internalise self-blame (and shame) for the violence they suffered. One victim, who left her husband after years of abuse, described how she rationalised his behaviour, believing, "I thought that it's not easy for him; he is a former soldier, struggling with post-traumatic stress disorder, sleeplessness, dissatisfaction because he does not have a job" (Savić 2013; Klaric et al. 2011). This deeply ingrained stigma reinforces silence, further amplifying women's vulnerability. Meanwhile, men remain largely unaccountable, and state institutions continue to evade their responsibility to act (Matić 2017).

Women in post-war Bosnia have faced distinct gendered vulnerabilities in accessing employment and livelihood opportunities, contributing to the rise of transactional sex with the gatekeepers – a phenomenon in which sex and the body are commodified as economic assets (Laudati and Mertens 2019). This trend is directly linked to the socio-economic constraints imposed on women within Bosnia's post-war economy. The material conditions underpinning violence against women stem from externally driven economic policies promoted by global economic governance structures. These policies have been implemented within an institutional and societal context profoundly shaped by the violent accumulation of capital by ethno-nationalist elites. As Gilbert and Mujanović (2015) argue, the resulting "political and economic order of inequity and dispossession of the means of dignified livelihood" has significantly eroded local society's ability to break this cycle of exploitation. Ultimately, the rise of transactional sex serves as a stark indicator of the ways in which women remain among the primary victims of these systemic economic and political processes.

## The material basis of gender-based violence: a political economy perspective

Post-conflict gender-based violence in Bosnia takes place at the intersection of normative change and deficient governance practices.[3] Despite its outward resemblance to the liberal market democracy, the country's post-war governance is dysfunctional. Normative change consists of reforms of domestic laws in compliance with international norms, aimed at addressing gender dimensions of public policy (CEDAW 2005: 6–12; O'Reilly 2012),[4] in general, and tackling domestic violence, in particular. State dysfunction manifests in the limited and uneven enforcement of these legal provisions aimed at protecting women and tackling gender-based violence. It also extends to related fields including legislation on small arms and organised crime. Reforms related to enduring socio-economic inequalities concern property legislation, which is consequential for women's access to economic opportunities. Flawed implementation of laws in the context of a weak post-conflict state is bound up with either non-existing or unreliable funding for policies that enhance women's welfare and protection because they are considered as second order priority (Pupavac 2005).

The failed implementation of the law on protection from domestic violence in both entities in Bosnia exemplifies the gap between normative change and governance practices (Puljek Shank 2017). The relevant laws comprise a series of protective measures, such as restraining or anti-stalking orders. However, on rare occasions when such measures were approved by the courts, they were not enforced (*Bljesak* 2017). A lack of legal protection impacts fundamentally on multiple forms of violence women suffer.

Since 2008, the provision of shelter in safe houses was introduced as an additional measure of protection (Muftić, Dejkić and Fansher 2019).[5] These measures are also rarely approved by the courts, in a clear violation of official legislation. In addition, the funding for safe houses is subject to complex procedures within multiple governance levels in Bosnia and is split between the state-level and local authorities (OSCE 2009: 13). A lack of commitment of the local authorities to tackle violence against women (Denda Borjan 2016) amplifies the absence of institutional remedies impacting women's vulnerability. It is illustrated by a respondent in the study by Babović et al. (2013: 97), who said, "If I divorced him, I would have nothing, my husband would take it all away from me, he would bribe the court, and then where would I go and what would I live off?"

The inconsistent enforcement of domestic violence laws reflects a larger pattern of state dysfunction in Bosnia, stemming from the financial constraints of this post-war state. Post-war rehabilitation involves numerous competing priorities, carefully monitored by international funders. As a result, resources for implementing gender laws – requiring increased taxation (Shaxson 2015) – remain insufficient. Ultimately, gender equality policies exist in name only, as Bosnia's weak economy, exacerbated by widespread tax evasion, undermines their effectiveness. In this context, gender budgeting, promoted by international actors to combat gender discrimination, amounts to little more than a token gesture (Bojicic-Dzelilovic and Hozić 2020).

### *Neoliberal reforms and violence against women*

Post-war economic development, which has led to precariousness among some sections of the Bosnian population, has disproportionately affected women who are disadvantaged by skewed labour market opportunities and outcomes. The gender gap in the activity rate and the employment rate in Bosnia and Herzegovina was the highest among the Western Balkan countries in 2018; activity rate and employment rate for men were 53% and 44.1%, respectively, compared to 34.4% and 25%, respectively, for women (World Bank 2019; Bosnia and Herzegovina Agency for Statistics n.d.). The rate of unemployment is higher among women than men, and is characterised by a high share of long-term unemployment (World Bank 2019). Women are disadvantaged by economic traditions that limit their ownership of assets/land to use as collateral – as much as 70% of land ownership is accounted for by men (Cancho and Elwan 2015: 36). Hence, the share of registered women entrepreneurs is lower than that of men (Efendić et al 2018b). These inequalities, along with women's limited access to education (Somun-Krupalija 2011), reinforce women's dependence on men and their marginal place and status in society, as evidenced in the context of the gendered division of household labour and in incidence of intimate partner abuse.

According to practitioners in non-governmental organisations (NGOs), about 90% of women who survived sexual violence in war have also experienced intimate partner and/or domestic violence (Sorguc 2015). Like other victims of violence, they may find it difficult to exit the relationship due to fear of destitution. As one survivor of sexual violence put it, "I spent 20 days in the camp where I was raped. Physical and psychological abuse in the marriage lasted much longer" (Sorguc ibid). While the women's movement in post-war Bosnia has organised around women's extraordinary resilience and self-sufficiency in the wake of sexual and gender-based violence and as a way of combating stigma (Helms 2013; Björkdahl 2012), women's economic precarity and continuing vulnerability have received less attention. Violence prevents women from participation in the labour market, while economic dependence and material insecurity increase the risk of violence. The inequalities in access to economic opportunities manifest as widespread feminisation of poverty in the post-war Bosnia and across the Western Balkans. The proportion of women among the poor has been rising everywhere except in Montenegro. Underinvestment in social infrastructure because of economic policy choices works to reinforce gender-based violence since it is foremost women who shoulder the negative effects of deteriorating health and education services provision, and of care services for the elderly and children.

### *Women and the informal economy*

The informal economy, which expanded during the war as the formal economy contracted, has continued to grow in the post-war period (Krstić and Sanfey 2007; Bojicic-Dzelilovic 2013; Ortlieb et al. 2019). As recently as 2018, it was estimated to account for approximately 30% of GDP, driven primarily by a weak institutional framework and low tax compliance (Efendic et al. 2018a: 80). Moreover, pervasive political corruption in post-war Bosnia has normalised rule-breaking, including tax evasion (Efendic et al. 2018a: 80), making it a widely accepted practice in everyday life (Jansen, Brković, and Čelebičić 2016). A 2018 survey revealed that roughly 40% of respondents believed tax evasion was justified in such circumstances.

The incentives for engaging in the informal economy vary, but the most significant factor is the lack of formal employment, which has pushed both men and women into informal work. Single mothers rely on informal jobs to support themselves and their children (Sorguc 2015). Additionally, women often face pressure to supplement household income, even when both spouses hold formal jobs. Many informal roles are distinctly gendered, particularly those in catering, retail, domestic services, and agriculture – sectors characterised by precarious employment opportunities and conditions. These jobs often entail low and irregular wages, poor working conditions, a lack of welfare protections, and the absence of formal contracts. Women in the informal workforce may also experience discrimination from male business owners yet remain trapped due to a lack of viable alternatives (Efendic et al. 2018a). This precarious employment has increased economic insecurity for women, especially vulnerable groups such as single mothers, war widows, and displaced persons.

Furthermore, men use women's marginal and vulnerable position to maintain labour market advantage and household dominance (Savić 2013). By withdrawing financial support, men force women into situations of dependence, and often onto neighbours and extended family. This can involve various forms of informal work, such as domestic cleaning and baby-sitting (*Bljesak* 2017; Babović et al. 2013; Efendić et al. 2018b). In the aftermath of the war, some women have been pressured into bearing more children regardless of financial limitations. Similarly, women are expected to look after elderly relatives in an extended family. This increases their involvement in unrecorded informal economy, resulting in them bearing a double burden— in the public and private spheres (Efendić et al. 2018b). Women's vulnerability emerges because of a complex mix of socio-economic and cultural processes related to the Bosnian war and pre-war social patriarchal practices.

Ultimately, the formal and informal economy routinely fail women pushing them to the black zone of the marketplace. It is an open secret that a job in the public administration requires access to personal networks and the distribution of bribes, which only exacerbates entry barriers for women who do not have access to such social capital and to such male-dominated networks (Brković 2015).

### *The post-conflict criminal economy, sex trafficking, and gender-based violence*

The material basis of continuing violence against women in the aftermath of a militarised conflict must be analysed alongside the evolution of Bosnia's criminal economy. As open violence gave way to latent threats, the nature and methods of criminal activity have changed. During the war, resource appropriation frequently involved extreme violence, including killings. In the post-war period, these methods were largely replaced by extortion, racketeering, and coercion – though politically motivated murders, as well as assassinations of prominent businessmen and independent journalists, have remained a regular occurrence. Persistent underdevelopment, widespread poverty, limited labour market opportunities, and weak rule of law have enabled criminal networks to establish powerful and enduring regional economies across the post-war Balkans (Haynes 2010, 1794; Festic and Rausche 2004). For example, one particularly prominent form of criminal activity has been sex trafficking, which has had a particularly adverse impact on women. It flourished during the war, intertwined with the trade of arms, drugs, and other high-value goods. A striking example is the trafficking operations through the infamous Arizona Market in northeastern Bosnia that was originally set up and endorsed by the international community to promote inter-ethnic reconciliation through commerce (Haynes 2010: 1795). The expansion of trafficking in the post-war period was initially driven by the presence of approximately 50,000 foreign troops, predominantly male. It established a lucrative market, drawing participation from international and local humanitarian workers, civil servants, diplomats, and businessmen – many of whom were connected to powerful local political and economic networks.

Porous borders in the region facilitate the operation of criminal networks which enjoy the protection of powerful local politicians and businessmen, while at the same time they are the sites of political contestation. Many of these networks involved in small arms and human trafficking were established before or during the war with direct involvement or approval of local political, economic and military elites. This is illustrated by the mushrooming of bars "employing" female victims of trafficking originally from outside Bosnia, specifically from Romania, Moldova, Ukraine and Russia (Isović 2012; Nikolić-Ristanović 2003). The effectiveness of criminal networks owes to a transnational dimension of their operation (through regional and international connections), enabled by Bosnia's inadequate legislation and institutional capacity to address the problem (Isović 2013). Despite the government's formal commitment to various regional and international initiatives targeting organised crime, in which human trafficking has been prominent, post-war Bosnia has become a favourable environment for illicit and illegal activities including women as victims.

Although trafficking and sexual exploitation of adolescents and women is generally less visible than in the immediate post-war period, it continues nowadays mostly in private flats, motels and petrol stations (Isović 2013; Jurilj 2016). Women are often subject to physical and psychological abuse within these sites; some have their documents confiscated by pimps, traffickers and police officials (Isović 2012). A further development in the evolution of criminal economy involving sex trafficking is the export of local Bosnian women and the selling of children for sex through channels operated by transnational criminal networks (Isović 2013; Brkanic 2016; Buka 2013). This illustrates the conflation of local and global dynamics in the continuing gender-based violence.

The post-conflict entrenchment of the criminal sector illustrates the interconnectedness between formal economic mismanagement and weak state institutions, against the background of the continuity of war and post-war actors who are in charge of neoliberal transition. As is the case with women engaged in informal economy, women's precarious socio-economic position makes them more vulnerable to, and dependent upon, illicit and illegal activities. According to an OSCE official, women accept options of sexual servitude in the absence of a range of legitimate employment opportunities (Isović 2013).

## Conclusion

This study contributes to analyses of gendered circuits of violence and capital by highlighting the "intimate connections between war, political economy, nationalism, and human displacement and their various impacts across scale" (Giles and Hyndman 2004: 314). We argue that structural accounts of gender-based violence often fail to capture the cumulative and intersecting effects of war and post-war transitions that perpetuate gender inequalities. Our analysis focuses on the material foundations of violence, emphasising the economic changes that occur during war and their lasting consequences, while challenging binary distinctions between global and local, as well as formal and informal post-war transition processes.

From a war and post-war political economy perspective, we demonstrate how economic incentives – created through violence as a means of resource extraction during war – have long-term detrimental effects, particularly on women's welfare and security. War economies defined as encompassing "organization and development of a society's legal and illegal resource flows in support or as a result of conflict and violence" (Kurtenbach and Rettberg 2018: 2), continue to shape local post-war conditions. These economies are complexly layered (Laudati and Mertens 2019), exhibiting contextual variations in how violence is used for production, distribution, and competition over resources with embedded structural violence as a shared feature.

In Bosnia, the war was waged as a transnationalised effort to build an (ethnic) nation-state, strengthening illegal and criminal economies and empowering domestic actors who operated through diffuse transnational networks. This reconfiguration of power has undermined post-war institution-building and resource governance. Steeped in systemic corruption and disregard for the rule of law, the post-war dispensation of power has nurtured conditions in which gender-based violence remains unchecked. Reordering the economy and the society through the violent extraction and control of resources, and maintaining an unequal and exclusionary economy, reproduces material conditions that sustain gender-based violence.

Building on this reconceptualisation, we have examined the various forms of violence against women in Bosnia and the failure of both local and international institutions to address their vulnerabilities. Our analysis is grounded in women's accounts of widespread insecurity, including their exclusion from essential services, education programmes, and labour markets. We argue that these conditions are not merely a consequence of war-inflicted destruction, or the currently poor socio-economic conditions shaped by neoliberal restructuring in a post-conflict setting. Rather, they stem from deep-seated institutional dysfunction, which, compounded by ethnic polarisation, has led to the systematic political and economic neglect of marginalised groups, particularly women. Furthermore, public policies – distorted by a skewed incentive structure and interests formed through war and influenced by global policy decisions – have had long-term, devastating consequences not only for women but also for men.

Our analysis seeks to illuminate how structural, direct, and symbolic forms of violence against women intersect along the war-to-peace continuum, shaped by enduring inequalities, patriarchal structures, and entrenched circuits of violence. Despite extensive scholarship on gender-based violence in Bosnia, this dimension remains underexplored (except see Nikolić-Ristanović 1999; Pupavac 2005; Đurić Kuzmanović and Pajvančić-Cizelj 2018). Given that many Bosnians recognise the political economy as a fundamental driver of violence across the war-to-peace continuum – as evidenced in our field research – addressing the material basis of structural gender-based violence is crucial for advancing conceptual frameworks and empirical analyses of these violent circuits in the feminist and post-conflict scholarship.

Above all, this study underscores the importance of situating post-war gender-based violence within the broader political and economic contexts of war-affected societies, whose material conditions remain shaped by conflict even after it ends. Moreover, global governance ideologies interact with these localised conditions and play a critical role in shaping the persistence of gendered violence against both men and women. The continued presence of coercive and exploitative relations – established through Bosnia's violent repositioning into global markets – reflects the lasting impact of the post-Yugoslav experience, highlighting the war economy as a mechanism that perpetuates the marginalisation of peripheral societies within the system of contemporary capitalism.

## Notes

1 The killer subsequently shot two other victims and committed suicide. Henceforth, we use Bosnia as a short form for Bosnia and Herzegovina.
2 This chapter is a significantly extended and developed analysis of the continuum of gender-based violence that was first published under the CC BY 4.0 license as Denisa Kostovicova, Vesna Bojicic-Dzelilovic, and Marsha Henry. 2020. "Drawing on the Continuum: A War and Post-war Political Economy of Gender-based Violence in Bosnia and Herzegovina." *International Feminist Journal of Politics* 22(2): 250–272. https://doi.org/10.1080/14616742.2019.1692686
3 For an extended discussion of empirical insights in this and in the following subsections, see Kostovicova, Bojicic-Dzelilovic, and Henry (2020).
4 Another example is a recognition of women victims of violence as a separate category in the state-level Action Plan for Employment for 2017 (Mucović 2017).
5 The total of nine safe houses in the entire country have been run by NGOs and dependent on external donor funding (Ministarstvo za ljudska prava i izbeglice Bosne i Herzegovine 2018).

## References


Alsaba, Khuloud, and Anuj Kapilashrami (2016) 'Understanding Women's Experience of Violence and the Political Economy of Gender in Conflict: The Case of Syria', *Reproductive Health Matters* 24(47): 5–17.

Babović, Marija, Olivera Pavlović, Katarina Ginić and Nina Karađinović (2013) 'Prevalence and Characteristics of Violence against Women in Bosnia and Herzegovina. Agency for Gender Equality of Bosnia and Herzegovina & Ministry for Human Rights and Refugees of Bosnia and Herzegovina'. Sarajevo: Gender Equality Agency of Bosnia and Herzegovina.

Björkdahl, Annika (2012) 'A Gender-Just Peace? Exploring the Post-Dayton Peace Process in Bosnia', *Peace & Change* 37(2): 286–317.

Bljesak (2017) 'Od samouništenja do mirnog života', Bljesak.info. 23 November. https://www.bljesak.info/obitelj/lifestyle/bebe-od-sest-mjeseci-savrseno-razumiju-roditelje/219440

Bojicic-Dzelilovic, Vesna (2013) 'Informality, Inequality and Social Reintegration in Post-War Transition', *Studies in Social Justice* 7(2): 211–228.

Bojicic-Dzelilovic, Vesna, Denisa Kostovicova and Ahmet Suerdem (2022) 'Persistence of Informal Networks and Liberal Peacebuilding: Evidence from Bosnia and Herzegovina', *Journal of International Relations and Development* 25: 182–209.

Bojicic-Dzelilovic, Vesna and Aida A. Hozić (2020) 'Taxing for Inequalities: Gender Budgeting in the Western Balkans', *Review of International Political Economy* 27(6): 1280–1304.

Boesten, Jelke and Marsha Henry (2018) 'Between Fatigue and Silence: The Challenges of Conducting Research on Sexual Violence in Conflict', *Social Politics: International Studies in Gender, State & Society* 25(4): 568–588.

Bosnia and Herzegovina Agency for Statistics (n.d.) www.bhas.gov.ba

Brkanic, Dzana (2016) 'Spike in Child Trafficking Causes Concern in Bosnia', *Balkan Insight*, November 21. https://www.balkaninsight.com/en/article/spike-in-child-trafficking-causes-concern-in-bosnia-11-16-2016

Brković, Čarna (2015) 'Management of Ambiguity: Favours and Flexibility in Bosnia and Herzegovina', *Social Anthropology* 23(3): 268–282.

Buka (2013) 'Trgovina ljudima u BiH: Najčešće žrtve su žene i djeca', *Byka*, March 4. https://www.6yka.com/novosti/trgovina-ljudima-u-bih-najcesce-zrtve-su-zene-i-djeca

Cancho, Cesar.A. and Elwan, Nihal (2015) *Gender Disparities in Endowments, Access to Economic Opportunities and Agency*. Washington DC: World Bank.

CEDAW (2005) *Consideration of reports submitted by States parties under article 18 of the Convention on the Elimination of All Forms of Discrimination against Women Combined initial, Second and Third Periodic Reports of States Parties Bosnia and Herzegovina*; CEDAW/C/BIH/1–3, https://documents-dds-ny.un.org/doc/UNDOC/GEN/N05/315/63/PDF/N0531563.pdf?OpenElement

Clark, Janine Natalya (2017) 'Masculinity and Male Survivors of Wartime Sexual Violence: A Bosnian Case Study', *Conflict, Security and Development* 17(4): 287–311.

Cockayne, James (2010) 'Crime, Corruption and Violent Economies', in *Ending Wars, Consolidating Peace: Economic Perspectives*, edited by Mats Berdal and Achim Wennmann, 189–219. London: Institute for Security Studies.

Cockburn, Cynthia (2004) 'A Continuum of Violence: A Gender Perspective on War and Peace', in *Sites of Violence: Gender and Conflict Zones,* edited by Wenona Giles and Jennifer Hyndman, 24–44. Berkeley: University of California Press.

Cockburn, Cynthia (2014) 'A Continuum of Violence: Gender, War and Peace', in *The Criminology of War,* edited by Ruth Jamieson, 357–377. London: Routledge.

Cramer, Christopher (2006) *Civil War Is Not a Stupid Thing*. London: Hurst & Company.

Denda Borjan, Jelena (2016) 'Žrtva porodičnog nasilja iz Trebinja', *Moja Herzegovina*. February 2. https://mojahercegovina.com/zrtva-porodicnog-nasilja-iz-trebinja-plasila-sam-se-svoje-sjenke-a-sada-sa-djecom-imam-srecan-dom/

Đurić Kuzmanović, Tatjana and Ana Pajvančić-Cizelj (2018) 'Economic violence against women: Testimonies from the Women's Court in Sarajevo', On-line: https://doi.org/10.1177/1350506818802425

Efendic, Nirha, Edin Pasovis and Adnan S. Efendic (2018a) 'Understanding the Informal Economy: Evidence from Bosnia and Herzegovina', *E-Finanse: Financial Internet Quarterly* 14(4): 77–89.

Efendić, Nirha, Dušanka Gavrilović, Vjollca Krasniqi, Orlanda Obad, Ines Prica and Tea Šošokić (2018b) Women's Entrepreneurship Between Production and Reproduction. Working Paper. https://www.formal-informal.eu/files/news/2018/Deliverables%202018/Ethnographic%20report_Women%E2%80%99s%20entrepreneurship%20reproduction.compressed.pdf.

Fena (2017) 'Svaka druga žena izložena nekoj vrsti nasilja', *Klix*, 2 December. https://www.klix.ba/vijesti/bih/svaka-druga-zena-u-bih-bila-je-izlozena-nekoj-vrsti-nasilja/171202026

Festic, Amra and Adrian Rausche (2004) 'War by Other Means: How Bosnia's Clandestine Political Economies Obstruct Peace and State Building', *Problems of Post-Communism* 51(3): 27–34.

Galtung, Johan (1990) 'Cultural Violence', *Journal of Peace Research* 27(3): 291–305.

Gilbert, Andrew and Jasmin Mujanović (2015) 'Dayton at Twenty: Towards New Politics in Bosnia-Herzegovina', *Southeast European and Black Sea Studies* 15(4): 605–610.

Goodhand, Jonathan (2004) 'Afghanistan in Central Asia', in *War Economies in a Regional Context: Challenges of Transformation*, edited by Michael Pugh, Neil Cooper with Jonathan Goodhand, 4591–4598. Boulder: Lynne Rienner Publishers.

Hansen, Lene (2000) 'Gender, Nation, Rape: Bosnia and the Construction of Security', *International Feminist Journal of Politics* 3(1): 55–75.

Isović, Maja (2012) 'Prostitucija u Banjaluci je javna tajna', *Byka*, 23 October. https://www.6yka.com/novosti/prostitucija-u-banjaluci-je-javna-tajna

Jansen, Stef, Čarna Brković and Vanja Čelebičić (2016) eds. *Negotiating Social Relations in Bosnia and Herzegovina: Semiperipheral Entanglements*. Abingdon: Routledge

Jung, Dietrich (2002) *Shadow Globalisation, Ethnic Conflicts and New Wars*. London: Routledge.

Jurilj, Zdenko (2016) 'Zastrašujući podaci - Iz BiH šalju žene i djecu na prisilni rad u Azerbajdžan', *Večernji list*, January 11. https://www.vecernji.ba/vijesti/zastrasujuci-podaci-iz-bih-salju-zene-i-djecu-na-prisilni-rad-u-azerbajdzan-1050924

Keen, David (2008) *Complex Emergencies*. Cambridge: Polity Press.

Kelly, Liz (1988) *Surviving Sexual Violence*. Cambridge: Polity Press.

Kelly, Liz (1987) 'The Continuum of Sexual Violence', in *Women, Violence and Social Control*, edited by Mary Maynard and Jalna Hanmer, 46–60. London: Palgrave Macmillan.

Klaric, Miro, Tanja Franciskovic, Aleksandra Stevanovic, Bozo Petrov, Suzana Jonovska and Iva Nemcic Moro (2011) 'Marital Quality and Relationship Satisfaction in War Veterans and their Wives in Bosnia and Herzegovina', *European Journal of Psychotraumatology* 2(1): 80–77.

Kondylis, Florence (2010) 'Conflict Displacement and Labor Market Outcomes in Post-War Bosnia and Herzegovina', *Journal of Development Economics* 93(2): 235–248.

Kostovicova, Denisa, Vesna Bojicic-Dzelilovic and Marsha Henry (2020) 'Drawing on the Continuum: A War and Post-war Political Economy of Gender-based Violence in Bosnia and Herzegovina', *International Feminist Journal of Politics* 22(2): 250–272.

Krause, Ulrike (2015) 'A Continuum of Violence? Linking Sexual and Gender-based Violence during Conflict, Flight, and Encampment', *Refugee Survey Quarterly* 34(4): 1–19.

Krstić, Gorana and Peter Sanfey (2007) 'Mobility, Poverty and Well-being among the Informally Employed in Bosnia and Herzegovina', *Economic Systems* 31: 311–335.

Kržalić, Armin (2011) *Oružano nasilje u Bosni i Hercegovini*, Centar za sigurnosne studije, Sarajevo, June. https://css.ba/wp-content/uploads/2011/06/images_docs_oruzano%20nasilje%20u%20bih.pdf

Kurtenbach, Sabine and Angelika Rettberg (2018) 'Understanding the Relation between War Economies and Post-war Crime', *Third World Thematics: A TWQ Journal* (3)1: 1–8.

Laudati, Ann and Charlotte Mertens (2019) 'Resources and Rape: Congo's (Toxic) Discursive Complex', *African Studies Review* 62(4): 57–82.

Lazarević, Milena and Katarina Tadić (2018) *Gender Issues in the Western Balkans*, CSF Policy Brief 4, European Fund for the Balkans and European Policy Centre. https://wb-csf.eu/docs/Gender_Issues.pdf.pdf

Le Sage, Andre L (1998) 'Engaging the Political Economy of Conflict: Towards a Radical Humanitarianism', *Civil Wars* 1(4): 27–55.

Matić, Milorad (2017) 'Toliko puta prepričana, ali nikad ispričana', *Byka*. 20 November. https://www.6yka.com/novosti/toliko-puta-prepricana-ali-nikad-ispricana-ovo-je-prica-o-mirjani-ovo-je-prica-o-zivotu-pored-neprijatelja-o-svima-nama

Ministarstvo za ljudska prava i izbjeglice Bosne i Herzegovine (2018) 'Grant sredstava za nevladine organizacije – Prevencija nasilja nad ženama i u porodici', Sarajevo, July 19. https://arsbih.gov.ba/grant-sredstva-za-nevladine-organizacije-prevencija-nasilja-nad-zenama-i-u-porodici/

Nikolić-Ristanović, Vesna. 2003. 'Sex Trafficking: The Impact of War, Militarism and Globalization in Eastern Europe,' *Michigan Feminist Studies* 17(1). https://quod.lib.umich.edu/cgi/t/text/text-idx?cc=mfsfront;c=mfs;c=mfsfront;idno=ark5583.0017.001;g=mfsg;rgn=main;view=text;xc=1.

Nikolić-Ristanović, Vesna. 1999. 'Living without Democracy and Peace: Violence against Women in the Former Yugoslavia', *Violence against Women* 5(1): 63–80

Ortlieb, Renate, Zijada Rahimić, Christian Hirt, Almina Bešić and Florian Bieber (2019) 'Diversity and Equality in Bosnia and Herzegovina: Limits to Legislation, Public Debate and Workplace Practices', *Equality, Diversity and Inclusion: An International Journal*, 1–17. https://doi.org/10.1108/EDI-10-2017-0231.

OSCE (2009) *Nasilje u porodici – odgovor nadležnih institucija i zaštita žrtava u Federaciji Bosne i Hercegovine i Republici Srpskoj; Zapažanja o primjeni Zakona o zaštiti od nasilja u porodici u praksi nadležnih institucija*. Sarajevo: Organization for Security and Cooperation; Mission to Bosnia and Herzegovina. July. https://www.osce.org/bs/bih/118943?download=true

Puljek-Shank, Randall (2017) 'Dead Letters on a Page? Civic Agency and Inclusive Governance in Neopatrimonialism', *Democratization* 24(4): 670–688.

Pupavac, Vanessa (2005) 'Empowering Women? An Assessment of International Gender Policies in Bosnia', *International Peacekeeping* 12(3): 391–405.

Rose, Eleanor (2016) 'Bosnian Arms Still Worryingly Available, Experts Say', *BIRN*. November 6. https://balkaninsight.com/2016/11/07/bosnian-arms-still-easy-to-obtain-11-04-2016/

*Sarajevo Times* (2024) "Let's stop Femicide': More than 60 Women have been killed in BiH', November 22. https://sarajevotimes.com/lets-stop-femicide-more-than-60-women-have-been-killed-in-bih/

Savić, Danka (2013) 'Nasilje je ozbiljan problem u BiH, ali nema statistike koja bi to dokazala!', *Slobodna Bosna*, February 14. https://www.slobodna-bosna.ba/vijest/5362/nasilje_je_ozbiljan_problem_u_bih_ali_nema_statistike_koja_bi_to_dokazala.html

SEESAC (2023a) 'Firearm Incidents in the Context of Domestic Violence in South East Europe in 2023', South Eastern and Eastern Europe Clearinghouse for the Control of Small Arms and Light Weapons and UNDP. Belgrade.

SEESAC (2023b) 'The Destruction of 820 pieces of SALW in Bosnia and Herzegovina', 10 November. https://www.seesac.org/News_1/the-destruction-of-820-pieces-of-salw-in-bosnia-and-herzegovina/

Shaxson, Nick (2015) 'Why Gender Equality Requires More Taxation', *Tax Justice Network*. 5 May. https://www.taxjustice.net/2015/05/05/why-gender-equality-requires-more-tax-revenue/

Somun-Krupalija, Lejla (2011) *Gender and Employment in Bosnia and Herzegovina: A Country Study*. Working Paper 4. Geneva: Bureau for Gender Equality International Labour Office. December. https://www.ilo.org/wcmsp5/groups/public/---dgreports/---gender/documents/publication/wcms_170832.pdf

Sorguc, Albina (2015) 'Domestic Violence Revives Bosnian Women's War Nightmares', *Balkan Insight*, May 19. https://www.balkaninsight.com/en/article/domestic-violence-revives-ex-prisoners-wartime-nightmare

Staniland, Paul (2012) 'States, Insurgents and Wartime Political Orders', *Perspectives on Politics* 10(2): 243–264.

The United Nations in Bosnia and Herzegovina (2024) 'Statement on the One-Year Anniversary of the Femicide in Gradačac', https://bosniaherzegovina.un.org/en/276434-statement-one-year-anniversary-femicide-grada%C4%8Dac#:~:text=In%20response%20to%20these%20deep,effectively%20prevent%20and%20eradicate%20femicide.

True, Jacqui (2010) 'The Political Economy of Violence against Women: A Feminist International Relations Perspective', *Australian Feminist Law Journal* 32(1): 39–59.

True, Jacqui (2012) *The Political Economy of Violence against Women*. Oxford: Oxford University Press.

UNDP (2014) *Progress towards Realisation of Millennium Development Goals in Bosnia and Herzegovina 2013*. New York: UNDP.

UNDP/SSEESAC/ (2007) *Posedovanje vatrenog oružja i nasilje u porodici na zapadnom Balkanu*: komparativna studija zakonodavstava i mehanizama za primenu. Beograd: Centar za kontrolu lakog naoružanja u jugoistočnoj i istočnoj Evropi, https://www.seesac.org/f/docs/Gender-and-Security/FIREARMS-POSSESSION-AND-DOMESTIC-VIOLENCE-IN-THE-WESTERN-BALKANS-SRB.pdf

Wennmann, Achim (2011) *The Political Economy of Peacemaking*. London: Routledge.

World Bank (2019) Western Balkans Labor Market Trends: 2019. Washington, DC: The World Bank.

Žurnal (2009) 'Inicijativa mladića: Sedmorica vole šamarati žene', *Žurnal.info*, December 19. https://www.zurnal.info/novost/898/inicijativa-mladica-sedmorica-vole-samarati-zene

# 6

# WOMEN AND UKRAINE'S ECONOMIES OF WAR AND PEACE

*Jennifer G. Mathers*

Ukraine's war effort relies heavily on its women. More than 67,000 women serve in the armed forces – all of them volunteers – with at least 10,000 in combat roles (Basmat 2024), while millions of civilian women maintain the country's war economy by serving as a flexible labour force to address a range of economic and social needs. Women are deployed to fill the gaps left by the men who are combatants or have been killed or seriously injured in the war, as well as continuing the everyday, reproductive labour that sustains households and civil society. Meanwhile, women (many accompanied by young children) who have found refuge in other countries also do their part: sending remittances back to family in Ukraine while ensuring that their children do not forget their native language and culture even as they make new homes for themselves in host countries. The Ukrainian government's plans for postwar economic recovery also identify key roles for women: as mothers to the next generation of Ukrainians and to contribute to achieving rapid economic growth in an economy where the private sector is dominant and the state largely exists to maintain a substantial military-industrial complex.

This chapter explores the impacts on women of Ukraine's wartime economic policies and plans for the country's postwar reconstruction. Drawing on insights from feminist security studies and feminist political economy, it argues that policies pursued by the Ukrainian government and by international actors since Russia's mass invasion of Ukraine in February 2022 continue and, indeed, exacerbate, the dependence of Ukraine's economy on the paid and unpaid labour of women. This pattern was established in the wake of the 2008 Global Financial Crisis and is accompanied by the systematic erosion of social welfare support that women themselves depend on for their own survival. The process of militarisation justifies and normalises placing extraordinary demands on women – and indeed on all members of society – to support the war effort. But while Kyiv needs women to do this work,

DOI: 10.4324/9781003571667-8

it also needs to demonstrate to audiences at home as well as to its international supporters that Ukraine is committed to Western, liberal values, especially capitalism, as well as gender equality. This is an important source of contradictory pressures. Ideals of political freedom, choice and democratic governance motivated the Maidan protests and the Revolution of Dignity in 2013–2014 and continue to inspire Ukrainian resistance to Russia's invasion. But these ideals are increasingly depicted, both by the ruling Servant of the People party and by Ukraine's international donors, as best realised through neoliberal economic policies alongside democratic institutions such as a free media and fair elections. Zelensky's government has therefore adopted policies that shift the balance towards privatisation and reducing workers' rights and protections in law as well as the capacity of the state to provide social safety nets. At the same time, the government compounds the economic insecurities experienced by the very women on whom it relies during this crucial period by ignoring or postponing formal, including legal, commitments to increase gender equality. The Ukrainian government's most recent plan for postwar reconstruction includes statements acknowledging the importance of incorporating gender equality and providing women with greater economic opportunities to "build back better," but there is a real danger that Kyiv will sacrifice the welfare and economic security of Ukraine's women to a neoliberal economic agenda.

The chapter begins with a discussion of some of the many ways that women are providing solutions to Ukraine's wartime labour shortages. The focus then turns to an analysis of two factors that have set the context for the wartime economic insecurity of women in Ukraine. The first is the austerity economic policies required by international financial institutions (IFIs) and implemented by successive Ukrainian governments. The second is an extensive slate of new legislation to address the demands of full-scale war. The chapter then considers how plans for Ukraine's postwar economic recovery have developed. These reconstruction plans have gone through several iterations already and have been shaped by the priorities of international donors. Although the most recent version of the recovery plan includes some gendered economic analysis thanks to the efforts of Ukrainian and international women's organisations, its provisions continue to be characterised by an intensification of Kyiv's commitment to expanding the private sector and shrinking the state in ways that are likely to extend the wartime economic insecurity of Ukraine's women into the postwar recovery. The chapter concludes by focusing on the example of the "Be Like Nina" movement, which illustrates the intersecting economic impacts of wartime policies on women, and the leading role that women are playing in challenging damaging government policies through civil society activism.

## Women as the solution to the problems of Ukraine's economy of war

There is no doubt that Russia's February 2022 full-scale invasion has had a devastating impact on Ukraine's economy. Russian attacks have destroyed homes, businesses and infrastructure throughout the country. In June 2022, the National Bank of Ukraine was reporting inflation of 21%, small and medium-sized enterprises (SMEs) were especially hard hit, with only 23% of them paying full salaries, 21% not paying salaries at all and 12% laying off staff (International Labour Organization 2022). By March 2024, the IMF described the impact of the war on the economy and infrastructure as "severe," with output 25% below pre-war levels and the capacity in agriculture and key industries "severely compromised" (International Monetary Fund 2024:5). The economy's need for labour has been particularly hard hit: 75% of Ukrainian employers surveyed in 2024 reported that they have experienced labour shortages (EBA 2024). The mobilisation of hundreds of thousands of men to serve in the armed forces combined with the departure of an estimated 1.5 million women who were previously in paid employment to find refuge abroad has created a significant deficit of skilled labour (Méheut 2024; Ukraine Facility 2023:18).

Ukraine's women are proving to be an important part of the solution to the country's labour needs. Women are the ultimate flexible workforce for a country at war and are being deployed to fill a wide range of needs for both paid and unpaid labour. To some extent, this is because women in Ukraine, unlike men, are not subject to compulsory military mobilisation. But women are also available for labour redeployment because they are disproportionately represented among the unemployed: during 2023, women made up 72% of those registered unemployed in Ukraine, as well as comprising 66% of those who found new employment (Ukrainska Pravda 2024). Many women in Ukraine have lost jobs due to war-related damage and disruption or the reduction in the number of public sector jobs in line with government's reformist agenda and IFI requirements. The ease with which women can be deployed from one employer to another is facilitated by reductions to the legal protections enjoyed by workers, as we will see in the next section.

The roles that women are now filling in critical industries include those that have traditionally been regarded as only suitable for men. The state has stepped in to enable this change by repealing Soviet-era legislation that banned women from doing physically demanding work that might reduce their fertility or endanger the unborn children of pregnant workers. The coal mining industry is one that has benefitted from this change in legislation, with women now being allowed to work underground for the first time. One news report identifies a coal mine hiring 100 women to help fill the gaps left by the more than 1000 of its male workers who left to fight in the war (Hunder 2023). The State Employment Service of Ukraine reported that in 2022–2023 the proportion of women in the mining industry accounted for 49% of all those employed, in comparison to 27% in 2021, while there were 1,200 women employed in the building and construction industry, representing 38% of the total workforce in that sector (compared with 20% in 2021) (Ukrainska Pravda 2024). Women are also entering other job roles that were previously all-male or heavily male-dominated, including driving heavy vehicles, such as buses and large trucks (Westerman 2024), and working in the steel industry (Koshiw 2024).

The war has also increased – almost infinitely so – the requirements for unpaid, reproductive labour. Much of this work is focused on women's own households and extended families. The temporary or permanent absence of so many husbands and fathers due to the war has significantly increased the number of households headed by women, while the reduction in state welfare services and other forms of social support has placed more of the work of caring for children, the disabled (including war veterans) and the elderly on women's shoulders (World Bank 2023). Women are also very active in community work and in civil society organisations, including voluntary work to support the war effort. Despite considerable resources from the Ukrainian state and international supporters, the war continues to be hungry for voluntary efforts to support the armed forces directly or indirectly, for example by collecting and delivering supplies to soldiers at the front, raising money for units to buy drones, as well as making camouflage nets and providing care packages. Over 71% of civilian society in Ukraine is estimated to have been involved in war-supportive voluntary work of this kind (Vincent 2025). This sort of practical support for the war by civilian society is widely regarded in Ukraine as normal and even unquestionable, and is a reflection of militarisation – a process defined by feminist scholars of International Relations and Security Studies as normalising the idea that the military and its needs should be prioritised over the needs of other institutions or communities (see Åhäll 2016; Enloe 2007; Sjoberg and Via 2010a).

And although millions of Ukrainian women have left the country in search of safe refuge from the war, they continue to support the war effort. The nature and extent of this support varies, but typically it includes working abroad and sending some of their earnings back home to support family members. Ukrainians have been working abroad on a temporary or even semi-permanent basis at least since the mid-1990s to overcome poor employment prospects and low wages at home and provide a better life for themselves and their families, for example by buying land, paying off debts and paying for their children's university education (Koshulko 2018:211). In 2023, Ukraine was second only to Uzbekistan among the countries of Europe and Central Asia in the value of remittances received, at $15.7 billion, representing 9.1% of Ukraine's GDP that year (Ratha et al. 2023:30). And while official statistics measure money transferred through the Ukrainian banking system, they do not reflect the full extent of remittances, which are also transferred through unofficial channels such as individuals carrying cash across state borders. Although there was a sharp dip in remittances in the spring of 2022, as the millions of Ukrainians who fled the country got themselves settled, by July 2022 the National Bank of Ukraine reported that remittances from abroad had increased to their pre-war levels (International Labour Organization 2022).

## Setting the context for Ukraine's economy of war

The discussion in this section focuses on two factors that create the context for the operation of Ukraine's war economy and shape its impact on women. The first is Ukraine's relationship with international financial institutions. Since the 2008 Global Financial Crisis, Ukraine has received a series of emergency agreements from IFIs worth tens of billions of US dollars (Ministry of Finance of Ukraine n.d.). While these funds have enabled Ukraine's economy to continue to function, their disbursement has also been conditional upon Kyiv's agreement to introduce measures to reduce real wages and employment rates to improve the price competitiveness of Ukrainian goods and services and to reduce the state budget deficit by increasing taxes and reducing spending, especially on social welfare. As we know from the work of feminist political economists such as Diane Elson (1989, 1991), there are gendered biases underpinning the ways that IFIs and states operate. The neoliberal macroeconomic medicine that they administer may be designed to strengthen and stabilise an economy by reducing the role of the state and increasing the role of markets, but it does not affect all members of society equally. Instead, these measures disproportionately increase the burden on women. As Celeste Montoya (2016:158) points out, "women absorb the costs and cuts in state expenditure" that result from austerity budgets. The analysis in this section builds on the work of Elson and Montoya and applies the concept of "feminization of survival" developed by Saskia Sassen, which offers the insight that not only households but whole communities and indeed governments are, as she puts it, "increasingly dependent on women for their survival" (2000:506).

Even before Russia's mass invasion, there was continuous pressure from IFIs on successive governments in Kyiv to introduce austerity measures. Although no Ukrainian government has implemented such measures as fully and quickly as the IFIs urged, there have nevertheless been substantial reductions in the scale and capacity of the social welfare system since 2008 (see Mathers 2020). These measures have affected households by, for example, reducing state fuel subsidies for domestic users of energy (WILPF 2017), reducing the availability of state-provided health care and child care, and cutting salaries and jobs in the public sector (Bogdan et al. 2017), all of which have a disproportionate effect on women, both as clients and as employees (WILPF 2017).

Changes to the health care sector in Ukraine encapsulate the way that women have been made more economically insecure both through changes to provisions in state-provided social services and through the knock-on effects of these changes on feminised roles in employment. In 2018, Ukraine began to introduce reforms to its healthcare sector, largely in response to pressures from IFIs to reduce social spending. The aims of the reforms were to create a more cost-efficient healthcare system that would allow the state to cut its expenditure in this area while also reducing the scope for corruption and making healthcare more accessible for ordinary Ukrainians. A key principle of the reform is patient choice, with state finance following the patient to ensure that those facilities that treat more patients receive proportionately more resources. But the new payment system disadvantages smaller and more specialised facilities, as well as those in smaller communities that are not able to attract large numbers of patients or even, in extreme cases, to attract enough patients to cover their costs. As a result of this reform, staff in some facilities report high workloads and unpaid wages, while some hospitals have closed. Healthcare workers also report that hospital directors intimidate those who speak out about their working conditions and take advantage of the ban on strikes and protests during martial law to push through measures that would otherwise be the catalyst for industrial action. Medical staff in roles that are dominated by women – such as social care nurses in residential homes for children or the elderly, or nurses working in schools – reportedly receive particularly low wages (Farbar 2023). Russia's full-scale invasion has exacerbated the issues created by the healthcare reform. In July 2022, the Ministry of Health reversed its previous policy guaranteeing a base level of income each month and instead ruled that hospitals outside conflict zones would only be paid for the services they provide to patients. This led to delays in the payment of wages to healthcare workers as hospitals scrambled for funds, just as the inflation of the early wartime period rose to 30% (Farbar 2022). Ukraine's reform to its healthcare system is therefore increasing the economic insecurity of the women who are employed by it as well as reducing the quality and availability of the service to patients.

Social spending in general is depicted in the analysis produced by IFIs as unproductive and wasteful, and as creating and sustaining damaging dependencies on the state. This attitude reveals a gendered bias in favour of the masculinised private sector, which, by contrast, is depicted as productive and the engine for generating wealth across the economy. It is the private sector that is presented as providing opportunity for individual self-improvement and driving the development of employability skills that provide a foundation for greater independence and self-realisation, thereby making society more resilient and able to withstand economic shocks. A further gendered aspect of IFI conditionalities is the exclusion of defence spending from the areas of the state budget that they cover. Both the IMF and the World Bank explicitly exclude national security from policy requirements on the grounds that this sector is "political" and therefore not an appropriate area for external interference (Leckow 2002; Boon 2007). The placement of national security into the category of political – and therefore untouchable – creates a privileged position for defence and the military and is, itself, a reflection of militarisation: regarding security as achieved primarily through the threat or use of force and equating the security of individuals and communities with the security of states (Cohn 2011; Sjoberg 2009). There is also a very practical effect of creating an exception for defence spending: any increases in spending on defence will place pressure on the level of state spending overall, further reducing the state's capacity to provide social welfare for its citizens. While this might be a moot point during peacetime, in wartime it becomes a very real consideration. It has certainly been a key factor in shaping Ukrainian state budgets since 2014 and even more so since February 2022.

In addition to allowing Kyiv to access much-needed funds, fulfilling IFI requirements demonstrates Ukraine's commitments to Western norms and values as well as its credibility as a future partner in Western international institutions such as the European Union and NATO. While these factors were important for Petro Poroshenko during his presidency (2014–2019), they have become even more crucial for Volodymyr Zelensky (2019 to present) during the mass invasion stage of Russia's war, when the continued flow of military as well as economic support depends upon persuading Western governments and Western-led international institutions that Ukraine shares core Western values such as a commitment to democracy, human rights and capitalism. A commitment to gender equality is among those shared values that Zelensky (and indeed Poroshenko) has been keen to emphasise although, as we will see in the discussion below, gender equality ranks well below the market in the hierarchy of values.

The IFIs have not relaxed their demands for Kyiv to continue cutting state spending and curbing inflationary pressures from rising wages despite the accelerating wartime needs in crucial areas such as health care and social care. In its third review of the extended arrangement under the Extended Fund Facility for Ukraine in March 2024, the IMF praised the Ukrainian government for its policies designed to "sustain fiscal, external, price and financial stability at a time of exceptionally high war-related uncertainty" (International Monetary Fund 2024:1). This same review confirms that the full-scale war has not significantly changed the priorities or the strategies of the loan-granting IFIs, or their determination to ensure that state spending is depressed to compensate for increases in defence expenditure:

> Lower than expected grants, import tax losses from border blockades, and high defense-related expenditures posed budget challenges in late 2023. However, tight control over other expenditure categories was nearly offsetting and contained the excess of the overall deficit relative to the Second Review's baseline.
> *(International Monetary Fund 2024:8)*

The IMF's review one year later indicates no major change: "the allocations in the 2025 Budget reflect the need for an adequate envelope for national defense, with other categories being tightly prioritized" (International Monetary Fund 2025:15–16).

Other passages in the 2024 report refer to the importance of the Ukrainian government gaining "more control over the costing of existing public services" (International Monetary Fund 2024:20) and plans to lift a moratorium on disconnecting consumers in arrears being necessary to "contribute to higher payment discipline" along with confirmation of plans to continue to liberalise the gas and electricity markets (reiterated in the 2025 report), although there is a nod to the importance of "establishing adequate safeguards to protect vulnerable groups as reforms proceed" (International Monetary Fund 2024:28).

The second factor that sets the context for Ukraine's war economy and its impact on women is an extensive slate of new legislation. There are two distinct categories for this legislation: new legal commitments to promote gender equality;

and provisions that make employment conditions more difficult for workers in general, but especially for women because of their impact on female-dominated roles. The two types of legislation are often mutually contradictory, with each speaking to different aspects of Ukraine's desire to develop in a more Western, and more specifically European, direction.

Women's activism has played a key role in influencing the decisions that successive governments have made to adopt legislation and policies intended to advance the cause of gender equality, building on the strong desire in Ukrainian society to join international institutions that champion democratic values. Women's advocacy was crucial in Ukraine's decision, during the war in the Donbas, to adopt its first National Action Plan (2016–2020) to implement United Nations Security Council Resolution 1325 on Women, Peace and Security. Pressure from Ukrainian and international women's groups ensured that the country adopted a second National Action Plan (2020–2025) (Manoilenko 2022; Peace Women n.d.). Thousands of women volunteering to serve in the armed forces raised the profile of gender equality in the armed forces, which was promoted by the removal of restrictions on women serving in combat roles in 2016, and the opening of all military roles to women in 2022 (Kuz and Soguel 2022). Women's groups lobbied successfully for Ukraine to sign the Council of Europe Convention on preventing and combating violence against women and domestic violence (the Istanbul Convention) in 2011, which was ratified in 2022 (Strelnyk 2025; Strasbourg 2022). In 2023, Ukraine's Economy Ministry announced a plan, to be implemented in cooperation with UN Women, to reduce the gender pay gap from 18.6% to 13.6% by 2030 ("Economy Ministry plans to reduce gender pay gap" 2023; UN Women 2024). Most far-reaching and ambitious of all is the State Strategy for Ensuring Equal Rights and Opportunities for Women and Men until 2030 and an operational plan for its implementation, approved in August 2022. The Strategy contains some very impressive terms, including calling for women's participation in recovery processes and involvement in decision-making at all levels from community to national, as well as gender mainstreaming in post-conflict recovery. One of the objectives of the Strategy is for women and men to participate equally in economic activity, to benefit from economic development, and to have equal access to economic resources. The provision for women's involvement in economic recovery is particularly important and would be a welcome correction to much of the discussions happening around Ukraine's postwar reconstruction, as we will see in the next section of this chapter, but for the fact that the implementation of these measures is explicitly delayed until after the end of martial law, and there is no defined budget to put them into practice (2023:3–4).

Martial law itself is one of the many legislative measures adopted by the Ukrainian government that tends to work against its own commitments to gender equality. Martial law was introduced in Ukraine on 24 February 2022, initially for 30 days, and has been extended and expanded since then. Under the provisions of martial law, organising strikes and holding public demonstrations or other mass gatherings is prohibited (Fremer 2022). To be sure, the ban on public demonstrations is not absolute. The wives of Ukrainian soldiers being held prisoner by Russia are permitted to protest without obstruction (Gilbody Dickerson 2024).[1] But the provisions of martial law do have direct implications for the traditional tools of organised labour to challenge the state and employers. And workers have had many reasons to want to make those challenges. Since the start of the mass invasion stage of the war, the Rada has passed a flurry of business-friendly changes to labour legislation that weight the balance of legal safeguards firmly in favour of employers.

In March 2022, the Rada passed a new law that suspended the employment contract, allowing employers to stop paying salaries to employees without formally dismissing them (Sandul 2023). Then in July 2022 a new law created the legal basis for zero-hour contracts. Employers are no longer required to provide work on a regular basis as long as the baseline of 32 hours per month is reached for those with the new contracts, and the employer issues them to no more than 10% of the workforce. And while employees on zero-hour contracts have the right to request a contract of employment with specified hours after 12 months, the employer has the right to refuse that request (Verkhovna Rada of Ukraine 2022). The law was presented by the government as providing greater safeguards for freelancers, who had previously worked effectively on zero hours contracts without any regulation, but in fact the law is applicable to any type of worker (Sandul 2023). Then on 17 August 2022 Zelensky signed Law 5371, which removes rights for those who work for organisations that employ fewer than 250 people to work under contracts negotiated by collective agreements with unions. Instead, these employees – comprising around 70% of workers in Ukraine – will be required to negotiate their contracts with their employers as individuals. Unlike the zero hours contract law, which is a permanent change, Law 5371 will only be in effect during the period of martial law, although this condition was only added at the insistence of trade unions. And although the government links this change in the law to addressing problems faced by business due to the onset of full-scale war, it first tried to introduce this law in 2021 (ODR Team 2022), indicating that this measure reflects a longer-standing political position.

For although the Ukrainian government has a clear incentive to demonstrate its pro-market, neoliberal credentials to its Western donors, Zelensky and his fellow elected representatives of the Servant of the People party also appear to favour the private sector in principle. Natalia Lomonosova of the Ukrainian think tank Cedos has argued that creating a more business-friendly environment in Ukraine is a long-term policy goal of this government, which is almost certainly intended to increase foreign investment (ODR Team 2022). This assessment is supported by the statement of a spokesperson for the Servant of the People party, who is quoted as saying "the extreme over-regulation of employment contradicts the principles of market self-regulation [and] modern personnel management" (ODR Team 2022).

In addition to having a clear disposition towards business-friendly policies, there are signs that key political figures are making rhetorical connections between neoliberal policies and modern, progressive and pro-European positions (that is, the chosen future of Ukraine). At the same time, state regulation is equated with the Soviet period and even, perhaps, with practices in contemporary Russia. As a leading member of the Servant of the People party and head of the parliament's finance committee Danylo Hetmantsev wrote on Telegram on 9 July 2022:

> A worker should be able to regulate his relationship with an employer himself. Without the state. This is what happens in a state if it's free, European and market-oriented. Otherwise, the country will be travelling with one leg on an express train to the EU, and with another inside a Soviet-era train going in the other direction.
>
> *(Rowley and Guz 2022a)*

This rhetoric reinforces the message often directed at international audiences that Ukraine shares the values of Western liberal democracy and a commitment to capitalism. Hetmantsev's remarks suggest that if Ukraine wants to enjoy a future with political freedoms and the economic benefits of EU membership, it must deregulate its markets and remove economic security for employees, especially those working as freelancers, those who are employed by smaller organisations and by the state itself – all of whom are disproportionately women. By equating a larger role for the state with the intrusive, controlling and authoritarian Soviet state, he implies that those who rely on the state for legal protections, social welfare and employment – also disproportionately women – are somehow suspect, backwards in their attitudes and under the influence of the Soviet past. In fact, the situation is quite the opposite. The European Union requires member states to include crucial safeguards for workers in their national legislation. A former EU commissioner for employment, social affairs and inclusion argued that wartime changes in Ukraine's labour legislation meant that Ukraine was going "in a completely different direction" from EU norms and that ignoring the views of trade unions was contrary to standard practice in EU member states (Rowley and Guz 2022a).

In a statement that closes the loop between IFI-mandated austerity measures to shrink the state and changes to labour laws, the head of the parliamentary committee on social policy has argued that the capacity of the Ukrainian state – after years of cutbacks – was not sufficient to undertake its obligations, for example to investigate breaches of social and employment rights, thereby justifying reducing the state's legal obligations in this area (Rowley and Guz 2022b). The changes that the Ukrainian government has made to labour legislation have made the working conditions for all workers more precarious, but these laws have a disproportionate effect on women because of the way that they are heavily concentrated in certain sectors of the economy. It is worth reflecting on the juxtaposition of these two categories of legal obligations that Ukraine has committed itself to: one that offers a more promising future for women, full of opportunities including greater economic security, while the other postpones that bright future and makes the material realities of everyday life more difficult.

## Looking for the women in plans for Ukraine's economy of peace

Even as the war continues with no clear end in sight, the extent of the war's damage to Ukraine's material and economic infrastructure means that planning for the postwar recovery has never been far from the minds of policymakers, not only in Kyiv but also in donor countries and among IFI decision makers. After the first recovery conference in Lugano in 2022, they have become an annual event, with one held in London in 2023, Berlin in 2024 and, at the time of writing, another planned in Rome in 2025. Their purpose is to raise awareness of the need for international support for Ukraine's reconstruction, bring together key stakeholders such as IFIs, national governments and the private sector and to gather pledges of funding. The annual recovery conferences also provide an opportunity for Ukrainian officials to articulate their priorities for reconstruction and, increasingly, for civil society organisations to lobby members of the policy and financial communities to mitigate some of the neoliberal economic assumptions that underpin plans for rebuilding postwar Ukraine. Ukrainian and international women's groups participate on the fringes of these conferences, and in the Ukrainian government's various consultation events, to raise the public profile of women's contributions to the wartime economy and their postwar economic needs and to lobby for the final recovery plans and spending commitments to be shaped by gender-informed analysis.

The Ukrainian government has so far produced two iterations of a recovery plan. The first was the *Draft Ukraine Recovery Plan* presented at the Lugano conference in July 2022. Produced by the National Council for the Recovery of Ukraine from the Consequences of War, the plan is the product of consultation among government agencies, the private sector and civil society and presents hundreds of pages of materials produced by 27 working groups. The second is the *Plan for the Implementation of the Ukraine Facility 2024–2027* (hereafter referred to as *The Ukraine Plan*), which was produced in 2023 and is much more succinct: just over 300 pages in total and explicitly oriented towards meeting the requirements of membership in the European Union. While both documents demonstrate a clear preference for neoliberal economic solutions to solve the problems of wartime destruction and postwar rebuilding, there are marked differences between them that are very revealing about the ways that Ukraine's policymakers are thinking about women and the gendered impacts of economic recovery measures.

The contribution to the 2022 *Draft Ukraine Recovery Plan* by the working group on economic recovery and development (NCRUCW 2022b) emphasises that the course set by the Ukrainian government towards more business-friendly, neoliberal policies was not expected to change during the period of economic recovery and beyond. Among constraints identified on economic development are "the excessive government apparatus (the share of government spending as a percentage of GDP) inherited from Soviet times," together with "low loyalty of workers to the reforms with an active position of resistance taken by trade unions, a lack of understanding of changes and needs of the modern labor market by trade unions" (NCRUCW 2022b:7–8). These statements demonstrate clear continuity with the government's wartime approach of restricting the rights of workers and trade unions. They are also consistent with the remarks quoted above by the head of the parliamentary finance committee that depict state-funded institutions in the image of Soviet-era repression. The private sector and the markets are instead regarded as the optimal solution to the problem of reconstructing postwar Ukraine, although this is likely to mean a heavy dependence on foreign investment. Private capital in Ukraine has been focused on the production of commodities (providing opportunities for the creation and consolidation of power bases by oligarchs) and in the financial services sector – neither of which has the experience or capacity to build infrastructure (Broder 2022). This suggests that Kyiv's political leaders will need to create and maintain an environment that is attractive to foreign investors, for example by ensuring that regulations such as those that protect the rights of workers and trade unions are kept to a minimum.

But while the 2022 *Draft Ukraine Recovery Plan* presents Ukraine's future as a place of opportunity for the market and the private sector, it is a future where women's economic agency is invisible outside of the household. While references are made to, for example, the importance of equal access to opportunities for all citizens, there is little mention of gender equality or indeed of women separately from their roles as mothers or future mothers. There is, however, considerable emphasis on the existence and welfare of children. Demographic trends, depopulation, fertility rates and birth rates are mentioned in several of the working groups' documents. Even the (very welcome) statement that domestic violence is inadmissible is made in the context of providing a secure and stable home for raising children. Key performance indicators for the protection of children's rights and the return of children temporarily displaced abroad include the number of couples still married after five years, the number of children born and the number of large families (NCRUCW 2022a).

In response to the tone and substance of the 2022 plan, international organisations with a remit to advocate for women were vocal in calling for Ukraine's economic recovery plans to incorporate gender-sensitive analysis, planning, funding arrangements and policymaking. As a September 2023 UN Women policy brief on gender-responsive recovery pointed out:

> Despite the disproportionate effect that the war is having on women, and the role that women are playing in the response, at the largescale international recovery conferences and in the National Recovery Plan 2022 there has been little attention to how recovery and construction can promote gender equality and women's empowerment, or alternatively, further deepen inequality and exclusion.
> *(UN Women 2023:2)*

But while the second Ukraine Recovery Conference in London in June 2023 focused heavily on the involvement of the private sector and paid little attention to gender equality, both Ukrainian and international women's advocacy organisations made interventions urging the adoption of a gender-informed approach to the economic reconstruction of the country (Prügl, Porobić and Dimitrova 2025:5–6). The 2023 *Ukraine Plan* was the beneficiary of these interventions, resulting from an extensive consultation process that included inviting proposed amendments from civil society groups and it demonstrates a much greater awareness of gender and the economic needs of women. The 2024 Berlin Recovery Conference was also different in tone and substance from its predecessors, with greater focus on the human dimension of recovery, although the discussions by policymakers and business elites about women's economic agency was framed in the context of their potential to contribute to economic growth (Prügl, Porobić and Dimitrova 2025:6). Once again, women's ability to strengthen the labour force – their role as the ultimate flexible workers – was revealed to be their most valuable attribute.

The most sustained engagement in *The Ukraine Plan* with ideas around gender equality and women's economic insecurity and agency is to be found in the "human capital" and "business environment" chapters. The importance of rebuilding schools and hospitals, providing childcare and attractive jobs are all acknowledged as essential steps towards encouraging the return of the millions of Ukrainian women who fled the war and found places of refuge abroad. There is a recognition of the range of barriers facing women entrepreneurs, from dismissive attitudes to difficulty in gaining the necessary credit to start and support their own businesses. The existence of reproductive labour is articulated, as is the fact that it falls predominantly on women and that withdrawing state support for social care without adequate substitutes increases the burden on households. At the same time, it is notable that women are *not* identified as a distinct category in the list of the most vulnerable populations in society (Ukraine Facility 2023:10–11, 119–120, 125–126, 127, 274). While women may be included among other categories of vulnerable citizens (war widows, the disabled, the elderly), the decision not to label all women as inherently vulnerable is a subtle recognition of their agency.

All these points, together with a lengthy paragraph explaining gender mainstreaming and indicating a commitment to it, indicate that the intense efforts of Ukrainian and international women's organisations to make policymakers more aware of the gendered impacts of economic policies are bearing fruit. But these very welcome signs of heightened awareness are embedded within a value system that privileges the market and the private sector and regards state funding as a remnant of the past, to be reduced or eliminated entirely, except when it comes to funding defence. The 425% increase in defence spending in 2022 alone is acknowledged in *The Ukraine Plan* to have contributed significantly to the state's budget deficit, although the remedy for that problem is depicted as a slowdown in non-military spending, together with higher tax collection – an indirect admission that the combination of IFI-mandated austerity policies and the war are creating a heavy burden on the civilian population (Ukraine Facility 2023:19). The sectors of the economy identified as having the greatest capacity to foster economic growth – energy, agriculture, transport, raw materials and information technology – are also male-dominated. And while health, education and social care are identified as fundamental for the development of society, increasing private investment in the institutions that provide those services is presented as the way to rebuild that capacity. There are lengthy discussions of the importance of reducing the number of state-owned enterprises, while the provision of childcare is linked to raising fertility levels and to freeing up women's time so that they can enter paid employment or start their own businesses (Ukraine Facility 2023:7–8, 10, 11, 13, 136–137).

### *Be Like Nina*

Despite the pressure for neoliberal solutions to the problems of Ukraine's economies of war and peace, women-led civil society actions are in the forefront of resistance. "Be Like Nina" is an excellent example of this practice. It is a social movement founded in 2019 and named for a nurse, Nina Kozlovska, who posted on Facebook about the working conditions of nurses, especially low salaries, overtime working and the lack of job security as a direct result of the government's healthcare reforms discussed in the previous section (Unions Helps Refugees 2023). Kozlovska's post inspired the hashtag #BeLikeNina (#БудьякНіна) and discussions on social media about and among healthcare workers across the country, as well as a group of the same name which, as of early January 2023, had more than 82,000 members who share problems and ideas as well as organise public events and protests to raise the profile of the problems. Protests organised by Be Like Nina were held in 2019, 2020 and in 2021 to coincide with Nurses' Day, receiving considerable attention in Ukraine's media. In November 2020 the group officially became the social organisation Medical Movement "Be Like Nina" and since then has become an umbrella organisation for local trade unions for healthcare workers. Organisations affiliated with Be Like Nina bring court cases, several successfully, for the reinstatement of unlawfully dismissed nurses and the payment of outstanding salaries. By November 2024, "Be Like Nina" had a presence in all of Ukraine's administrative regions including occupied territories (Global Union 2024).

Although the descriptions of "Be Like Nina" and the organisations affiliated with it emphasise that these are organisations for health care workers in general, images used to illustrate media stories about them tend to show protests and other actions that are either all women or clearly women-dominated – typically a group of women facing a man in a suit, described in the caption to the image as a hospital director or regional official.

The suspension of protests under martial law has restricted the scope of some of the activities of "Be Like Nina" organisations, but they have responded by focussing on other activities, such as training for health care workers across Ukraine, including raising awareness of legal rights and avenues to pursue claims. They provide humanitarian assistance to medical workers, for example helping to provide housing and psychological support for those who have been displaced or injured by the war. Members also network with trade unionists and labour activists in other parts of Europe to share experiences and strategise, hold press conferences to raise awareness of hospital closures among Ukrainian society and make public appeals to government ministries to address low salaries and other issues (Be Like Nina 2024).

## Conclusions

Women are essential to Ukraine's war economy and are expected to play a crucial role in its postwar recovery, but there is a fundamental tension between the government's commitments to Western liberal values including gender equality and the neoliberal economic policies that it champions. In practical terms, this means that women receive few of the promised benefits of greater rights and opportunities. The laws that are implemented immediately, such as the removal of restrictions preventing women from doing especially dangerous jobs and the ones that reduce employment rights, have the effect of making working life more difficult and precarious. The laws that hold out the hope for a better, more equal future with more opportunities for women are the ones that are postponed, perhaps indefinitely, until times are more settled and other, more pressing needs have been met. There is a large gap between Ukraine's legal and rhetorical commitments to women's rights, opportunities and economic security and women's everyday experience of material realities. This situation is reminiscent of Cynthia Enloe's comment on the difficulties that women have in getting their needs taken seriously during struggles for national liberation:

> the more imminent and coercive the threat posed by an outside power – a foreign force or the local government's police – the more successful men in the community are likely to be in persuading women to keep quiet, to swallow their grievances and their analyses.
>
> *(Enloe 2000:56)*

Women are urged to postpone their demands for gender equality until independence has been achieved or, in the case of modern-day Ukraine, until the military threat from Russia has been dealt with. Even in the government's plans for postwar rebuilding, women are represented primarily as contributors to economic growth and encouraged to find their future in the private sector, with little or no support envisaged from the state. But the danger of postponing the delivery of promises for a more equitable future is that by the time the national struggle has been won, it will be too late. The patterns that maintain men's political, social and, in the case that we are concerned with, economic, dominance have already been set and are difficult to unpick.

But while the moment of possibility and fluidity, when fundamental structures can be reshaped, passes quickly, there are many signs that Ukraine's women are seizing every opportunity to make good use of that time by resisting damaging policies and articulating their needs. Sustained lobbying by women-led civil society groups, sometimes working with international partners such as UN Women, is already shifting the government's economic narrative of postwar recovery to incorporate more, and more meaningful, acknowledgements of the gendered impact of economic policies and on the importance of gender-sensitive planning and preparation for the postwar period. Initiatives such as "Be Like Nina" demonstrate the persistence and effectiveness of women-led activism that works on behalf of the needs and the security of civilian society as a whole. If Ukraine relies on women to support its economies of war and peace, then women are relying on each other to make sure that their country's opportunity to build a more equitable society after the horrors of war is not squandered.

## Note

1 The author is grateful to Marnie Howlett for pointing out this example.

## References

Åhäll L (2016) 'The dance of militarisation: A feminist security studies take on "The Political"', *Critical Studies on Security* 4(2):154–168.

Basmat D (12 July 2024) *Ukraine sees surge in female soldiers with over 10,000 women serving on the front lines, Deputy PM says*, The Kyiv Independent. https://kyivindependent.com/ukraine-sees-surge-in-female-soldiers-with-over-10-000-women-serving-on-front-lines-deputy-pm-says/

Be Like Nina (30 December 2024) *Ukraine: Be Like Nina: A year of activities*, Europe Solidaire Sans Frontières. https://www.europe-solidaire.org/spip.php?article73148

Bogdan T, Landesmann M, Harlik P and Gligorov V (2017) *From fiscal austerity towards growth-enhancing fiscal policy in Ukraine*. The Vienna Institute for International Economic Studies Research Report 417.

Boon KE (2007) 'Open for business: International financial institutions, post-conflict economic reform, and the rule of law', *Journal of International Law and Politics* 39(3): 513–581.

Broder D (3 August 2022) *To Help Ukraine, Cancel Its Foreign Debt: An Interview with Alexander Kravchuk*, Jacobin. https://jacobin.com/2022/03/ukraine-cancel-foreign-debt-imf-economic-conditions

Cohn C (2011) 'Feminist security studies: Toward a reflexive practice.' *Politics & Gender* (4):581–586.

Elson D (1989) 'The impact of structural adjustment on women: Concepts and issues', in Onimode B (ed) *The IMF, the World Bank and the African Debt. Volume 2: The Social and Political Impact*, Zed Books.

Elson D (1991) 'Male bias in macro-economics: The case of structural adjustment', in Elson D (ed) *Male bias in the development process*, 2nd edition, Manchester University Press.

Enloe C (2000) *Bananas, Beaches and Bases: Making Feminist Sense of International Politics*, University of California Press.

Enloe C (2007) *Globalization and Militarism: Feminist Make the Link*, Rowman & Littlefield Publishers, Inc.

EBA (Evropeis'ka Bisnes Asotsiatsiya) (24 April 2024) *Tri chverti robotodavtsiv vigchyvayut' defitsit kadriv v Ukraini.* https://eba.com.ua/try-chverti-robotodavtsiv-vidchuvayut-defitsyt-kadriv-v-ukrayini/

Farbar K (29 November 2022) *Ukraine's nurses face brutal winter as health austerity collides with war*, openDemocracy. https://www.opendemocracy.net/en/odr/ukraine-hospital-staff-nurses-unpaid-reform-russia-war/

Farbar K (3 August 2023) *Ukraine's medics are calling for change – but nobody is listening*, openDemocracy. https://www.opendemocracy.net/en/odr/ukraine-doctors-nurses-healthcare-reforms-low-wages-layoffs-demand-change-unions/

Fremer I (2022) *Ukraine: Martial Law introduced in Response to Russian Invasion.* https://www.loc.gov/item/global-legal-monitor/2022-03-03/ukraine-martial-law-introduced-in-response-to-russian-invasion/

Gilbody Dickerson C (16 May 2024) *Ukraine war: How wives of imprisoned Azovstal fighters are honouring them,* Sky News. https://news.sky.com/story/ukraine-war-how-wives-of-imprisoned-azovstal-fighters-are-honouring-them-13136185

Global Union (26 November 2024) *Ukrainian care workers' union growth shows strength, resilience during war*, UNI. https://uniglobalunion.org/news/ukrainian-care-workers-organize-in-war/

Hunder M (22 November 2023) *Ukraine's coal mines turn to women to solve wartime staff shortages*, Reuters. https://www.reuters.com/world/europe/ukraines-coal-mines-turn-women-solve-wartime-staff-shortages-2023-11-22/

International Labour Organization (28 July 2022) *How does the war against Ukraine impact employment and migration?: Interview with Nataliia Slaviuk, Economist and Assistant Professor National University Kyiv-Mohyla Academy*. https://www.ilo.org/budapest/whats-new/essential-questions/WCMS_852649/lang--en/index.htm

International Monetary Fund (March 2024) *Ukraine: Third review of the extended arrangement under the extended fund facility*, IMF Country Report No. 24/27.

International Monetary Fund (March 2025) *Ukraine: Seventh review under the extended arrangement under the extended fund facility*, IMF Country Report No. 25/78.

Koshiw I (19 May 2024) *Ukrainian women wanted in factories as men drafted into army*, Financial Times. https://www.ft.com/content/8880fe18-0830-41e2-a62f-dea64d532b85

Koshulko O (2018) 'Personal remittances of labor migrants to Ukraine: Benefits for the country', *Ekonomičnij vìsnik unìversitetu,* 36 (1):207–214.

Kuz M and Soguel D (23 February 2022) *"We want to keep Ukraine free." Why women rise in Ukraine army*, The Christian Science Monitor. https://www.csmonitor.com/World/Europe/2022/0223/We-want-to-keep-Ukraine-free.-Why-women-rise-in-Ukraine-army

Leckow R (2002) *Conditionality in the International Monetary Fund.*

Manoilenko H (10 October 2022) *The continuing relevance of the "women, peace and security" agenda in the context of Russia's War on Ukraine*, PRIF Blog. https://blog.prif.org/2022/10/10/the-continuing-relevance-of-the-women-peace-and-security-agenda-in-the-context-of-russias-war-on-ukraine/

Mathers JG (2020) 'Women, war and austerity: IFIs and the construction of gendered economic insecurities in Ukraine.' *Review of International Political Economy,* 27(6): 1235–1256.

Méheut C (20 August 2024) *War is draining Ukraine's male-dominated workforce. Enter the women*, New York Times. https://www.nytimes.com/2024/08/20/world/europe/ukraine-women-workforce-war.html

Ministry of Finance of Ukraine (n.d.) *International monetary fund.* https://mof.gov.ua/en/mvf

Montoya C (2016) 'Exploits and exploitations: A micro and macro analysis of the "DSK affair"', in Hozić A and True J (eds) *Scandalous Economics: Gender and the Politics of Financial Crises*, Oxford University Press.

NCRUCW (The National Council for the Recovery of Ukraine from the Consequences of the War) (2022b) *Draft Ukraine recovery plan: Materials of the 'economic recovery and development' working group.* https://assets-global.website-files.com/621f88db25fbf24758792dd8/62c6d289b1ec3b714442a9eb_Economic%20recovery%20and%20development.pdf

NCRUCW (The National Council for the Recovery of Ukraine from the Consequences of the War) (2022a) *Draft Ukraine recovery plan: Materials of the 'Protection of children's rights and the return of children temporarily displaced abroad' working group.* https://assets-global.website-files.com/621f88db25fbf24758792dd8/62d81572bcbd290c70893809_Protection%20of%20children_s%20rights%20and%20return%20of%20children%20temporarily%20displaced%20abroad.pdf

ODR Team (25 August 2022) *Ukraine's anti-worker law comes into effect*, openDemocracy. https://www.opendemocracy.net/en/odr/ukraine-labour-law-wrecks-workers-rights/

Peace Women (n.d.) *Ukraine*, Peace Women. https://1325naps.peacewomen.org/index.php/country/ukraine/

Prügl E, Porobić N and Dimitrova M (2025) *Planning for (Post-)war Recovery in Ukraine: A Feminist Political Economy Perspective*, Paper presented at the Annual Meeting of the Swiss Political Science Association, University of Geneva.

Ratha D, Chandra V, Kim EJ, Plaza S and Shaw W (2023) *Migration and development brief 39: Leveraging diaspora finances for private capital mobilization.* https://www.knomad.org/sites/default/files/publication-doc/migration_development_brief_39.pdf#page=32

Rowley T and Guz S (20 July 2022a) *Ukraine uses Russian invasion to pass laws wrecking workers' rights*, openDemocracy. https://www.opendemocracy.net/en/odr/ukraine-draft-law-5371-workers-rights-war-russia/

Rowley T and Guz S (9 August 2022b) *Ukraine could abandon key labour principle as part of EU drive*, openDemocracy. https://www.opendemocracy.net/en/odr/ukraine-new-labour-law-social-dialogue/

Sandul G (10 February 2023) *A full-scale attack on Ukraine's labour rights*, IPS. https://www.ips-journal.eu/topics/democracy-and-society/a-full-scale-attack-on-ukraines-labour-rights-6501/

Sassen S (2000) 'Women's burden: Counter-geographies of globalization and the feminization of survival', *Journal of International Affairs,* 53(2):503–524.

Sjoberg L (2009) 'Introduction to security studies: Feminist contributions', *Security Studies*, 18(2):183–213.

Sjoberg L and Via S (2010) 'Introduction' in Sjoberg L and Via S (eds) *Gender, war, and militarism: Feminist perspectives*, Praeger.

Strelnyk O (6 February 2025) *The Feminist Movement in War-Torn Ukraine: Challenges and Opportunities*, ZOIS. https://www.zois-berlin.de/en/publications/zois-spotlight/the-feminist-movement-in-war-torn-ukraine-challenges-and-opportunities

Strasbourg (18 July 2022) *Ukraine ratifies the Istanbul Convention*, Council of Europe. https://www.coe.int/en/web/istanbul-convention/-/ukraine-ratifies-the-istanbul-convention

The Kyiv Independent (14 October 2023) *Economy Ministry plans to reduce gender pay gap*. https://kyivindependent.com/economy-ministry-plans-to-reduce-gender-pay-gap/

Ukraine Facility (2023) *Plan for the Implementation of the Ukraine Facility 2024-2027*. https://www.ukrainefacility.me.gov.ua/

Ukrainska Pravda (12 January 2024) *Women assume "male" roles amidst full-scale war in Ukraine*. https://www.pravda.com.ua/eng/news/2024/01/12/7436878/

UN Women (2023) *Policy brief: A gender responsive recovery for ukraine: Introduction*, https://ukraine.unwomen.org/sites/default/files/2023-09/policy_brief_recovery_long_version_sept_2023_0.pdf

UN Women (18 September 2024) *Reducing the gender pay gap from 18.6% to 13.6% and launching the national campaign "Of Course You Can!" – how is Ukraine moving towards women's economic empowerment in times of great war?*. https://ukraine.unwomen.org/en/stories/pres-reliz/2024/09/skorochennya-hendernoho-rozryvu-v-oplati-pratsi-z-186-do-136-ta-start-natsionalnoyi-kampaniyi-zvisno-zmozhesh-yak-ukrayina-rukhayetsya-do-ekonomichnoho-upovnovazhennya-zhinok-u-chasy-velykoyi-viyny

Unions Help Refugees (3 January 2023) '"Be Like Nina!", Unions Help Refugees'. https://uhr.org.pl/en/be-like-nina/

Verkhovna Rada of Ukraine (18 July 2022) *Law of Ukraine: On making changes to some legislative acts of Ukraine regarding the regulation of labour relations with non-fixed working hours*. Signed by President Zelensky. https://zakon.rada.gov.ua/laws/show/2421-IX#Text

Vincent F (6 April 2025) *The invisible army of Ukrainian volunteers: "Without them, the country's defense and society would have suffered enormous losses"*, Le Monde. https://www.lemonde.fr/en/international/article/2025/04/06/the-invisible-army-of-ukrainian-volunteers-without-them-the-country-s-defense-and-society-would-have-suffered-enormous-losses_6739885_4.html

Westerman A (21 July 2024) *Women in Ukraine are taking over traditionally male-dominated work as the war goes on*, National Public Radio. https://www.npr.org/2024/07/21/nx-s1-5041604/women-in-ukraine-are-taking-over-traditionally-male-dominated-work-as-the-war-goes-on#:~:text=Weekend%20Edition%20Sunday-,Women%20in%20Ukraine%20are%20taking%20over%20traditionally%20male%2Ddominated%20work,who%20is%20available%20to%20work.

WILPF (Women's International League for Peace and Freedom) (2017) *The effects of intervention by international financial institutions on women's human rights in Ukraine*, Joint Shadow Report, CEDAW Committee.

World Bank (2023) *Ukraine – Third Rapid Damage and Needs Assessment February 2022–December 2023*, World Bank Group.

# 7

# GENDERED CIRCUITS OF VIOLENCE AND STATES OF AUSTERITY IN SOUTHERN EUROPE

*Iratxe Perea Ozerin*

In a joint statement released in February 2024 by the United States and Greece, within the framework of the Strategic Dialogue between both states, the former commended the Southern European country for spending over 3.5% of its GDP on defence. The document underlines this collaboration to promote peace and prosperity in Europe, "particularly in the wake of the October 7 attack on Israel, violent actions by the Houthis that threaten shipping and navigational rights and freedoms in the Red Sea, and Russia's ongoing war against Ukraine." It also refers to the "challenges" that Greece and "frontline countries in the Mediterranean face when receiving large numbers of migrants and asylum seekers while ensuring effective protection of the EU external borders."[1] The statement circumvents the reasons for these people to migrate, precisely, war, violence, and impoverishment. It also fails to mention how, parallel to the increase in military spending, which reached a record of 4% of GDP in 2022,[2] Greece keeps suffering the consequences of a deep social restructuring since 2010, including massive cuts of the minimum wage, job losses, cutbacks in social protection, and rising poverty. Neighbouring countries in the Mediterranean, Portugal, Spain, and Italy, have endured similar austerity-driven adjustments (Perez & Matsaganis, 2018).[3]

Indeed, the fleeting shift from austerity in Europe after the COVID-19 pandemic, including the temporary suspension of the Stability and Growth Pact (SGP) and the activation of the Next Generation EU (NGEU) funds in 2020, has made way for a landscape of war economies across the region that rest in further harm. The transfer of resources from social spending to preparation for war was clear in the EU Economic and Financial Council's (ECOFIN) announcement in December 2023.[4] Budgetary rules would be reintroduced, involving EU member states to collectively cut their budgets. Flexibility in these rules depends on commitments to reforms in pension systems, labour markets, and wages. Aditionally, these reforms

DOI: 10.4324/9781003571667-9

may require further cuts in public services, while military expenditures are secured and excluded from expenditure ceilings (Botenga, 2024). Fiscal reform was effectively adopted in April 2024. According to these rules, members exceeding a public deficit of 3% must follow a fiscal adjustment period to reduce government debt.[5]

This chapter explores the ways in which restructuring through austerity in Southern Europe has actually rested in the (re)production of everyday gender violence, exposing how austerity, and its gendered violent logics underpin the current militarisation of the region. At the same time, just like responses to the GFC in the 2010s, intensification of war economies in Europe is particularly useful to secure austerity. These interconnections between spaces of scarcity, militarisation and gender violence put forward the specific operative in this context of transnational gendered circuits of violence (True & Hozić, 2020: 1194) that run through the intimate and the international, across "private" and "public" spaces, contexts of war and alleged peace, and which connect traditionally compartmentalised sites of security and economy, in this case, of war, everyday violence, and austerity.

Feminist scholars in IR have long made these links, by doing feminist gender analysis and centring everyday lives and experiences (Enloe, 2016: 15–32). Indeed, taking the gendered violences and insecurities in the ground as a starting point reveals "how the security of the state and the prosperity of the global economy are frequently dependent on the insecurity of certain individuals', often women's, lives" (Tickner, 2006: 27). Global data on gender-based violence (GBV) corroborates this feminist premise. According to the UN Office on Drugs and Crime (UNODC) and UN Women, 60% (51,100) of the nearly 85,000 women intentionally killed in 2023 were murdered by their intimate partners or other family members. The proportion for men was significantly lower, at 12% (UNODC & UN Women, 2024). So, "private," allegedly "secure," sites such as the home are particularly dangerous for women. Still, defence and security policy dismiss sites of gendered insecurity like the household, as it constitutes a basic pillar of the global political economy.

Certainly, dominant conceptions of security, particularly in IR, tend to direct the attention of scholars and practitioners toward war and inter-state conflict. These perspectives prioritize state security within a self-help international system, often at the expense of the security of individuals and the natural environment (Tickner, 2018: 22). This approach is misleading on what should be the role of states and international institutions in providing security. It conveniently excludes security threats such as inequality, poverty, racism, and gender subordination, as well as their relation with international processes like war and economic crises, ignoring individuals and communities rendered vulnerable by these insecurities (Sjoberg, 2009, 2010: 4–5). As a result, states build their security on individuals' insecurity and, specifically, on women's bodies. Feminist global secureconomy is well equipped for grasping this logic, as these scholars prioritise bottom-up analyses that centre everyday gendered violences and insecurities in the study of the global political economy (see Elias, 2015; Elias & Rai, 2019; Meger, 2017). The chapter, thus, approaches from this lens the gendered circuits of violence that connect austerity politics, militarisation and war, and everyday insecurities.

Narratives of the GFC in 2008 eased pressure on the financial system from which it originated and reoriented attention towards the public sector and the household. In doing so, they concealed the "opportunity for contesting the normal, masculine ways of governing the global economy" (Hozić & True, 2016: 13), blocking, thus, transformative, inclusive economies and feminist solutions for violence (Cohn & Duncanson, 2021). Instead, austerity states and institutions directed the response towards cutbacks in public services and social policy, dismantling public gender regimes that in the case of Southern European social models, traditionally rooted in the family and women's unpaid care work, were already a source of gendered insecurities. This path has, more recently, facilitated the transfer of resources towards war preparedness. The current war economy-oriented scenario in Europe clearly exposes how gendered circuits of violence connect sites of scarcity and precarisation in Southern Europe, with militarised streets and borders in the region, and spaces of war such as Ukraine and Palestine.

To uncover how these circuits operate, the chapter first outlines the contribution of a feminist secureconomy perspective. Second, it examines the interconnections between spaces of austerity and war economies. Third, it analyses specific sites of GBV – namely the household, workplace, and street – within the austerity landscapes of Southern European countries since 2010 and considers how these contexts have secured the emergence and expansion of war economies in the region. The chapter concludes with some reflections on the operation of transnational gendered circuits of violence, as analysed in the context of Southern Europe since the GFC.

## Austerity from a feminist global secureconomy lens

Feminist global secureconomy reflects the combined approach of Feminist International Political Economy (FIPE) and Feminist Security Studies (FSS). FIPE has deepened into the material aspects of gender inequality and its connection with the global political economy, centring productive *and* reproductive economies. These scholars have addressed the gender dimension of crisis and readjustment (Bakker, 1994; Benería & Feldman, 1992; Elson, 2010, 2013), a research area that gained new interest after the crisis of 2008 (Hozić & True, 2016; Karamessini & Rubery, 2014; Walby, 2015). FSS, in turn, have critically engaged with international violence and security in IR, unpacking their discursive dimensions and examining how narratives and discourses construct gendered subjects and forms of resistance (Shepherd, 2007, 2008; Sjoberg, 2010).

Building on classic feminist works in IR, conversations between these sub-fields have emphasised the relevance of this integrated approach (see: Elias 2015; Hudson 2018; Weldes & Wynne-Hughes 2017). Indeed, it allows us to trace the circuits that interconnect spaces of scarcity, war and everyday gender violence outlined above.

Certainly, war and conflict greatly intensify gendered insecurities. But even the extreme, systematised and mass gender violence of war is elusive in traditional analyses of in/security in IR, particularly the attack on social reproduction as a consistent strategy of war. At the same time, these analyses further underestimate the scope of gender violence, as they ignore the continuum of gender violence that women still face "when no war has been declared, and life goes on in a state of everyday hostilities" (MacKinnon, 1994: 5–6). The violence within this continuum and its underlying logics are interconnected, and "to consider one moment in this flux in the absence of the next is arbitrary" (Cockburn, 2004: 43). This is particularly the case during crises, where narratives tend to exceptionalise and individualise violence, isolating it from structural inequalities and discrimination (True & Tanyag, 2019). At the same time, the dismantling of transnational gendered circuits of violence in traditional IR approaches, provides with limited understandings of violence and security across time and space.

Tracking these circuits is particularly relevant given that a key feature of capitalism has been its ability to hide the violence it produces, naturalising the suffering of some and valorising some lives over others (Hozić, 2021: 174). Austerity follows this logic. We can actually distinguish in its operative three key interconnected violent logics that create or exacerbate gender violence: dispossession, devaluation and discipline (Perea Ozerin, 2024).

First, austerity constitutes a mechanism persistently reactivated in times of crises of capitalism that deepens into processes of accumulation by dispossession (Federici, 2004: 125–126; Harvey, 2003: 142–146). It requires and secures gender orders based on the "housewifization" of women (see Mies et al., 1988; Mies, 2014). In the aftermath of the GFC in 2008, women did not leave paid work (Walby, 2015), they went through a combination of shock-absorbing in the household and more precarity in the labour market. This involves maintaining the relationship between "housewife" and salaried worker, and structuring women's time considering our responsibility in care. More than women's access to employment, this precludes women's access to professionalisation, to secure, better paid, permanent employment (Bennholdt-Thomsen 1988: 123–28). It pushes women to part-time, temporary, and informal work, limiting our access to social insurance and creating gendered insecurities. Such gendered and racialised hierarchies in work and access to resources, involving (violent) exclusions from formal, secure, paid work, or relegating groups of people to lower paid or lower status work, also condition social reproduction processes in households, communities, and neighbourhoods. Currently, broad sectors of the population -those relegated to the margins of paid work, periodic exclusions or subordinated positions- face limited access to resources and find it increasingly difficult to obtain the necessary means of subsistence (Bhattacharyya, 2018).

Second, austerity facilitates dispossession, generating "coping economies" for survival and social reproduction *also* in "peaceful" times. Coping strategies often involve resorting to informal insecure activities. Most often, these economies are feminised, so they result in a devaluation of the feminine that fuels and normalises violence, as it translates into underestimating/naturalising the burdens on women and the insecurities they experience, devaluating "women's work" and feminised skills, neglecting women's healthcare and reproductive issues, limiting women's participation in the "public" sphere, or prioritising male issues and employment (Peterson, 2008: 15). In particular, precarity due to austerity enables and condones practices that stereotype and devaluate women in employment (Weissman, 2004). Mechanisms such as stereotyping -which constitutes a form of indirect violence that can lead to direct violence (EIGE, 2013)- have actually *made* cheap women's work (Enloe, 2016, pp. 19–38). Disinvestment in social reproduction also devalues women's social position (Federici, 2013: 160–176). Such processes of devaluation and dehumanisation of women fuel and condone GBV.

Third, austerity politics encounter wide opposition, and states resort to discipline for its implementation. Austerity programmes have been described as a "shock doctrine" that exploits situations of crisis to advance the neoliberal project (Klein, 2007, 2018). Neoliberal globalisation has required a coercive role of states and the intensification of authoritarian tendencies in international institutions such as the EU after 2008 (Bruff & Wöhl, 2016; Tansel, 2017). Discipline targets those groups (women, feminists, activists, migrant people, refugees, racialised people or minorities) most affected by dispossession, and which constitute the bulk of opposition to austerity policies. These groups are subjected to devaluation and criminalisation to justify and facilitate dispossession and discipline. Austerity narratives render some bodies "vulnerable, precarious-even socially dead," while others are represented as entitled, "even as they may be economically disentitled by austerity measures" (Carastathis, 2015: 4). The "harshness" and "scarcity" of austerity politics naturalise hostility and the precarity and violence suffered by the "undeserving" (Carastathis, 2015). These narratives sustain the political economy of austerity, representing some groups as "not deserving" public policies and resources. This violent classification between "entitled" and "not entitled" secures cutbacks in public resources, as well as the ideology that sustains them (Ali & Whitham, 2021: 192), devaluating and dehumanising those most affected by the politics of austerity, and neutralising their demands. Such processes operate to facilitate the maintenance and intensification of war economies. There is a bidirectional relationship between both projects that we explore in the next section.

## War economies and austerity in Southern Europe

Instead of valuing security considering criteria such as food security or access to decent housing, dominant conceptions in IR involve a militarisation of national security (Enloe, 2016). This theory has guided international politics, advising states and governments to arm and prepare for war, under the narrative that this is the only valid, serious, strategy to prevent threats from outside their borders. Such a proposal involves states allocating an important part of public resources to this type of defence and military spending. Ultimately, the function of the armed forces and all the systems around them is to prepare for war, whether as deterrence, in defensive, or offensive ways. In this sense, we can talk about a *war economy* in a state, even if it is not *wartime* or if that territory is not directly *at war*. Its public institutions, policies and budget are still subordinated to war preparedness (Ortega, 2019). This is the case of Southern European countries in the current European scenario, where even though unemployment, precarity, authoritarian governance, and resulting insecurity greatly increased because of the GFC, the consolidation of permanent austerity has facilitated the prioritisation of militarism and the intensification of war economies.

Indeed, in the aftermath of the GFC, austerity became one of the hegemonic projects in Europe. As the sovereign debt crisis extended across the Eurozone in 2010, the "troika" of the European Commission, European Central Bank (ECB) and IMF demanded austerity in countries increasingly unable to pay their debt, as a condition for financial support. Formally (by signing Memoranda of Understanding) or through implicit conditionality by the ECB, Southern European countries, Portugal, Spain, Italy, and Greece, were required to implement austerity measures involving minimisation of fiscal deficits, inflation and import tariffs, and maximisation of privatisations and liberalisation of finance (Perez & Matsaganis, 2018; Blyth, 2013). Austerity programmes increased poverty in the four countries compared to pre-crisis levels and reversed the trends toward greater equality and inclusion observed in the previous decades (Perez & Matsaganis, 2018). Even though the scope and form of the crisis and its austerity responses varied across these countries, austerity politics exacted a heavy human toll in all of them. Following what has been described as a "lost decade" in the region, Southern Europe entered the pandemic in 2020 with severely under-resourced health systems, which contributed to higher mortality rates compared to their European neighbours. Despite a more supportive response from EU institutions to the COVID-19 crisis, which enabled spending on job retention schemes and limited the impact on employment, these measures did little to assist those who had been most affected by austerity during the previous decade. Poverty continued to rise during those months, and sectors of the population on the margins of paid employment, who had already fallen into social exclusion, were particularly affected by the cost-of-living crisis resulting from the war in Ukraine and the rising energy prices (Pérez, 2023).

Against this backdrop, and in parallel with the expanding austerity project, military spending has increased to record levels over the past decade. In Europe, it totalled $588 billion in 2023, 16% more than in 2022 and 62% more than in 2014 (Tian et al., 2024). NATO's 2023 European military spending (adding non-EU members Norway and the United Kingdom) amounted to $366,623 billion, coming in second place only to the world's top military spender (the United States), above China, and tripling Russia's military spending (Brunet et al., 2024). Effectively, this funding generates a military economic cycle that starts with states' budgets and the allocation of resources to Ministries or Departments of Defence, responsible to maintain armed forces, but also including public spending set aside for research and development of weapons and equipment, or funding for the military industries that produce them. This cycle is self-feeding as these companies end up selling their products to the state (Ortega, 2019: 13–14). Indeed, these economies do not have a positive impact in society and public opinion is generally not favourable to military spending.

As a result, and despite the existence of NATO criteria to measure military expenditures, which are also used by the Stockholm International Peace Research Institute (SIPRI), governments apply different measurement methods depending on their interests in the matter, so it is difficult to know exactly the costs of militarisation. States like Spain, and also the United States, Russia, or China, exclude from their calculation's military-related items that, for technical or political reasons, are not included in the Ministry of Defence budget but are instead allocated under other budgetary headings. These include, for instance, funds for military-oriented research and development (R&D) through industry ministries, expenditures on foreign military missions, or costs associated with internal security, including allocations to paramilitary forces such as the Spanish Civil Guard, or in Italy's case, the Carabinieri (Ortega, 2019). In fact, beyond established criteria, states or international institutions such as NATO can unilaterally redefine what counts as military according to their own interests.

On the one hand, the strategy of camouflaging the cost of militarisation (Ortega, 2019) reveals that governments are concerned with justifying resource allocations that are not necessarily popular, especially in societies affected by poverty and unemployment. In Southern Europe, after a "lost decade," military spending has not been significantly reduced to prioritise social needs. To the contrary, in all the cases the share of GDP for military expenditure in 2023 is higher than in 2010. At the same time, as NATO members, all these countries must reach the arbitrary 2% of GDP in military spending required by the organisation. Recently, NATO's Secretary-General Mark Rutte has called for a new spending target of 3%, arguing that "it is time to shift to a wartime mindset."[6] Likewise, US President Donald Trump has stated that this percentage should reach 5%[7]. Such statements place pressure on member states to continue increasing military spending.

In the case of Greece, as we have seen, expenditures have already reached record levels, doubling NATO's current requirements, but Italy, Spain and Portugal are regarded as laggards. Given current pressures, though, Italy announced a new historic high in military spending for 2025, $32,000 million, reflecting a 12.4% increase compared to the previous week, and a 60% increase over the past decade (Vignarca, 2024). Spain and Portugal also committed to reach the 2%. Portugal requested the activation of the national escape clause from the Commission to spend more on defence without violating deficit rules. And, according to the Spanish government, its military spending in 2025 will be $33,123 million, representing a 70% increase in the last decade.[8] The Centre Delàs d'Estudis per la Pau in Barcelona, specialised in disarmament and peace, has actually indicated that Spain's military spending, measured through NATO's criteria, already reached 2.17% of GDP in 2023 (Ortega et al., 2022) and will reach 2.48% in 2025, $40,457 million (Rodríguez, 2025).

In this context, social needs are once again devalued and sidelined, not due to a global financial crisis, but because of a prioritisation of militarised security. As noted above, alongside the historic surge in military spending, the EU has reinstated its fiscal rule limiting member states' budget deficits to 3% of GDP, following its temporary suspension in 2020 due to the COVID-19 crisis. According to a study by the European Trade Union Confederation (ETUC), the fiscal rules adopted in 2024 will lead to cuts worth over $100 billion for the first year only, while the EU would need additional public investment to meet their own social and green goals. Most of EU members will not be able to meet their targets for public investment in schools, hospitals and housing, including Southern European countries. The European Commission's own figures show a disinvestment in social infrastructure of $192 billion a year. This would need to be raised annually by $120 billion in health, $57 billion in affordable housing and $15 billion in education (Mang & Caddick, 2024).

As a recent European Economy Discussion Paper shows (Cepparulo & Pasimeni, 2024), advocates of military investment link it to economic growth. But the type of circular economy that it creates within the military industrial complex is better described as antisocial (Ortega, 2019; Ortega et al., 2022). As mentioned earlier, this is a source of public opposition to military expenditures, and austerity seems to intensify this rejection. However, representations of external threats can reorient citizens' perceptions, even when facing the social burdens created and exacerbated by austerity policies (DiGiuseppe et al., 2024). Transfer of resources from social policies to military spending is legitimated through specific depictions of external threats and security needs. This is clear in the above-mentioned joint document by Greece and the United States, which represents migration as a "challenge" related to the defence of Europe's external borders.

Indeed, Southern European countries adopting austerity policies have become "Europe's shield," a term used by the Commission's president Ursula von der Leyen in 2020 to praise Greek efforts in preventing refugees from crossing the highly militarised steel wall-border with Turkey on the Evros river, once again, shifting focus away from asylum rights and humanitarian crises resulting from armed conflicts in Syria, Afghanistan, or Iraq, towards narratives of "threats," "invasion" and the need of "border protection" (Vasilaki, 2020). Southern Europe effectively functions as a violent and *technologised* shield in the Mediterranean borders of the EU, collaborating with Frontex (the European Border and Coast Guard Agency) and NATO in a militarised European regime of migration (Ruiz Benedicto, 2019) that the austerity politics of scarcity, differentiation, and exclusion help to normalise. Delegitimization of social needs through austerity, is also instrumental for a prioritisation of military needs.

Militarism expands beyond armed forces and military bases, resulting in militarised individuals, groups, and societies, at material, cultural, and ideological levels.

Feminist scholars in IR have exposed how these spaces are particularly masculinised, reinforcing gender orders and roles, and are especially hostile for women and anyone transgressing these values (Enloe, 2016). At the same time, this process involves a prioritisation of war preparedness, to the detriment of a social use of public resources, that induces or exacerbates gendered insecurities. In that sense, we can say that interconnected war economies and austerity politics are built over the bodies of women. The following section delves into sites of everyday gender violence created or intensified under these dynamics.

## Sites of everyday gender violence in Southern Europe

The context described above is particularly concerning for Southern European women, given that these countries share a social model in which the family plays a central role as the guarantor of the welfare state (Karamessini, 2007: 2). They present most of the characteristics of a family-based care regime in which the male breadwinner has traditionally played a key role, enjoying high employment protection and job stability, while other groups like women, young people or migrants suffer from high unemployment and are disproportionally involved in informal work. Care of children and elderly has been traditionally provided by the unpaid work of women, and labour market segmentation has created gaps and inequalities in employment and social protection (Karamessini, 2007: 2–4). Even if the social protection system had improved immediately before the GFC, it was still oriented towards the protection of male breadwinners temporarily or definitively laid off. The state had increased its role in childcare, but the family or paid domestic care remained the rule, also in the case of the elderly. In both cases, the carers are predominantly women (Karamessini, 2007: 15–25).

Given the socioeconomic and cultural conditions produced by this model, both austerity and war economy pose dangers in terms of gendered insecurities. Indeed, war economy contributes to shifting security concerns from "private" to "public," traditional, sites of violence, redirecting attention towards militarised forms of security. Moreover, Southern Europe's role as the militarised border of the EU in the Mediterranean further reinforces these dynamics. Considering these factors, this section explores three specific sites of everyday gender violence: the household, the workplace, and the street.

### *Household*

The household is a central site to understand the violence of the global political economy and of austerity politics. Firstly, because, as the pillar of social reproduction and life, the household is a main target in plans for social restructuring, also in connection with war economies. Control and/or destruction of means for social reproduction is a political and strategic choice in global capitalism, it is not collateral. Austerity is a mechanism to intensify and legitimise such destruction in times of crises. Second, as the "private" place where intimate partner violence (IPV), the most prevalent form of GBV, mostly occurs, it constitutes a particularly dangerous place for women, where violence has been traditionally, and strategically, silenced and depoliticised. As noted above, this devaluation of women's security needs intensifies in the war economy.

Indeed, IPV is about power and control. Rachel Pain has framed it as "intimate war" (Pain, 2015) and "everyday terrorism" (Pain, 2014), putting forward the severity, complexity, and political character of this form of violence. This frame locates "global war/terrorism" and "everyday war/terrorism" in the same complex. These violences share a common objective to exert political control through fear. Violence happening in the private sphere of the household is also *measured* violence that operates through emotions and psychology as well as physical violence. It involves a psychological and emotional warfare that instills fear (Pain, 2014, 2015). Pain's analysis depicts the household as a site of recurrent, political, and strategic violence against women. This violence serves to sustain a specific social model rooted in women's unpaid labor. Feminist research has revealed the correlation between IPV and high levels of economic stress within the household, resulting from austerity measures that increase unemployment and precarity (True, 2012: 105). This research further demonstrates how austerity reinforces this model and its associated violence.

In its reports on the post-crisis period, the CEDAW Committee highlighted the prevalence of IPV in Portugal, Spain, Italy, and Greece, as well as its underreporting and the low numbers of prosecutions and convictions. The Committee pointed, for example, to the deterioration of protection services for women victims of domestic violence in Spain, the number of children killed during the visitation rights, and "the limited access to civil courts for women victims of domestic violence who seek restraining orders" in Italy (CEDAW, 2015a, 2015b, 2017, 2013).

Despite these scenarios of violence in the household, austerity policies in Southern Europe targeted resources directed at this site, which had the objective of socialising care and reversing the family-based social model. Initiatives such as the Ministry of Equality or the Dependency Law to de-familiarise care in Spain were suspended (González Gago & Segales Kirzner, 2014: 228–247). In Greece, in a very short period, there were massive cutbacks in public services and social benefits, important reductions in the salaries of the public sector, cuts of pensions, and high rises of taxes. The National Program for Gender Equality was not enough to absorb the effects of the extreme austerity measures imposed in the country (Karamessini, 2014: 164–185). There were also cutbacks in policies to prevent and combat IPV that, for example in the case of Portugal, had been reinforced in 2007 (Ferreira, 2014: 207–227; Karamessini & Rubery, 2014). Financialisation of housing, as well as private pension schemes, and privatisation of health or private provision of care for people with dependency intensified since 2008, constituting another mechanism for dispossession in the reproduction sphere (Wöhl, 2017).

Dispossession of means for social reproduction and socialisation of care was accompanied by a matching narrative, to displace the responsibility for the crisis towards the household. Such reorientation requires to reinforce narratives on the traditional family and the role of women as guarantors of reproduction. As an example, in 2014, the Spanish Minister of Justice Alberto Ruiz Gallardón tried to reform the law on abortion towards a restrictive model, deploying a conservative discourse in defence of the "family" as "a natural reality" that "cannot abdicate their obligation to educate their children," nor should they delegate this responsibility "in favor of public powers or private institutions" (Europapress, 2014). Landscapes of widespread unemployment and precarity, like those described in the next section, have also condemned a whole generation of young people to remain economically dependent on their parents, often forced to live in the family home well into their thirties. Like Theodoros Karyotis reflects, especially in countries with social models based on the family, once again "this reinforces the moral authority of the patriarchal family over the dependent family members" (Karyotis, 2020), with a specific effect of reinforcing gender stereotypes and gendered insecurities.

### *Workplace*

Feminist scholars and activists have long established a correlation between gender violence and workplace hierarchies. The European Trade Union Confederation (ETUC) highlights how the world of work is connected with *all* forms of gender violence, in particular, sexual harassment, IPV, third-party violence and cyber-violence, with a centrality in this space of related-economic violence and harm (ETUC, 2024). Recently, the #MeToo movement has put forward the scope of the everyday sexualised violence that women suffer in their jobs across different industries. According to testimonies, "men who harass and rape women [do not] pick any 'random' woman," they target women who are made vulnerable because they are young, just starting their professional careers, or have precarious contracts (see: De los Reyes, 2023: 37). This depicts, once again, scenarios of measured and controlled violence, which function to subordinate and discipline women while limiting our professional possibilities. In these contexts, austerity-induced precarity, insecurity, and individualisation in employment prevent workers from defending their rights and making collective demands (De los Reyes, 2023), thereby creating gendered insecurities.

There is also an interconnection between IPV and gender violence in the workplace. Normalised everyday gendered and racialised violence in employment determines workers' subjectivities beyond the workplace, while, at the same time, women exposed to IPV experience work-related impacts such as barriers to employment, lost wages or decreased working capacity. This interdependence reinforces the heteronormative male breadwinner/female carer family model that sustains traditional social reproduction systems (De los Reyes, 2023). Unemployment is also a key factor in gendered insecurity, as it significantly disrupts social relations within the household. Furthermore, stereotyping and the devaluation of women workers fuel gender-based violence beyond the workplace (Weissman, 2004).

Austerity in Southern Europe generated sharp increases of unemployment, facilitating a reserve army of labour and worsening working conditions. It has also attacked frameworks and tools for safer working conditions and rendered workplaces more insecure for women. Labour market reforms were justified as mechanisms to reduce labour segmentation, particularly in Spain and Portugal, where temporary contracts were widespread. However, these measures led to overall wage reductions and more precarious employment conditions (Perez & Matsaganis, 2018). If we look at the evolution of unemployment rates for women and men in these countries since 2000, considering as well other indicators of precarity such as part-time employment and informal work, the "shock" and the landscape of insecurity generated by austerity clearly emerge.

In terms of unemployment, there were peaks between 2013 and 2014 in the four countries, with huge disruptions such as in the case of women in Greece, rising from 11.5% to 31.3% between 2008 and 2013, after a period (2000–2008) in which this indicator was in decline. In Spain, the trend also reversed. It decreased between 2000 and 2008, but it rose from 12.8% to 26.7% between 2008 and 2013. In the case of men, both in Spain and Portugal unemployment had been rising from 2000 to 2008, still, there was also a sharper growth between 2008 and 2013[9]. Both women and men's unemployment have declined since then. However, despite optimistic narratives, the numbers have barely gone back to 2008. If we look at percentages of unemployed women in January 2024, the rates were 6.9% in Portugal, 13.2% in Spain, 13.2% in Greece and 8.2% in Italy, while unemployment in men amounts to 6.1% in Portugal, 10.1% in Spain, 6.5% in Italy and 8% in Greece.[10]

In the aftermath of the GFC, the European labour market also resented from an increase in layoffs, around 25% between 2008 and 2015. Italy accounted for around 45% of laid-off workers in the EU in both years. The share of part-time employment has also increased in recent decades and accentuated after 2008. Women constitute most of the part-time work with very short hours (four out of five part-timers in the EU), but the share of male part-timers has also increased. The growing share of involuntary part-time work is especially worrying. Together with Cyprus, Greece and Spain were the countries where involuntary part-time work grew most after 2008, and this is correlated with an increase in unemployment, exposing poor labour market performance. The labour slack rate increased to very high levels in the four countries between 2008 and 2015: from 9.8% to 28.8% in Greece, from 16.7% to 24% in Italy, from 10.2% to 19.1% in Portugal, and from 16.4% to 28.4% in Spain. Italy has also a very high share of "discouraged workers," or working-age individuals who are available but not seeking work, reaching more than one in three of the EU total in 2015 (Eurofound, 2017).

Such precarity required discipline. In fact, labour reforms can also be understood in this light. They involved atomisation of employment contractual relations and the erosion of collective bargaining and labour legislation (Clua-Losada &

Ribera-Almandoz, 2017). Furthermore, these reforms have not been reversed, reaffirming the structural logic of austerity. In Italy, for example, there has been a continuity in liberalisation of the labour market, with the post-pandemic National Recovery and Resilience Plan (NRRP) from 2021 deepening into neoliberalisation. Dismantling of employment protection legislation has not been reversed, and the Plan continues dynamics of union disempowerment, with a dominance of employer interests. It shows a neoliberal approach to gender equality, allocating resources for female entrepreneurship and women-led start-ups, while structural gendered insecurities related with the labour market, like low female participation, stagnant wages and high incidence of informal and precarious employment remain (Tassinari, 2022). In this context, the ETUC states that austerity should be recognised as a form of economic violence against women, and underlines collective bargaining as a tool to address GBV (ETUC 2024). Feminist scholars also stress labour international standards and national labour laws, weakened as a result of austerity policies, as key intervention areas (Weissman, 2004).

### *Street*

Gendered insecurity in public spaces is often linked to sexual and street harassment. From this perspective, feminist scholars have examined how limitations in public services, such as street lighting or public transport, create or exacerbate gendered insecurities in public spaces (Gálvez Muñoz, 2013). They have also highlighted how austerity measures lead to cutbacks in public policies and programmes aimed at tackling violence against women (Karamessini & Rubery, 2014). These measures devaluate women's experiences of insecurity and feminist solutions, sending the message that this is not a priority in times of crisis. At the same time, like other types of GBV, sexual harassment is also about control over women and our access to political, economic and social resources. This violence is anticipated and recurrent, normalised and accepted "when the power to define the situation resides with those who are not experiencing it." Those who experience it learn from a very young age that the public sphere is not for them, and struggle to reclaim it (Lundqvist et al., 2023: 224). Such power is used to discipline feminist activism and limit women's participation in public forums, and this struggle intensifies in times of austerity, combining with state coercion.

Indeed, as a tool for advancing the neoliberal project, austerity undermines the state's role in promoting welfare and gender equality, while simultaneously relying on force and coercion to implement such measures. This coercive role is further legitimised within the war economy, where militarism is both expanded and revalorised. Authoritarian neoliberalism began to intensify in Europe after 2008, with policies such as the restriction of EU member states' parliamentary capacity to define national budgets, a measure that, as previously noted, was suspended in 2020 but reinstated in 2024. Hard law adopted as a result of the GFC, such as the Fiscal Compact, the so-called Six Pack legislation and the Euro-Plus Pact, increased the capacity of the EU to require from state members economic reforms, correction of macroeconomic imbalances or the implementation of austerity measures if necessary, including sanctions for members not following these guidelines (Bruff & Wöhl, 2016).

Wide opposition to these measures in Southern European streets has been contained through state force and legal instruments such as the so-called Gag Laws in Spain, including the reform of the Penal Code and the Citizen Security Law, still in force despite changes of government. Since 2015, these laws have been used to criminalise activism and protests, including anti-austerity movements (Escaño, 2024). The feminist group *Asamblea Feminista de Valencia*, for example, accumulated more than $11,000 in fines, based on these laws, for non-violent actions related to the feminist strikes on March 8, 2018 and 2019 (Simón, 2022). An additional provision in the Citizen Security Law also legalises summary expulsions, which combined with the use of force by authorities in the border, resulted in 470 forced returns, 37 people dead and at least 76 disappeared in the case known as the "massacre of Melilla" on June 24, 2022 (Escaño, 2024).

Indeed, the politics of contention since 2010 have sought to neutralise the legitimate demands and protests of those most affected by austerity, including refugees and migrant people. In this period, Greece saw an increase in gendered and racialised attacks against refugees and migrants that have been connected to austerity politics. Indeed, the securitisation and dehumanisation of migration in Europe results in massive loss of life and extreme suffering, without these lives even being mourned, officially or even socially in our streets (Carastathis, 2015; Miralles, 2019: 31).

Suffering and unrest in this period were also caused by housing dispossession, which became a central problem in the aftermath of the crisis. Research on Lisbon points at the facilitation of evictions and liberalisation of rents as a result of austerity measures, which together with lack of social housing, has resulted in housing exclusions and increasing occupation for economic hardship and inaccessibility to other forms of housing, being single low-income mothers "a clear majority of these occupiers" (Saaristo, 2022). As a result of the crisis and austerity policies, non-performing mortgages in Greece went from 5% of all mortgages in 2008 to 45% in 2019. Many renters in the neighbourhood of Koukaki in Athens, for example, have been thrown out, being their homes bought by foreign or local investors and turned into touristic flats. Anti-Airbnb demonstrations in Koukaki, or in the socially organised Exarcheia, have been met with violent repression (Karyotis, 2020). The anti-evictions Platform for People Affected by Mortgages (PAH) in Spain, one of the most active movements against austerity, has been criminalised and targeted through the Gag Laws (La PAH, 2022). As well as gendered insecurities resulting from housing dispossession and repression against collective care and action in this context, we should also consider that increasing rents – often higher than the average wage – resulting from austerity-driven commodification and financialisation of housing, interconnected with gentrification and tourism, drive locals out of their neighbourhoods, disrupting social relations and community networks, and exacerbating gendered insecurities in the street.

## Conclusion

The study of transnational gendered circuits of violence in Southern Europe since the GFC reveals how austerity politics and militarisation in the region rest in GBV. Gender violence serves to reinforce the heteronormative family structure, along with the gender stereotypes and values that underpin austerity-driven, depleted economies. These economies reproduce, and rely on, gender-based violence because of widespread precarity in employment and housing. They expropriate common goods, weaken workers' collective mechanisms for demanding safe labour conditions, and contain and militarise spaces of contestation and feminist resistance in the streets. Everyday gendered insecurities in these sites are exacerbated by a (re)orientation of security towards traditional, militarised frameworks and policies. Gendered circuits of violence, thus, connect spaces of alleged peace to the logics and materials of war, seeking to discipline and control those groups especially targeted by the exclusions and harms of the global political economy.

While austerity policies might intensify public opposition to military spending, the consolidation of this project, both materially and ideologically, facilitates the diversion of social resources toward war preparedness by devaluing social needs and enabling the militarisation. Likewise, war economy functions to secure austerity, dismissing feminist conceptions of security and solutions to GBV that rely on the socialisation of care, the provision of social services, and public gender regimes. It also legitimises, and materially supports, the state's coercive role in disciplining anti-austerity and feminist resistance.

## Notes

1 I would like to thank the editors of the book, Aida Hozić and Jacqui True, for their valuable insights and comments on previous drafts of the chapter. I am also thankful to Ian Bruff, Burak Tansel, Julia Hartviksen, Alison Johnston, Catherine Eschle, and participants in the workshop on "Global Entanglements of the Neoliberal Security State" at EWIS 2023, for their encouragement and suggestions.
2 Joint Statement on the U.S.-Greece Strategic Dialogue, February 9, 2024, https://www.state.gov/joint-statement-on-the-u-s-greece-strategic-dialogue-2/.
3 See SIPRI Military Expenditure Database, https://www.sipri.org/databases/milex.
4 Economic and Financial Affairs Council, 8 December 2023, https://www.consilium.europa.eu/en/meetings/ecofin/2023/12/08/.
5 Council of the EU, "Economic governance review: Council adopts reform of fiscal rules", 29 April 2024, https://www.consilium.europa.eu/en/press/press-releases/2024/04/29/economic-governance-review-council-adopts-reform-of-fiscal-rules/.
6 POLITICO, "NATO's Rutte wants a return to Cold War-level military spending", 12/12/2024,https://www.politico.eu/article/nato-secretary-general-mark-rutte-cold-war-military-spending-defense-budgets-russia/.
7 Euractiv, "Trump asks Europe again for more defence cash, leaves NATO strategy elusive", 13/03/2025, https://www.euractiv.com/section/defence/news/trump-asks-europe-again-for-more-defence-cash-leaves-nato-strategy-elusive/.

8 Swissinfo, "Portugal y España se comprometen a aumentar su gasto militar en el marco de la OTAN", 27/01/2025, https://www.swissinfo.ch/spa/portugal-y-espa%C3%B1a-se-comprometen-a-aumentar-su-gasto-militar-en-el-marco-de-la-otan/88788292; Swissinfo, "Portugal pedirá a UE acogerse a cláusula para aumentar gasto en defensa sin subir déficit", 23/04/2025, https://www.swissinfo.ch/spa/portugal-pedir%C3%A1-a-ue-acogerse-a-cl%C3%A1usula-para-aumentar-gasto-en-defensa-sin-subir-d%C3%A9ficit/89202284.
9 See: OECD Factbook 2015–2016; Eurostat.
10 Data from Eurostat: Unemployment by sex and age – annual data, https://ec.europa.eu/eurostat/databrowser/view/UNE_RT_A__custom_6710001/default/table?lang=en.

## References


Ali, N., & Whitham, B. (2021). Racial Capitalism, Islamophobia, and Austerity. *International Political Sociology*, *15*(2), 190–211.

Bakker, I. (Ed.). (1994). *The Strategic Silence. Gender and Economic Policy*. ZedBooks and the North-South Institute.

Benería, L., & Feldman, S. (Eds.). (1992). *Unequal Burden: Economic Crises, Persistent Poverty, And Women's Work*. Westview Press.

Bennholdt-Thomsen, V. (1988). The future of women's work and violence against women. In M. Mies, V. Bennholdt-Thomsen, & C. Von Werholf (Eds.), *Women: The last colony* (pp. 113–130). Zed Books.

Bhattacharyya, G. (2018). *Rethinking Racial Capitalism: Questions of Reproduction and Survival*. Rowman & Littlefield.

Blyth, M. (2013). *Austerity: The History of a Dangerous Idea*. Oxford University Press.

Botenga, M. (2024, January 25). *Europe's Leaders Are Addicted to Austerity*. Jacobin. https://jacobin.com/2024/01/european-commission-austerity-working-class

Bruff, I., & Tansel, C. B. (2019). Authoritarian Neoliberalism: Trajectories of Knowledge Production and Praxis. *Globalizations*, *16*(3), 233–244.

Bruff, I., & Wöhl, S. (2016). Constitutionalizing Austerity, Disciplining the Household—Masculine Norms of Competitiveness and the Crisis of Social Reproduction in the Eurozone. In A. A. Hozić & J. True (Eds.), *Scandalous Economics. Gender and the Politics of Financial Crises* (pp. 92–108). Oxford University Press.

Brunet, P., Calvo, J., Font, T., Ortega, P., & de Vries, W. (2024). *Peace and disarmament in Europe. For shared détente, peace and security* (65). Centre Delàs D'Estudis Per la Pau. https://centredelas.org/publicacions/peaceanddisarmamentineurope/?lang=es

Carastathis, A. (2015). The Politics of Austerity and the Affective Economy of Hostility: Racialised Gendered Violence and Crises of Belonging in Greece. *Feminist Review*, *109*(1), 73–95. https://doi.org/10.1057/fr.2014.50

Cepparulo, A., & Pasimeni, P. (2024). *Defence Spending in the European Union* (199; Discussion Paper). Publications Office of the European Union. https://economy-finance.ec.europa.eu/publications/defence-spending-european-union_en

Clua-Losada, M., & Ribera-Almandoz, O. (2017). Authoritarian neoliberalism and the disciplining of labour. In C. B. Tansel (Ed.), *States of Discipline. Authoritarian Neoliberalism and the Contested Reproduction of Capitalist Order* (pp. 29–46). Rowman & Littlefield.

Cockburn, C. (2004). The continuum of violence: A gender perspective on war and peace. In W. Giles & J. Hyndman (Eds.), *Sites of Violence: Gender and Conflict Zones* (pp. 24–44). University of California Press.

Cohn, C., & Duncanson, C. (2021). Create just, inclusive feminist economies to foster sustainable peace. In M. MacKenzie & N. Wegner (Eds.), *Feminist Solutions for Ending War* (pp. 181–199). Pluto Press.

Committee on the Elimination of Discrimination against Women (CEDAW). (2013, March 26). *Concluding observations on the seventh periodic report of Greece adopted by the Committee at its fifty fourth session (11 February – 1 March 2013)*.

Committee on the Elimination of Discrimination against Women (CEDAW). (2015a). *Concluding observations on the combined eighth and ninth periodic reports of Portugal*.

Committee on the Elimination of Discrimination against Women (CEDAW). (2015b, July 29). *Concluding observations on the combined seventh and eighth periodic reports of Spain*.

Committee on the Elimination of Discrimination against Women (CEDAW). (2017). *Concluding observations on the seventh periodic report of Italy*.

De los Reyes, P. (2023). Depleted bodies: Intersectional perspectives on workplace violence. In M. Lundqvist, A. Simonsson, & K. Widegren (Eds.), *Re-Imagining Sexual Harassment.Perspectives from the Nordic Region* (pp. 33–47). Policy Press.

DiGiuseppe, M., Aspide, A., & Becker, J. (2024). Threats and the Public Constraint on Military Spending. *British Journal of Political Science*, *54*(3), 649–666. https://doi.org/10.1017/S0007123423000443

Elias, J. (2015). Introduction: Feminist Security Studies and Feminist Political Economy: Crossing Divides and Rebuilding Bridges. *Politics & Gender*, *11*(2), 406–408. https://doi.org/10.1017/S1743923X15000100

Elias, J., & Rai, S. M. (2019). Feminist Everyday Political Economy: Space, Time, and Violence. *Review of International Studies*, *45*(2), 201–220. https://doi.org/10.1017/S0260210518000323

Elson, D. (2010). Gender and the Global Economic Crisis in Developing Countries: A Framework for Analysis. *Gender and Development*, *18*(2), 201–212.

Elson, D. (2013). Economic crises from the 1980s to the 2010s: A gender analysis. In G. Waylen & S. M. Rai (Eds.), *New Frontiers in Feminist Political Economy* (pp. 189–212). Routledge.

Enloe, C. (2016). *Globalization and Militarism. Feminists Make the Link* (Second). Rowman & Littlefield.

Escaño, C. (2024, January 7). *Leyes Mordaza: Análisis de 9 años de restricciones y libertad de expresión en España*. https://www.es.amnesty.org/en-que-estamos/blog/historia/articulo/ley-mordaza/

ETUC (European Trade Union Confederation). (2024, June 25). *Adopted Resolution—On the offensive to combat gender-based violence in the world of work | ETUC*. https://etuc.org/en/document/adopted-resolution-offensive-combat-gender-based-violence-world-work

Eurofound. (2017). *Estimating Labour Market Slack in the European Union*. Publications Office of the European Union.

Europapress. (2014, 11). *Gallardón dice que le producen 'asco' los motivos para retirar la reforma de la ley del aborto | España | EL MUNDO*. https://www.elmundo.es/espana/2014/11/14/546648aa268e3e65098b456c.html

European Institute for Gender Equality (EIGE). (2013). *Gender Equality Index: Report*. Publications Office of the European Union.

Federici, S. (2004). *Caliban and the Witch: Women, the Body and Primitive Accumulation*. Autonomedia.

Federici, S. (2013). La Reproducción de la Fuerza de Trabajo en la Economía Global y la Inacabada Revolución Reminista. In *Revolución en Punto Cero. Trabajo Doméstico, Reproducción y Luchas Feministas* (pp. 153–180). Traficantes de Sueños.

Ferreira, V. (2014). Employment and Austerity: Changing welfare and gender regimes in Portugal. In M. Karamessini & J. Rubery (Eds.), *Women and Austerity: The Economic Crisis and the Future for Gender Equality*. Routledge.

Gálvez Muñoz, L. (2013). Una lectura feminista del austericidio. *Revista de Economía Crítica, 15*, 80–110.

González Gago, E., & Segales Kirzner, M. (2014). Women, Gender Equality and the Economic Crisis in Spain. In M. Karamessini & J. Rubery (Eds.), *Women and Austerity: The Economic Crisis and the Future for Gender Equality*. Routledge.

Harvey, D. (2003). *The New Imperialism*. Oxford University Press.

Hozić, A. A. (2021). Follow the Bodies: Global Capitalism, Global War, Global Crisis and Feminist IPE. *International Relations, 35*(1), 173–177. https://doi.org/10.1177/0047117821992418

Hozić, A. A., & True, J. (Eds.). (2016). *Scandalous Economics: Gender and the Politics of Financial Crises*. Oxford University Press.

Hudson, H. (2018). Close(d) encounters: Feminist security studies engages feminist (I)PE. In J. Elias & A. Roberts (Eds.), *Handbook on the International Political Economy of Gender* (pp. 127–141). Elgar.

Karamessini, M. (2007). *The Southern European social model: Changes and continuities in recent decades*. International Labour Organization.

Karamessini, M., & Rubery, J. (2014). *Women and Austerity: The Economic Crisis and the Future for Gender Equality*. Routledge.

Karyotis, T. (2020, July 1). *Repression, Eviction and Dispossession in New Democracy's Greece*. ROAR Magazine. https://roarmag.org/essays/squat-eviction-house-dispossession-greece/

Klein, N. (2007). *The Shock Doctrine: The Rise of Disaster Capitalism*. Knopf Canada.

Klein, N. (2018). *The Battle for Paradise. Puerto Rico Takes on the Disaster Capitalists*. Haymarket Books.

La PAH. (2022, February 11). *Movilización contra la Ley Mordaza*. Plataforma de Afectados por la Hipoteca (PAH). https://afectadosporlahipoteca.com/2022/02/11/movilizacion-contra-la-ley-mordaza/

Lundqvist, M., Simonsson, A., & Widegren, K. (Eds.). (2023). *Re-Imagining Sexual Harassment. Perspectives from the Nordic Region*. Policy Press.

MacKinnon, C. A. (1994). Rape, Genocide, and Women's Human Rights. *Harvard Women's Law Journal, 17*, 5.

Mang, S., & Caddick, D. (2024). *Navigating Constraints for Progress: Examining the Impact of EU Fiscal Rules on Social and Green Investments*. ETUC. https://www.etuc.org/en/pressrelease/study-social-cost-austerity-rules

Meger, S. (2017, September 3). Introducing Feminist 'Secureconomy'. *Progress in Political Economy (PPE)*. https://www.ppesydney.net/introducing-feminist-secureconomy/

Miralles, N. (2019). *Gender and Security Policies. A Feminist Look into the Impacts of Militarization in the West*. Centre Delàs d'Estudis per la Pau. https://centredelas.org/publicacions/informe-36-genero-y-politicas-de-la-inseguridad-una-mirada-feminista-hacia-los-impactos-de-la-militarizacion-de-occidente/?lang=en

Ortega, P. (2019). *The War Economy*. Centre Delàs d'Estudis per la Pau.

Ortega, P., Bohigas, X., & Moya, X. (2022). *El colosal aumento del presupuesto militar del Estado de 2023. El mito del 2% de gasto en Defensa queda superado* (58). Centre Delàs D'Estudis Per la Pau. https://centredelas.org/publicacions/despesamilitarreal2023/?lang=es

Pain, R. (2014). Everyday Terrorism: Connecting Domestic Violence and Global Terrorism. *Progress in Human Geography, 38*(4), 531–550. https://doi.org/10.1177/0309132513512231

Pain, R. (2015). Intimate War. *Political Geography, 44*, 64–73. https://doi.org/10.1016/j.polgeo.2014.09.011

Perea Ozerin, I. (2024). La violencia de género en las relaciones internacionales: Las lógicas violentas de la austeridad desde la secureconomía global feminista. *Revista Electrónica de Estudios Internacionales, 47*, Article 47. https://doi.org/10.36151/reei.47.04

Perez, S. A., & Matsaganis, M. (2018). The Political Economy of Austerity in Southern Europe. *New Political Economy*, *23*(2), 192–207. https://doi.org/10.1080/13563467.2017.1370445
Peterson, V. S. (2008). 'New Wars' and Gendered Economies. *Feminist Review*, *88*, 7–20.
Rodríguez, O. (2025, April 28). "España destinará este año 40.457 millones a gasto militar, casi medio punto más de lo que calcula el Gobierno", *eldiario.es*, https://www.eldiario.es/internacional/espana-destinara-ano-40-457-millones-gasto-militar-medio-punto-calcula-gobierno_1_12249225.html.
Ruiz Benedicto, A. (2019). *Guarding the Fortress. Frontex role in the militarisation and securitisation of migratory flows in the European Union*. Centre Delàs d'Estudis per la Pau. https://centredelas.org/publicacions/informe-40-custodiar-la-fortalesa-el-paper-de-frontex-en-la-militaritzacio-i-securititzacio-dels-fluxos-migratoris-a-la-unio-europea/?lang=en
Saaristo, S.-M. (2022). Informal Modes of Governance: Negotiating Evictions and Housing Rights in Lisbon, Portugal. *Radical Housing Journal*, *4*(1), 9–31. https://doi.org/10.54825/SKGV4690
Shepherd, L. J. (2007). 'Victims, Perpetrators and Actors' Revisited: Exploring the Potential for a Feminist Reconceptualisation of (International) Security and (Gender) Violence. *The British Journal of Politics and International Relations*, *9*(2), 239–256. https://doi.org/10.1111/j.1467-856x.2007.00281.x
Shepherd, L. J. (2008). *Gender, violence, and security. Discourse as practice*. Zed Books.
Simón, P. (2022, February 22). Mordaza contra las feministas. *Pikara Magazine*. https://www.pikaramagazine.com/2022/02/mordaza-contra-las-feministas/
Sjoberg, L. (2009). Introduction to Security Studies: Feminist Contributions. *Security Studies*, *18*, 183–213.
Sjoberg, L. (Ed.). (2010). *Gender and International Security: Feminist Perspectives*. Routledge.
Tansel, C. B. (Ed.). (2017). *States of Discipline: Authoritarian Neoliberalism and the Contested Reproduction of Capitalist Order*. Rowman & Littlefield.
Tassinari, A. (2022). Labour Market Policy in Italy's Recovery and Resilience Plan. Same Old or a New Departure? *Contemporary Italian Politics*, *14*(4), 441–457. https://doi.org/10.1080/23248823.2022.2127647
Tian, N., Lopes da Silva, D., Liang, X., & Scarazzato, L. (2024). *Trends in World Military Expenditure, 2023*. SIPRI. https://www.sipri.org/publications/2024/sipri-fact-sheets/trends-world-military-expenditure-2023
Tickner, J. A. (2006). Feminism meets International Relations. In *Feminist Methodologies for International Relations* (pp. 19–41). Cambridge University Press.
Tickner, J. A. (2018). Rethinking the state in international relations: A personal reflection. In S. Parashar, J. A. Tickner, & J. True (Eds.), *Revisiting Gendered States. Feminist Imaginings of the State in International Relations* (pp. 19–32). Oxford University Press.
True, J. (2012). The political economy of violence against women. In *The Political Economy of Violence against Women*. Oxford University Press.
True, J., & Hozić, A. A. (2020). Don't Mention the War! International Financial Institutions and the Gendered Circuits of Violence in Post-Conflict. *Review of International Political Economy*, *27*(6), 1193–1213. https://doi.org/10.1080/09692290.2020.1732443
True, J., & Tanyag, M. (2019). Violence against women/violence in the world: Toward a feminist conceptualization of global violence. In C. E. Gentry, L. J. Shepherd, & L. Sjoberg (Eds.), *The Routledge handbook of gender and security* (pp. 15–26). Routledge. https://www.unwomen.org/en/news-stories/in-focus/2023/10/in-focus-the-conflict-in-gaza
UNODC, & UN Women. (2024). *Femicides in 2023: Global estimates of intimate partner/family member femicides*. https://www.unwomen.org/en/digital-library/publications/2024/11/femicides-in-2023-global-estimates-of-intimate-partner-family-member-femicides.

Vasilaki, R. (2020, March 10). How Greece became Europe's "shield" against refugees. *Jacobin*. https://jacobin.com/2020/03/greece-refugees-european-union-migrants-turkey-border.

Vignarca, F. (2025, October 30). Esplosione per le spese militari italiane: nel 2025 a 32 miliardi (di cui 13 per nuove armi). *MIL€X (Osservatorio Sulle Spese Militari Italiani)*. https://www.milex.org/2024/10/30/esplosione-per-le-spese-militari-italiane-nel-2025-a-32-miliardi-di-cui-13-per-nuove-armi/

Walby, S. (2015). *Crisis*. Polity Press.

Weissman, D. M. (2004). The Political Economy of Violence: Toward an Understanding of the Gender-Based Murders of Ciudad Juarez. *North Carolina Journal of International Law*, *30*(4), 795–868.

Weldes, J., & Wynne-Hughes, E. (2017, September 10). Beyond Binaries with Feminist Secureconomy. *Progress in Political Economy (PPE)*. https://www.ppesydney.net/beyond-binaries-feminist-secureconomy/

Wöhl, S. (2017). The gender dynamics of financialization and austerity in the European Union—The Irish Case. In J. Kantola & E. Lombardo (Eds.), *Gender and the Economic Crisis in Europe: Politics, Institutions and Intersectionality* (pp. 139–159). Springer International Publishing.

# 8

# WHY IFI PRESCRIPTIONS FOR POST-WAR ECONOMIC RECOVERY CANNOT BRING SUSTAINABLE PEACE

## A feminist analysis[1]

*Carol Cohn and Claire Duncanson*

The contemporary world is characterised by entrenched war economies, local and transnational, where militarisation and profit-seeking mutually reinforce each other, resulting in a complex web of vested interests that make it ever harder to transition from war to peace. Unfortunately, the policy prescriptions for war-affected countries coming from the international financial institutions (IFIs) and other members of the donor community do little to facilitate this transition. Instead of helping build a foundation for a just peace that could be politically and environmentally sustainable, their policy prescriptions tend to: (a) neglect what is needed to address the destructions, disruptions and distortions caused by war and (b) deepen the social and economic inequalities that contributed to war in the first place.[2] In this chapter, we illustrate these extremely problematic dynamics by focusing on one of the central strategies promoted by the IFIs, the extraction and export of natural resources, drawing on examples from Guatemala and Liberia.

We argue that the flaws of the IFIs' approach to natural resources – like other elements of the IFI's recipe for "post-war" recovery[3] – can only be fully understood by employing a feminist political economy (FPE) analysis. An feminist political economy (FPE) analysis reveals that the problem is not just in the IFIs' neoliberalism, but in the profoundly gendered neoclassical economic model underlying it. Thus, feminist economic perspectives that challenge the gendered assumptions of neoclassical economics must become the basis for radically new solutions for the economic reconstruction of war-affected countries. We show how adopting the work of feminist economists and ecologists who emphasise care and social reproduction, human rights, and our interdependence with nature, though not without its challenges, can offer radically new visions for these economies, creating conditions which will make peace more sustainable.[4]

DOI: 10.4324/9781003571667-10

## Post-war recovery and IFI economic policy: An FPE critique

Feminist economists have long drawn attention to the flaws in neoliberal policies and the neoclassical economics that underpins them (see e.g., UN Women 2014, 2015). But they have rarely applied those critiques to post-war recovery. Critical peace and security scholars, meanwhile, have also criticised the neoliberal policies of IFIs (see, e.g., Peterson 2014; Pugh 2006), but rarely from a feminist perspective. In this section, we analyse some of the main strands of critique of IFI post-war economic recovery policy, before laying out our feminist approach.

Our emphasis is on the IFIs because in most war-affected states it is simply not possible to grasp the gendered realities of people's experience, nor, indeed, the contours of the states themselves, without an understanding of the macroeconomic context (Jacobson 2012). And whilst there are many other economic actors in post-war contexts, including other lenders and donors, they tend to accept and work within the same overall macroeconomic assumptions that shape IFIs' prescriptions for recovery and development (True and Svedberg 2018; Woodward 2013).

In any assessment of IFI policies in war-affected countries, it is important to note that the IFIs' approach has not stayed static. Over the post-Cold War period, the World Bank and IMF have increasingly recognised that war-affected contexts pose a set of distinctive challenges. From the mid-1990s, the Bank began to advocate for more of a role for states and institutions in planning and regulating economic policy in order to tackle the inequalities which lead to violence (Woodward 2013:141–142). This is evident in Bank reports such as *Breaking the Conflict Trap* (Collier et al. 2003), the *World Development Report* on *Conflict, Security and Development* (World Bank 2011), and its more recent work on Fragility, Conflict, and Violence. Meanwhile, the IMF produced a 2011 policy paper concluding that in the past it had possibly been "too bold" and "too optimistic" in its prescriptions – e.g., its standard macroeconomic adjustments including cutting state spending, privatisation, and orienting the economy to export – for "countries in fragile situations" (IMF 2011), and also endorsed a bigger role for governments to manage post-war recovery.[5]

Despite these efforts to adapt and improve their response to states attempting to recover from war, the IFIs' approach to recovery has continued to be criticised. We can identify three strands of literature critical of the IFIs' approach to post-war countries. One strand of critique focuses on relatively technical issues, such as sequencing and timing, flexibility and coordination (see, e.g., del Castillo 2017; Langer and Brown 2016). In this account, the IFIs fail because, despite the shifts in recent years, they have continued to insist on implementing neoliberal "development as usual" policies too early, instead of postponing them until after efforts to focus on peacebuilding objectives such as providing jobs for ex-combatants.

An overlapping but slightly different strand of the literature criticises the IFIs as still, despite the aforementioned shifts, not sufficiently recognising how their policies exacerbate the inequalities and violence of the war economy contexts (see, e.g., Berdal and Wennmann 2013; Walter 2015). There is a greater recognition, in this second strand, that it just not an issue of timing or coordination, but that there may need to be an enhanced role for the state in order to ensure the smooth running of the economy. In this critique, neoliberal economic policies are seen as sound in general, but further institutional reform and strengthening are required to tackle the way profits are subject to elite capture and corruption in war-affected contexts. Neither of these strands questions the IFIs' pursuit of economic growth as the goal and measure of post-war economic recovery.

A third set of scholars argue that it is the neoliberal model of the IFIs itself which is the problem (see, e.g., Peterson 2014; Pugh 2006; Pugh et al. 2008; Woodward 2013). For these critics, however much the IFIs' approach to post-war societies has been modulated in recent years, what remains the same is that the IFIs aim to create a state that facilitates private sector, market-led growth. And the IFIs continue to be motivated more by the state's capacity to service its foreign debt than the well-being of its citizens or its ability to enact the social, economic, and political transformations which are required for peace to be sustainable. The role for the state envisioned in the IFIs' version of "good governance" is "that which is considered necessary for markets and the private sector to function and no more" (Woodward 2013:144).

We find much to agree with in the third strand's critique but still find it lacking in important ways. We agree that the problem is rooted in the IFIs' continuing commitment – despite shifts in rhetoric and modifications to policy and practice – to neoliberal views as to what leads to and counts as economic success. We agree with the analysis that although the IFIs have shifted to endorse a role for governments and government policies for post-war economic recovery, the role they envisage for governments remains relatively limited, restricted to ensuring markets operate fairly and efficiently (i.e., "good governance") and to providing safety nets for the most marginalised and excluded. And we agree that the shifts have not included any deviation from a commitment to economic growth as the route to poverty reduction, nor any questioning of deeper integration into the global capitalist economy as the surest formula for economic growth.

However, we think that integrating a feminist analysis reveals two critical insights which are even more fundamental. The first concerns the question of whose recovery is being prioritised, or what the "subject" of recovery is. The second looks beyond the critique of neoliberalism to explore the way that the IFIs' neoliberal approach to post-war recovery is based on a neoclassical economics, which, as many feminist political economists, economists, and ecologists have pointed out, is profoundly gendered.

### *Whose recovery?*

A basic, but critical, feminist move when confronting the social sciences has been to ask the deceptively simple question: who, or what, is this theory about? Upon whose experience has it been based? A feminist approach to IFI post-war economic recovery prescriptions, then, leads us to ask the fundamental question, what does post-war "economic recovery" mean? To whom or what does it refer? A layperson hearing the phrase might start by thinking about *recovery from war*, and ask what are the economic dimensions of that recovery? However, in the way the term is used by economists, it means something quite different – the *recovery of the economic system,* or the health of the economy as measured by indicators such as GDP. So how are these two meanings different, and why is it important to our discussion?

An FPE approach, which starts from the perspective of the most marginalised, helps reveal that the economic dimensions of recovery from war are multiple and significant. When we centre the day-to-day experiences of people who have survived the war, what economic needs become most salient? First, there is the need to rebuild and restore what war too often destroys. Although these needs will always be context specific, the rebuilding will likely include needs such as: homes; tools, markets, workshops, factories, and other means of livelihood; bicycles, carts, cars, buses, and other forms of mobility; roads, bridges, railways, power grids, schools, hospitals and clinics, and more. Restoration needs will likely include not only domestic animals and agricultural plots, but the ecosystems that wars disrupt and despoil, and upon which communities depend.

Second, beyond the rebuilding and restoration of what war has destroyed, war creates an entirely new set of needs, including: gaps caused by war's disruption of health care and education which need to be remedied; both individuals and families dealing with the injuries and traumas of war need systems of care; roads and fields need to be de-mined; widow- and child-headed households need new forms of livelihood and support, as will people disabled by the violence; and large numbers of people who have been displaced need to be resettled.

Third, there will need to be a transformation from a war economy, in which some of a country's most violent actors control and exploit both licit and illicit goods, to a peacetime economy which does not simply continue channelling economic rewards into the pockets of violence's perpetrators.

Importantly, though, the economic dimensions of *recovery from war* go beyond these repairs to war's destructions, disruptions, and distortions. If peace is to be sustainable, recovery also requires the transformation of the inequalities, marginalisations and exclusions that underlie and fuel wars (see, e.g., Stewart 2008). Not only does this mean that there must be full funding for the implementation of the peace agreement's provisions (e.g., DDR, SSR, land reform, etc.) – something that all too often does not materialise. But more fundamentally, it means that economic policy must be measured against its impact on those pre-existing inequalities – does it deepen them, ameliorate them, or even create new ones? In other words, we would argue, the economic dimensions of *recovery from war* include not only tremendous needs for repair of the material conditions, structures and physical and social services that make people's lives liveable, but also, and crucially, the need for the transformation of the economic inequalities that underlie structural violence and war itself.

This understanding of the economic dimensions of recovery from war is in stark contrast to what is typically meant by "post-war economic recovery" as the term is used in the international policy community, including by the IFIs. Here, it is neither the conditions of people's lives nor a society's recovery from war that are centred, but rather the *recovery of the economic system,* or the health of the economy. A healthy economic system, for the IFIs, is one where countries are fully integrated into the global capitalist economy, with minimal barriers to the profit-maximising goals of transnational corporations and finance.[6]

One of the crucial points in our critique of the IFIs, then, is this: despite the different purposes of the two institutions, and despite change over time, neither the IMF nor the World Bank is *directly* focused on a society's recovery from war and creating the conditions for sustainable peace. The IMF's remit is to protect the stability of the international monetary and financial system. The Bank's aim of poverty reduction could possibly suggest a focus on society's recovery and the conditions for peace, but in practice it addresses them only indirectly, in its assumption that economic growth will be good for everyone (if institutions are in place to ensure markets are non-corrupt, transparent, and efficient). And perhaps unsurprisingly, then, the IFIs' economic recovery policies often work against social recovery and peacebuilding, or what we refer to as *recovery for sustainable peace*.

In other words, we are arguing that what an FPE approach does here is more than focus attention on the specific needs of post-war repair and transformation; by starting from that ground-up question, it reveals the disjunction (indeed, some might say "chasm") between *recovery for sustainable peace* and *recovery of the economic system.* In so doing, it highlights and destabilises the meaning of "post-war economic recovery" as it is used by the IFIs. And it begins to provide the basis for a different conceptualisation of economic health – where the measure would not be GDP, but the extent to which the post-war economic needs outlined above are met. We believe that feminist economists' alternative approaches provide a fertile source for this reconceptualisation, an argument we go on to make in our final section below.

### *Neoclassical economics and post-war recovery*

The second strand of our FPE critique of IFI post-war recovery policies is that their flaws stem not just from neoliberalism per se, but from a profoundly gendered neo-*classical* economics. We argue that the gendered assumptions embedded in neoclassical economics are central to explaining how IFI post-war economic recovery policy can be so distant from and antithetical to real, society-wide recovery from war, and can harm the prospects for sustainable peace.

Neoclassical economics' conception of what counts as economic activity, and of what should be included in its accountings of how to maximise efficiency and GDP growth, are based on a series of exclusions, and those exclusions both draw on and reinforce an extremely distorted representation of economic life (see, e.g., Benería et al. 2015). At the most fundamental level, it excludes non-market activities. What is then not counted in this scheme is caring labour, reproductive labour, subsistence labour and other labour outside the formal market economy (see, e.g., Folbre 2001; UN Women 2015), as well as the work done by and value of ecosystems (see, e.g., Merchant 1980; Leach 2015). These are all, somehow, simultaneously devalued, assumed nevertheless to always be there, and ignored. The failure in neoclassical economics, then, is double: it is a failure to value these forms of activity in and of themselves, but it is also, by not attending to them, a failure to understand that they are integral to the economic relationships that neoclassical economics *does* focus on – i.e., a failure to see that the formal economy *relies* on all of them, cannot function without them, and is constructed through its relation to them.

This wildly inaccurate representation of economic life embedded in neoclassical economics has several highly problematic impacts when it becomes the basis of economic policy. Here we highlight two of them, as they are particularly relevant to the challenges of countries recovering from war: the first is that it fails to count, and/or to take serious action to avoid, the harms to anything in its exclusion zone, i.e., "non-market activities." And the second is that it then mis-codes potential investment of financial resources in *recovery for sustainable peace* as "non-productive," inefficient, and thus unnecessary and undesirable.

The first issue has been well-documented by feminist economists. The neoclassical framework ignores or denies that the (part of) the economy it is counting is intertwined with and relies on the parts it is ignoring (e.g., caring labour, subsistence labour, other forms of unpaid work). When that's the case, economic institutions can aim for "structural adjustments" in the formal economy without ever noticing the increased burdens that puts on women (who bear so much responsibility for reproductive, caring and subsistence labour) and without counting those burdens as economic harms to the women or to the economic system itself. Hence, the extensive feminist literature demonstrating SAPs' harmful impacts on women and other subordinated groups (e.g., Elson 1991; Çağatay and Özler 1995).

A related dynamic is at work in relation to neoclassical economics' exclusion of the costs of the environmental degradation, toxic pollution and climate disruption that result from the IFIs' post-war economic recovery policies, including the large-scale extraction of natural resources. Corporations are not required to pay these costs, which lie outside neoclassical accounting of efficiency and measures such as GDP. And, since there is no accounting of the caring, subsistence, and provisioning labour done by women and poor people, the fact that these environmental costs make their work so much more burdensome in the present and far into the future is unremarked, and certainly not guarded against. The effect is to deepen gender and other intersectional inequalities, thus immiserating large swathes of the population, and to exacerbate the ecological crises of climate change and nature loss, further attenuating the prospects for sustainable peace.

The second issue arising from neoclassical economics' blindness to the ways that the market activity it measures *relies* on "non-market" activities is that it then mis-codes potential investment of financial resources in *recovery for sustainable peace* as non-productive, inefficient, and thus unnecessary and undesirable. That is, because caring, subsistence and other forms of non-market activity are not acknowledged as the very foundation upon which market activity depends, they do not appear as a sensible or necessary place to invest financial resources. So any of the multiple economic needs for remedy and repair of war's harms that we discussed above tend to be seen as largely irrelevant to "economic recovery." As we've seen, IFIs may recognise that a few of those issues need some (typically minimal) attention (such as employment for some ex-combatants) before the real business of economic recovery policy proceeds. Or they may accept that there should be a minimalist social safety net for the poorest of the poor. But because of the assumptive framework of neoclassical economics, putting resources into the social infrastructure that could begin to repair war's harms is (mis)understood and accounted for as "consumption" (!) – rather than as an "investment" in what makes the economy tick (Seguino 2016).[7]

And that, we think, is the crux of it. The problem is not just a lack of government revenue to finance the social infrastructure that could repair war's damages, enhance human security, and support the ecosystems on which human security depends. It is that such investment is completely deprioritised, indeed prevented, by policies such as the limits the IMF imposes on a country's public debt relative to GDP (see Seguino 2016), which are based on the fundamental misconception of human reproductive, caring and subsistence labour, and of nature, as external to the economy, rather than as central to the ability of the economy to function.

## Natural resource extraction in Guatemala and Liberia

This section illustrates our arguments by examining one common element of the IFIs' approach to post-war economic reconstruction – the promotion of large-scale extraction and export of natural resources – in two war-affected countries. Our aim is to demonstrate the particular insights an FPE approach provides.

The IFIs promote the large-scale extraction and export of natural resources because it is an obvious means of economic growth and a way to bring in foreign currency which will enable the country to service its debt. This suits the extractive industries, which often see countries emerging from armed conflict as attractive targets, the last frontier – in contrast to countries not affected by war, where rights to oil, gas, minerals, and other resources have already been largely allocated (see, e.g., Bruch et al. 2016; Klare 2012; Pugh et al. 2008). From the perspective of the countries themselves, however, having a wealth of natural resources which can be extracted is rather more complicated, especially since, in many cases, the wealth generated by those resources has both fuelled and funded decades of war.[8] Despite this troubled past, the IFIs, committed to their faith that good governance will prevent a repeat of history, prescribe large-scale extraction for export as a key plan for the economic growth they believe to be the route to, and representative of, recovery.

In Guatemala, the country's orientation to extraction and export had begun before the war ended, but the peace accords offered the opportunity for IFIs, other transnational economic actors, and domestic elites to speed up the process (see, e.g., Jonas 2000; Robinson 2000; Short 2007). With World Bank blessings and support, Guatemala immediately reformed and rehabilitated national laws to facilitate large-scale mining, primarily in gold and nickel (see, e.g., Dearden 2012; Granovsky-Larsen 2017; Hale 2011). Liberia also had an extractives industry before the end of the war, but despite the ways gold, diamond, timber, and rubber extraction fuelled the armed conflict (Sawyer 2005), the IFIs encouraged revitalisation of the natural resources sector as a central plank of Liberia's post-war economic recovery strategy. Liberia's post-war Poverty Reduction Strategy, designed by the World Bank in partnership with the Liberian government, prioritised opening up the country to foreign investment, mostly to be channelled into palm oil, forestry, rubber, and iron ore, which would be extracted for export (see Paczynska 2016:298; O'Mahony 2019).

### *Natural resource extraction as a route to recovery from war's harms?*

When we look at these cases to assess the impact of the extraction and export of natural resources on the prospects for social recovery and the repair of war's harms, three main issues stand out. First, this strategy is simply not oriented toward or designed to meet war-affected countries' needs of social and physical repair, nor to improve the physical and economic security of the nation's citizens; that is not its goal. Instead, the aim is to "strengthen the economy" by making the country as attractive as possible to global corporate finance. This is accomplished through, inter alia: making sure there is little in the way of labour or environmental protections; removing barriers to foreigners amassing huge tracts of land or taking ownership of national natural resources; and making sure the state prioritises using its revenue to pay international lenders the interest on its (often inherited, odious) debt. However much the neoliberal assumption is that economic growth will trickle down and be good for all, the reality is that heavily-indebted war-affected states, if they are being pressed to service their debt, are unlikely to be able to invest in the remedy and repair of war's damages.

Second, to the extent that the extraction and export of natural resources is promoted as meeting any of the country's specific war-recovery needs (such as providing employment or government revenue), it tends to under-deliver on those promises. The two main war-recovery benefits extractivism promises are increased revenue to the state via both royalties and taxation, and increased employment. The promised increase in revenue is undercut, however, by the IFIs' prescriptions for how to attract foreign corporations in the first place. In Guatemala, for example, World Bank-approved "reforms" that facilitated large-scale mining included corporate tax exemptions and a reduction in the royalties rate from 6% to 1%

(Dearden 2012:15), thus depriving the Guatemalan government of significant revenue much-needed for development. In 2004, the International Finance Corporation (IFC) (the branch of the World Bank that lends to private companies) gave $45 million support to Goldcorp for work on the Marlin gold mine, claiming that the mine's "taxes and royalties would equal 7% of the government's annual tax revenue" (Dearden:2012). Things turned out differently. In 2007, for example, royalties and taxes from the Marlin mine amounted to nearer 0.3% of total government revenue (Dearden 2012; also see Zarsky and Stanley 2013:138); to put it another way, that means that almost 96% of the funds the post-war government was supposedly going to receive from Goldcorp's exploitation of this highly lucrative mine did not materialise.

In Liberia, the IFIs argued natural resource extraction would provide the government with tax revenue that it could utilise to improve public services, estimating that the royalties and corporate taxes generated by concessionary deals with foreign investors could bring in two billion dollars over ten years (IMF 2010:14). The World Bank and other donors concerned about Liberia's experience with extraction and export of natural resources launched the Governance and Economic Management Assistance Programme (GEMAP) to try and ensure wealth stayed in the country and was more evenly shared (see Benner and Oliviera 2013). Despite GEMAP, and despite foreign direct investment (FDI) flowing in considerable amounts, however, firms have avoided paying their full tax and royalties obligations (see Paczynska 2016:305; Global Witness 2017; Watkins 2013:63).

As for the promise of jobs, the record has been little better. In Liberia, one of the key rationales for encouraging FDI was the promise of new employment opportunities and improved living standards. Neither objective was accomplished, even before the Ebola crisis exacerbated the situation. Secure, well-paying jobs did not materialise (Beevers 2016; Paczynska 2016; O'Mahony 2019). Many were employed on the basis of the Sime Darby concession: on short term, three-month contracts that did not include health benefits, on salaries of three US dollars per day (Paczynska 2016:310). The same story of failure to provide good jobs or raise living standards can be seen in relation to extractives in Guatemala (see Deonandan and Ortiz Loaiza 2016).

Of equal, if not greater, concern than the failure of the extraction-and-export strategy to deliver on its promises, is the fact that it frequently makes things much worse. This can be seen in many different aspects of what people need for recovery.

There is no human security without livelihoods – the means of securing the necessities of life. And as those means are often destroyed in war, reconstructing livelihoods, whether they are subsistence livelihoods linked to the land, or livelihoods in the form of paid employment, is a crucial part of recovering from war. But development of extractive industries frequently has disastrous effects on subsistence livelihoods, since it is a model that is imposed largely through land dispossession, and because it pollutes surrounding land and waters. All of this impacts women, the rural poor and indigenous communities disproportionally.

In Guatemala, mining, along with the expansion of biofuel production, has forced people from their subsistence plots, eliminated the option of renting land, and eliminated access to the mountains, where food has been traditionally gathered or hunted (Méndez Gutiérrez and Carrera Guerra 2015). This undermines food security and makes life particularly challenging for those who are assigned the task of providing food for families and communities – predominantly women (Méndez Gutiérrez and Carrera Guerra 2015; also see Hale 2011).

In Liberia, as in Guatemala, the invitation to foreign-owned corporations to extract the country's natural resources has resulted in significant land dispossession for ordinary people (see The Rights and Resources Group 2013; O'Mahony 2019). Extensive land-grabbing has been facilitated by an approach that classifies land without visible development as "idle and useless," and deems it available for concessionary agreements (Buntzel and Topor 2013:27). This is a breath-taking instantiation of the neoclassical economics blinders that feminist economists and ecologists have described. When all it counts as being part of the economy are forms of production that are paid and add goods and services to the GDP, neoclassical economics wilfully fails to perceive and acknowledge that "idle" land, and the ecological systems it supports, is actually active and useful. And it equally fails to perceive and acknowledge all of the ways that land *is* actively being used – for the informal, unpaid, and subsistence forms of economic activity, often undertaken by women, which are central to household livelihoods and community survival and identity. Such land-grabbing means water resources for fishing, forests for hunting and gathering herbs, and marshes for rice growing are claimed from local people (Buntzel and Topor 2013), undermining food security, already at crisis levels due to the war (Paczynska 2016:304), and increasing women's burdens.[9]

Extractive industries undermine recovery for sustainable peace not only through land dispossession, but also through despoiling and fouling the physical environment. In Guatemala, for example, at the Fenix nickel project, indigenous communities in the municipality of El Estor allege that land productivity and thus food availability have decreased due to airborne emissions from the mine (Deonandan et al. 2017:408). Local water supplies, too, have been reduced by overuse, or contaminated by the toxic chemicals used to extract minerals, causing health problems[10] and generating additional burdens on those responsible for finding clean water sources for drinking, cooking and cleaning – again, predominantly women (Deonandan et al. 2017:408). In Liberia, as in Guatemala, the environmental impacts of extractivism are often severe and further exacerbate the challenge for women to provide for their families and maintain their own and their children's health (see, e.g., Paczynska 2016:309).

Equally disturbingly, extractive industries are often antithetical to human security at the most basic level of physical violence, including sexual violence. In Liberia, people protesting the expansion of Golden Veroleum (GVL), a palm oil company, are reported to have been beaten, threatened and arrested (Global Witness 2015; Brownell 2019; O'Mahony 2019). In Guatemala, decades after the Guatemalan military employed sexual violence to get Indigenous Mayan communities to flee and yield their land during the civil war, the Guatemala Nickel Company, a subsidiary of Canadian Hudbay Mining, used it on the same communities to undermine community resistance to mining (Méndez Gutiérrez and Carrera Guerra 2015).

### *Natural resource extraction as a route to address the inequalities underlying war?*

Recovery from war requires not only the repair of the material conditions, structures and physical and social services that make people's lives liveable, but also the transformation of the economic inequalities that underlie structural violence and war itself. Extractivism, however, tends to deepen inequalities and even create new ones, by: denying the state the revenue it needs to invest in the services and social infrastructure which would bring equality; failing to provide decent jobs for any but a small minority; exacerbating the burdens of those charged with care and social reproduction; or undermining land reform and other efforts to distribute a state's resources more equitably.

The accounts above made clear the way in which the IFI-promoted legislation around extractive industries robbed the Guatemalan and Liberian governments of considerable revenue, despite IFI rhetoric about the importance of good governance. What the IFI approach misses is the inevitability of foreign corporations exporting as much wealth derived from extractives as possible, even in best case scenarios of good governance; this is, after all, the purpose of their investment. Whilst this dynamic makes extractivism a disastrous strategy in many countries in the global south, it is particularly harmful in war-affected contexts, where inequalities are urgently in need of transformation if a return to war is to be avoided. The missing wealth undermines post-war governments' abilities to invest in that which could address inequalities, including universal, free, quality education and healthcare, childcare, social care for the elderly and people with disabilities, and a transformative justice system.

When it comes to employment, the problem is not only that extractive industries deliver far fewer decent jobs than promised; it is also the ways that the allocation of those jobs deepens inequalities. By privileging certain social groups over others, often along pre-existing lines of power and patronage, they risk inflaming tensions and fuelling communal violence. They can also exacerbate gender inequalities which, whilst perhaps not directly contributing to reigniting armed conflict, contribute to violence in its broader sense. In Guatemala, mining employment opportunities have been predominantly open only to men, deepening women's economic dependence on men, and driving a rise in drinking, prostitution, and other disruptions to family life (Deonandan et al. 2017:410). A similar account emerges from most areas of the world where large-scale mining operates (Eftimie et al. 2009).

The deepening of inequalities through extractive production is not limited to the effects of their employment practices. They too often exacerbate the poverty of the already-poor by undermining the livelihoods women and indigenous people once had, as outlined above. This deepens inequalities as it is the poor and marginalised who suffer most from depleted and degraded physical environments, especially those who are charged with care, social reproduction, and provisioning for their families.

Extractivism also undermines processes which are often initiated at war's end to address inequalities, such as land reform, justice and reconciliation programmes, and security sector reform. In Liberia, for example, the granting of long-term concessions to transnational extractive corporations risks rendering the Land Rights Act impotent (see, e.g., O'Mahony 2019).

This section has been but a brief look at one of the common elements of IFI post-war economic recovery prescriptions – the large-scale, privatised, FDI-led extraction of natural resources for export. Looking at how this approach has played out in two war-affected contexts well-illustrates, we think, our two key points. First, it shows not only the disjuncture between IFI post-war economic recovery policy and recovery for sustainable peace, but also how the former actually frequently undermines the latter, as it too often leads to land dispossession, the undermining of livelihoods, physical violence, the despoiling of the environment, with concomitant effects on people's health and increasing burdens of care, and the deepening of inequalities. Second, we've argued that the failure of IFI post-war economic recovery policy to facilitate recovery for sustainable peace is rooted not only in its neoliberalism, but deeper, in neoclassical assumptions about what the economy is for and its silences about care and nature. A feminist political economy approach, attentive to those who are most marginalised, to all forms of violence, and to the gendered assumptions at the core of mainstream political and economic thought, is required to see the source of the shortcomings. Fortunately, it also generates the solutions.

## Feminist alternatives for recovery from war

Feminist scholarship outlining alternatives to extractivism, and to neoliberal policies more generally, is vast and extraordinarily rich (see Balakrishnan et al. 2016; Bauhardt and Harcourt 2018; Leach 2015; Raworth 2017). It is thus somewhat surprising that there have not been more attempts to apply the insights of feminist economists and ecologists to the specific context of countries recovering from war. For, as much as war-affected contexts present significant challenges, as outlined in our earlier discussion of what is required for recovery for sustainable peace, they also offer "windows of opportunity" (Rees and Chinkin 2015): typically, external support flows in; constitutions are drafted, infrastructure is (re)built; economic plans are drawn up; and the social, political, and economic arrangements that will structure the post-war society are being set. While these windows of opportunity might be small, unstable and contested, we believe that this "post-war moment" is a crucial time to aim for a truly transformative vision of post-war economic recovery.

And that applying some of the central ideas of feminist economic and ecological thought can point the way.

If we return, for example, to one key insight of feminist economics – that unpaid work, especially unpaid care work, is as important as paid work in determining the well-being not only of individuals and families, but also of the economy itself – how might that insight transform the priorities of economic recovery policy?

The benefits of an approach to economic recovery that privileges care – and the infrastructure to support it – are obvious given the widespread needs outlined above. Providing state-funded care for the injured and disabled – and for children and the elderly – would improve the lives of men and women, war-wounded and their care-givers alike, provide jobs, would enable those with dependents to combine their caring roles with paid employment; and would help societies recover from the impacts of widespread violence. Investing in education, in health, in the justice system – a transformative social infrastructure – would rebuild lives damaged by war and address the inequalities underlying war. Such investments in Guatemala and Liberia could have produced a new social contract, which could in turn have enhanced the legitimacy of the post-war state, contributing to the sustainability of the peace.

And, if we return to one key insight of feminist ecologists – that natural resources, like unpaid labour, also need to be revalued, to be seen as part of an ecosystem upon which humans depend – how might that insight similarly transform the priorities of economic recovery policy?

It would mean a turn away from the large-scale extraction and export of natural resources, especially fossil fuels. Instead, feminist alternatives could include renewable energy programmes, structural transformations to everything from transport to food production and distribution, and massive reforestation[11] – a move from extraction to restoration, regeneration, and replenishment. Many war-affected countries in the poorest regions of the world have comparative advantages in renewable energy and have the opportunity to leapfrog to climate-friendly urbanisation and transport strategies (Klasen 2013; UN Women 2014). If attention to justice and equality are built-in (which does not always happen with "green economy" proposals but is central to feminist ecological thinking (see Nelson 2009; Leach 2015; Raworth 2017; UN Women 2014)), reforestation, renewable energy, and sustainable agriculture could provide plentiful employment and livelihood opportunities, vital for addressing gender inequalities and the inequalities underlying war. There might be extraction of natural resources in that feminist future, but it would likely be of a radically different model, involving small-scale extractive activities driven by local and regional interests and demands; inclusive of community and women's rights of participation, control, and ownership; and which supports societies to organise work on a collective, shared, and equitable basis, such as that proposed by the Mining Working Group at the UN (Mining Working Group at the UN 2014).[12]

The massive physical infrastructure projects created to facilitate the efficient export of extracted goods, currently prioritised by IFIs and governments in war-affected states, would be replaced by the social infrastructure designed to support care, well-being and harmony with nature. Corridors of extraction, in other words, would be replaced by webs of provisioning. Feminist-inspired models would not use GDP growth or repayment of debts as a measure of whether a war-affected country is recovering. Rather, the measures would relate to recovery for sustainable peace, whether the percentage of people receiving the care and the food they need, or the number of acres rewilded or rivers running free of pollution.

Feminist economists and ecologists draw attention to a range of mechanisms through which such a transformation could be financed. Aid transfers to war-affected countries can be significant but IMF rules preclude post-war governments from spending it to support an infrastructure of care; this could be changed. If investment in social infrastructure was classified as "investment" rather than "consumption," to recognise its "public goods quality," war-affected states could invest more freely without infringing IMF limits on public debt (see Seguino 2016; UN Women 2015). More resources for an infrastructure of care would also be available if donors decided to forgive odious debts, an appropriate action especially because those debts were often racked up by the corrupt regime a war was fought to overthrow. Transforming taxation practices offers multiple opportunities: controls could be applied to cross border short term capital flows (e.g., Financial Transaction Tax); tax loopholes could be closed; and more progressive tax regimes enacted (corporate tax dodging costs poor countries at least $100 billion every year) (see Oxfam 2019). Redirecting just a fraction of the resources spent on militaries and military equipment, some $1.7 trillion in 2018 (SIPRI 2018), to war-affected countries would enable significant investment in the transition from extractivism to an economy of restoration and care (WILPF 2018).

Not only is the financing *possible* if the international community had the will to do it and were willing to throw off their neoclassical blinders, but there is also basis in law for adopting feminist economists' proposals, as many feminists point out (Chinkin and Kaldor 2017; Rees and Chinkin 2015). The International Covenant of Economic and Social Rights puts obligations on states and, potentially, the IFIs themselves, to meet the economic and social rights enshrined in the Universal Declaration of Human Rights of 1948, including the right to work, the right to leisure, the right to a decent standard of living and the right to an education. In fact, they are not only obligated to meet these rights, but to use "the maximum of their available resources" with a view to "progressively achieving the full realization of economic, social and cultural rights."

Although space does not permit exploration of additional elements of feminist economic and ecological thought, we hope the above examples demonstrate that it opens a rich vein of possibilities for developing post-war economic recovery policy that supports peace that is just and sustainable.

Applying the insights of feminist economists to economic recovery from war would not be without major challenges, of course. Among others, they assume a strong role for the state to create, support, and finance an infrastructure of care, uphold social and economic rights, and regulate environmental impacts, but in countries emerging from war, states are often weak, fragmented, and beset by corruption. Whilst the IFIs have partly recognised this with their push for good governance, we are arguing that good governance means far more than providing a stable environment for markets; it should mean an active, interventionist state that puts care and environmental principles at its heart. How you get from states which have been weakened by decades of structural adjustment policies, austerity measures and warfare, and which privilege patriarchal patronage relations over public services, to stronger states which prioritise social provisioning and environmentally sustainable forms of development presents a considerable challenge, for sure, but we would suggest that it is a challenge that feminists must take on.

## Conclusion

In this chapter, we have used an FPE approach to show how the IFIs' approach to economic recovery from war undermines the prospects for transitioning away from war economies and towards just and sustainable peace. We have focused on just one strand of the IFIs' approach – an encouragement of large-scale extraction and export of natural resources – in order to demonstrate the flaws. We have argued that even if the IFIs' attempts to instate "good governance" were successful, extractivism would not facilitate just and sustainable peace. This is because extractivism – along with other strands of the IFIs' approach such as their emphasis on privatisation, their insistence on fiscal balancing, and their encouragement of private investment in massive infrastructure projects – is geared towards recovery of the economic system, and not the recovery of people, communities, or ecosystems. A key to understanding how *economic recovery policy* can be so antithetical to *recovery for sustainable peace* can be found, we have argued, in the gendered assumptive framework of neoclassical economics. Therefore, feminist economic thinking, which denaturalises those assumptions and offers alternative visions of the functioning and purpose of an economy, must become an integral part of our imaginings of how it is possible to enhance human security in war-torn countries and to build peace that is transformative enough to be sustained.

## Notes

1 This chapter is a shortened and lightly edited version of a previously published article: Cohn, C., & Duncanson, C. (2020). Whose recovery? IFI prescriptions for postwar states. *Review of International Political Economy, 27* (6), 1214–1234. https://doi-org.eux.idm.oclc.org/10.1080/09692290.2019.1677743

2 They typically also contribute to climate change, biodiversity loss and other ecological destruction, further undermining the prospects for peace, a point we address more fully elsewhere (Cohn and Duncanson 2020).

3 In this chapter, we try as much as possible to avoid the term "post-war"; as feminists have long pointed out, it is problematic for several reasons. First, wars do not have straightforward beginnings, middles and ends. Indeed, Cynthia Cockburn's concept of "the continuum of violence" reminds us that in states recognized officially as "at war," there are many people for whom the violence does not end with the declaration of a ceasefire. And there

are other states with protracted high levels of violence that are not officially considered to be "at war" at all, even though violence and fear suffuse the lives of their citizens. Even when thinking about what is commonly recognized as war, it remains problematic to think of war as a temporally and spatially discrete event; wars require a wider war system, the complex range of social, political, and economic relationships that make fighting a war possible, and even alluring. There are very few countries where the end of war also brought a commitment to move away from a war system; in most "post-war" states, that system continues to engage so much of a country's economic, political and social life that war is a constant presence, even when the guns are quieted. Thus, we think that while "post-war" may be intended as a temporal marker, it has the effect of simplifying and distorting the realities that people face after an outbreak of armed violence has formally been concluded by a political settlement. In this chapter, then, we opt as much as possible for the more accurate "war-affected states," but we maintain the use of "post-war" when it is the term used by the IFIs and other institutions whose recovery policies we are describing.

4 It should be clear from this introduction that in our Feminist Political Economy approach, we employ gender as an analytical tool; it helps us see what is privileged, what is devalued, and what is rendered invisible in societies and systems of thought.

At the same time, because these systems – here, our specific focus is on neoclassical economics and neoliberal policies – are built on gendered assumptions, they have differential gendered impacts, affecting men, women and other gender categories differently, *as groups*, even whilst other intersecting inequalities create differential impacts *within* each of those groups. In this chapter, our focus is on how they affect women as a group, whilst recognising that this is a diverse and contested category, as well as on how they affect other inequalities and the prospects for the sustainability of peace.

5 These shifts can be seen as part of the move to a "Post-Washington Consensus" (PWC), the extent and significance of which, of course, is much contested (see Krogstad 2007; Peterson 2014; Pugh, 2006).

6 Notwithstanding the fact that there is a lot more variety of individual belief and motivation within the IFIs than blanket accounts of their institutional goals give you.

7 Seguino (2016) discusses this point in relation to the question of how the Sustainable Development Goals may be financed (not the financing of post-war recovery), but we think her arguments have much to offer for war-affected contexts.

8 The so-called "resource curse," in both war-torn and post-war countries, has now been the subject of a considerable literature (for overviews, see, e.g., Benner and Oliviera 2013; Bruch et al. 2016; Lujala et al. 2016).

9 The recently adopted Land Rights Act (2018) may restrict future land grabbing, but Liberia's experience indicates that provisions on paper are not always followed in practice (Paczynska 2016; Brownwell 2019; O'Mahony 2019). The law also cannot be applied retro-actively and so cannot help those who have already been dispossessed (see O'Mahony 2019).

10 Specific illnesses mentioned to be plaguing community members, because of effluent from the mine's refinery polluting Lake Izabal, a major source of the area's water supply, were said to be hair loss, rashes, and gastrointestinal problems, all occurring more frequently for children (see Deonandan et al. 2017, p. 208).

11 Building on Wangari Mathai's inspirational GreenBelt Movement.

12 Of course, any move away from extractivism also requires tackling cultures of consumerism, built-in obsolescence in technological goods, and other harmful ecological practices, which are situated predominantly in the global north.

## References

Balakrishnan R, Heintz J and Elson D (2016) *Rethinking Economic Policy for Social Justice: The Radical Potential of Human Rights,* Routledge, Abingdon, Oxon.

Bauhardt C and Harcourt W (eds) (2018) *Feminist Political Ecology and the Economics of Care: In Search of Economic Alternatives*, Routledge, Abingdon, Oxon.

Beevers MD (2016) 'Forest Governance and Post-conflict Peace in Liberia: Emerging Contestation and Opportunities for Change?', *The Extractive Industries and Society*, 3(2):320–328.

Benería L, Berik G and Floro M (2015) *Gender, Development and Globalization: Economics as If All People Mattered* (2nd ed.), Routledge, New York.

Benner T and de Oliviera RS (2013) 'Statebuilding and the Political Economy of the Extractive Industries in Post-conflict States', in Berdal M and Zaum D (eds.) *Political Economy of Statebuilding: Power after Peace*, Routledge, Abingdon, Oxon:122–136.

Berdal M and Wennmann A (2013) *Ending Wars, Consolidating Peace: Economic Perspectives*, Routledge, Abingdon, Oxon.

Brownell A (17 May 2019) *OPINION: The Struggle for Land Security in Liberia is Just Beginning*, Thomas Reuters Foundation News. https://news.trust.org

Bruch C, Muffett C and Nichols SS (2016) *Governance, Natural Resources and Post-conflict Peacebuilding*, Routledge, Abingdon, Oxon.

Buntzel R and Topor WE (2013) *Large-Scale Land Acquisitions in Liberia: Case Studies and Some Legal Aspects on the Palm Oil Sector*, Bread for the World – Protestant Development Service, Brot für die Welt. https://www.brot-fuer-die-welt.de/fileadmin/mediapool/2_Downloads/Fachinformationen/Analyse/Analyse_39_large_scale_land_acquisitions.pdf

Çağatay N and Özler S (1995) 'Feminization of the Labor Force: The Effects of Long-term Development and Structural Adjustment', *World Development*, 23(11):1883–1894.

Chinkin C and Kaldor M (2017) *International Law and New Wars*, Cambridge University Press, Cambridge, UK.

Collier P, Elliot VL, Hegre H, Hoeffler A, Reynal-Querol M and Sambanis N (2003) *Breaking the Conflict Trap: Civil War and Development Policy*, The World Bank and Oxford University Press, Washington, DC.

Consortium on Gender, Security and Human Rights (2017) *What Kind of Growth?: Economies that Work for Women in Post-War Settings (Workshop Report)*, Consortium on Gender, Security and Human Rights, Boston, MA. https://genderandsecurity.org/feminist-roadmap-sustainable-peace

Dearden N (2012) *Generating Terror*, Jubilee Debt Campaign, London. https://jubileedebt.org.uk/report/generating-terror

del Castillo G (2017) *Obstacles to Peacebuilding*, Routledge, Abingdon, Oxon.

Deonandan K and Ortiz Loaiza P (2016) 'Mining, Taxes, and Development in Guatemala: The State and the Marlin Mine', *Latin American Policy*, 7(2):288–310.

Deonandan K, Tatham R and Field B (2017) 'Indigenous Women's Anti-Mining Activism: A Gendered Analysis of the El Estor Struggle in Guatemala', *Gender & Development*, 25(3):405–419.

Eftimie A, Heller K and Strongman J (2009) *Gender Dimensions of the Extractive Industries: Mining for Equity*, Extractive Industries and Development Series No. 8, The World Bank, Washington, DC. https://openknowledge.worldbank.org/handle/10986/18236

Elson D (1991) 'Male Bias in Macro-economics: The Case of Structural Adjustment', in Elson D (ed.) *Male Bias in the Development Process*, Manchester University Press, Manchester:164–190.

Folbre N (2001) *The Invisible Heart: Economics and Family Values*, New Press, New York.

Global Witness (2015) *The New Snake Oil: Violence, Threats, and False Promises at the Heart of Liberia's Palm Oil Expansion*, Global Witness, London, UK. https://www.globalwitness.org/en/campaigns/land-deals/new-snake-oil/

Global Witness (2017) *Holding the Line*, Global Witness, London, UK. https://www.globalwitness.org/en/reports/liberia-holding-line/

Granovsky-Larsen S (2017) 'The Guatemalan Campesino Movement and the Postconflict Neoliberal State', *Latin American Perspectives, 44*(5):53–73.
Hale CR (2011) '*Resistencia para que?* Territory, Autonomy and Neoliberal Entanglements in the 'Empty Spaces' of Central America', *Economy and Society*, 40(2):184–210.
IMF (International Monetary Fund) (2010) *Liberia: 2010 Article IV Consultation and Fifth Review Under the Three-Year Agreement Under the Extended Credit Facility-Staff Report; Public Information Notice and Press Release on the Executive Board Discussion; and Statement by the Executive Director for Liberia,* Country Report No. 10/373, Washington, DC.
IMF (International Monetary Fund) (2011) *Macroeconomic and Operational Challenges in Countries in Fragile Situations,* Policy Paper, Washington, DC. https://www.imf.org/external/np/pp/eng/2011/061511A.pdf
Jacobson R (2012) 'Women "After" Wars', in Cohn C (ed.) *Women & Wars,* Polity Press, Cambridge, UK:215–241.
Jonas S (2000) *Of Centaurs and Doves: Guatemala's Peace Process*, Westview Press, Boulder, CO.
Klare MT (2012) *The Race for What's Left: The Global Scramble for the World's Last Resources*, Henry Holt & Company.
Klasen S (2013) 'Gender, Growth and Adaptation to Climate Change', in Cela B, Dankelman I and Stern J (eds.) *Powerful Synergies: Gender Equality, Economic Development and Environmental Sustainability,* UNDP, New York:49–59. https://www.undp.org/content/undp/en/home/librarypage/womens-empowerment/powerful-synergies.html
Krogstad E (2007) 'The Post-Washington Consensus: Brand New Agenda or Old Wine in a New Bottle?', *Challenge*, 50(2):67–85.
Langer A and Brown GK (eds) (2016) *Building Sustainable Peace: Timing and Sequencing of Post-Conflict Reconstruction and Peacebuilding*, Oxford University Press, Oxford, UK.
Leach M (ed) (2015) *Gender Equality and Sustainable Development*, Routledge, Abingdon, Oxon.
Méndez Gutiérrez L and Carrera Guerra A (2015) *Clamor for Justice: Sexual Violence, Armed Conflict and Violent Land Dispossession*, Equipo de Estudios Comunitarios y Acción Psicosocial (ECAP), Guatemala.
Merchant C (1980) *The Death of Nature: Women, Ecology, and the Scientific Revolution*, HarperOne, San Francisco.
Mining Working Group at the UN (2014) *A Rights-Based Approach to Resource Extraction in the Pursuit of Sustainable Development* (Advocacy Brief). https://miningwg.files.wordpress.com/2014/05/advocacy-brief.pdf
Nelson JA (2009) 'Between a Rock and a Soft Place: Ecological and Feminist Economics in Policy Debates', *Ecological Economics*, 69(1):1–8.
O'Mahony J (22 March 2019) *Liberia's New Land Rights Law Hailed as Victory, But Critics Say It's Not Enough*, Mongabay. https://www.mongabay.com
Oxfam (2019) *Public Good or Private Wealth?* Oxfam Briefing Paper, Oxfam GB, Oxford, UK. https://oxfamilibrary.openrepository.com/bitstream/handle/10546/620599/bp-public-good-or-private-wealth-210119-en.pdf
Paczynska A (2016) 'Liberia Rising? Foreign Direct Investment, Persistent Inequalities and Political Tensions', *Peacebuilding*, 4(3):297–316.
Peterson JH (2014) *Building a Peace Economy? Liberal Peacebuilding and the Development-security Industry*, Manchester University Press, Manchester.

Pugh M (2006) 'Post-war Economies and the New York Dissensus', *Conflict, Security & Development*, 6(3):269–289.

Pugh M, Cooper N and Turner M (eds) (2008) *Whose Peace? Critical Perspectives on the Political Economy of Peacebuilding*, Palgrave Macmillan, Basingstoke.

Raworth K (2017) *Doughnut Economics: Seven Ways to Think Like a 21st-Century Economist*, White River Junction, Chelsea Green Publishing, Vermont.

Rees M and Chinkin C (2015) 'Exposing the Gendered Myth of Post Conflict Transition: The Transformative Power of Economic and Social Rights', *New York University Journal of International Law and Politics*, 48:1211–1226.

Robinson WI (2000) 'Neoliberalism, the Global Elite, and the Guatemalan Transition: A Critical Macrosocial Analysis', *Journal of Interamerican Studies and World Affairs*, 42(4):89–107.

Sawyer A (2005) *Beyond Plunder: Toward Democratic Governance in Liberia.* Boulder, Lynne Rienner Boulder, CO.

Seguino S (2016) *Financing for Gender Equality in the Context of SDGs,* Working Paper Series No. 426, PERI, Boston MA. https://www.peri.umass.edu/media/k2/attachments/WP426_Seguino.pdf

Short N (2007) *The International Politics of Post-conflict Reconstruction in Guatemala*, Palgrave Macmillan, New York.

SIPRI (Stockholm International Peace Research Institute) (2 May 2018) *Global Military Spending Remains High at $1.7 Trillion*, SIPRI. https://www.sipri.org/media/press-release/2018/global-military-spending-remains-high-17-trillion

Stewart F (2008) *Horizontal Inequalities and Conflict: Understanding Group Violence in Multiethnic Societies*, Palgrave Macmillan, Basingstoke.

The Rights and Resources Group (2013) *Investments into the Agribusiness, Extractive and Infrastructure Sectors of Liberia: An Overview*, The Rights and Resources Group, Washington, DC. https://rightsandresources.org/wp-content/exported-pdf/countryreportliberiafinal.pdf

True J and Barbro S (2019) 'Women, Peace and Security and International Financial Institutions', in Davies SE and True J (eds) *The Oxford Handbook on Women, Peace and Security,* Oxford University Press, New York.

UN Women (2014) *World Survey on the Role of Women in Development 2014: Gender Equality and Sustainable Development*, UN Women, New York. https://www.unwomen.org/en/digital-library/publications/2014/10/world-survey-2014

UN Women (2015) *Progress of the World's Women 2015–2016: Transforming Economies, Realizing Rights*, UN Women, New York. https://progress.unwomen.org/en/2015/pdf/UNW_progressreport.pdf

Walter BF (2015) 'Why Bad Governance Leads to Repeat Civil War', *Journal of Conflict Resolution*, 59(7):1242–1272.

Watkins K (2013) *Equity in Extractives: Stewarding Africa's Natural Resources for All,* Africa Progress Report 2013, Africa Progress Panel, Geneva, Switzerland. https://reliefweb.int/report/world/africa-progress-report-2013-equity-extractives-stewarding-africa-s-natural-resources

WILPF (Women's International League for Peace & Freedom) (2018) *Move the Money from War to Peace.* https://www.wilpf.org/move-the-money/

Woodward SL (2013) 'The IFIs and Post-conflict Political Economy', In Berdal M and Zaum D (eds) *Political Economy of Statebuilding: Power After Peace*, Routledge, Abingdon, Oxon.

World Bank (2011) *World Development Report 2011: Conflict, Security, and Development.* https://openknowledge.worldbank.org/handle/10986/4389

Zarsky L and Stanley L (2013) 'Can Extractive Industries Promote Sustainable Development? A Net Benefits Framework and a Case Study of the Marlin Mine in Guatemala', *The Journal of Environment & Development*, 22(2):131–154.

# PART III

# Gendered Circuits (III)

## Movements

# 9

# TRACING THE GENDERED INTERSECTIONS OF INTERNATIONAL INTERVENTIONS AND SOCIOECONOMIC JUSTICE IN BOSNIA AND HERZEGOVINA

*Daniela Lai*

During the first wave of COVID-19, in the Spring of 2020, Bosnia and Herzegovina (BiH) made international headlines after a raspberry producer (F.H. Srebrena Malina) was given a lucrative state contract for importing much-needed respirators from China, despite not having a licence for the import of medical equipment, nor previous experience in the medical sector (Djugum et al. 2020). The scandal, which was later investigated by the Bosnian judiciary and led to the conviction of the former PM of the Federation of Bosnia and Herzegovina (one of the two entities of Bosnia and Herzegovina, alongside Republika Srprska) (Kurtić 2024), became emblematic of the mismanagement of healthcare and corruption that Bosnian citizens were in fact very familiar with. Only seven years prior to this, Bosnian citizens had organised mass protests after the ethnonationalist state's dysfunctional bureaucracy prevented newborns from receiving a registration number that was needed to get travel documents, resulting in the preventable death of a three-month-old baby who required treatment abroad (Kurtović 2018). And even before 2013, Bosnians had been experiencing the effects of 20 years of neoliberal reforms that had undermined the welfare state they had known and valued under socialism. Scandals such as the respirator case are thus only one, most visible, aspect of the mismanagement of the pandemic in BiH. The country suffered from one of the highest per capita death tolls in the world (at least in terms of officially registered deaths; WHO 2023). The healthcare system came under immense strain, with many Bosnian healthcare workers having emigrated or being prompted by the pandemic itself to leave the country. As elsewhere in the world, COVID-19 was also seen as an opportunity for the state and its security apparatus to strengthen societal control (Veličković 2020) while also ignoring the gendered crisis of care gripping communities (Hozić 2024). Internationally sponsored reforms since the end of the Bosnian War had been conducive to the unfolding of these events, by

DOI: 10.4324/9781003571667-12

prioritising liberalisation, privatisation and macroeconomic stability over addressing socioeconomic harms and injustice that were deeply gendered and rooted in the political economy of the war and post-war transition.

This chapter is thus primarily concerned with showing how a neglect of justice issues – and chiefly gender justice – has long been constitutive of international interventions into Bosnia and Herzegovina's multiple "transitions" and underpins the current shift towards a war economy. As highlighted by the volume editors and many chapter authors, this shift is global, but also firmly connected to the localised implementation of economic and security policies in countries such as Bosnia and Herzegovina. In my research on international intervention in BiH, I showed how economic reforms promoted with the goals of liberalisation formed part of gendered circuits of violence that connected the wartime political economy of conflict and violence and peacetime politics of privatisation and austerity (Lai 2020a). It is now apparent that these circuits are extending into a post-pandemic gendered crisis and a geopolitical and ecological crisis that are becoming constitutive components of the war economy. The chapter thus traces the links connecting the gendered injustice of socioeconomic reforms following the Bosnian War of 1992–1995, which was allowed by extensive international intervention into virtually every aspect of the country's political and economic life, and our current moment.

The disregard of socioeconomic justice, and especially its gendered dimensions, is rooted in the tendency of international organisations working in post-conflict or otherwise "transitional" countries to treat justice issues and the economy as distinct spheres of intervention. This is due, on the one hand, to technocratic and depoliticised views of economic interventions and, on the other, to narrow conceptions of what "justice" means for communities experiencing war and post-war transitions. In this chapter, I suggest that in order to better understand and respond to gendered harms stemming from war we need to centre notions of gender justice. It is by following women and their gendered experiences of violence and injustice that we are able to see how international interventions formed part of gendered circuits of violence that connect the wartime political economy of conflict and violence and the peacetime politics of privatisation and austerity, but also hardwired injustice into the management of subsequent crises, both acute – such as the management of the COVID-19 pandemic – and chronic (emigration, poverty, and mismanagement of the economy and natural environment).

Bosnia and Herzegovina provides a privileged vantage point for observing how these dynamics are constitutive of a war economy that, while global in scope, can only be fully understood, seen, and felt through localised histories and struggles. The case of BiH makes explicit and visible the links between justice claims, women's wartime experiences, socioeconomic violence in war, and the economic legacies of the conflict, characterised by a complex overlapping of ethnic cleansing, destruction of property and accumulation of wealth through war profiteering, trafficking, and market fragmentation (Pugh and Cooper 2004; Andreas 2009). In the two Bosnian communities I researched more in-depth, Prijedor (Republika

Srpska) and Zenica (Federation of Bosnia and Herzegovina), the process of economic reform sponsored by international actors that resulted in the decline of the iron ore and steel industries, rising unemployment, and emigration was experienced as a deeply gendered form of socioeconomic injustice. In addition to this continuing post-industrial decline, today the country's political and institutional landscape continues to be marked by the same divisive and dysfunctional system that was set up at the 1995 Dayton Peace Agreement. In this context, ethnonationalist elites continue to profit from political privilege while threatening the integrity of the country and livelihoods of its citizens, and unaccountable international actors continue to exercise significant and controversial powers over Bosnia's politics (Brezar 2022; OSCE 2024; RFE/RL 2024). BiH and its neighbouring countries are also locked into increasingly confrontational talk of rearmament (Ejdus et al. 2023), at a time when we have global geopolitical tensions and interests from global and regional powers (from the United States to Russia and Turkey) that have the potential to cause further instability. As Danijela Majstorović (2021) explains, BiH is not constituted just by its post-socialist or post-war condition, but more broadly by a condition of peripherality – a peripherality inhabited by peripheral subjects encompassing, among others, those outside EU borders, migrants, women, and feminist and labour activists. The Bosnian War thus casts a long shadow: not only over the country's political and economic present, but over prospects for escaping gendered injustice and insecurity that were locked in from the 1990s. BiH thus starkly illustrates how complex transitions are experienced by communities and the injustice embedded in the policies that accompany them, and serves as a warning to resist the steady slippage towards the entrenchment of injustice that characterises the rise of a global war economy.

Feminist political economy remains best placed to comprehensively map the relationship between economic reforms and justice issues in contexts of crises, wars and their transformation (Hozić and True 2017). Two issues make such analysis particularly urgent. First, the characterisation of the global economy as a "war economy," as noted by the editors in their introduction, is leading to policy decisions across a growing number of sectors to be subordinated to security and military considerations, even in zones of apparent peace. Second, in the context of growing calls for militarisation, we face the risk that calls for meaningful gender justice will be once again compartmentalised and sidelined in favour of narrower (and shallower) approaches to justice claims that are incapable of addressing complex and intersecting forms of harm. A feminist framework that links together the political economy of war and post-war transformation on the one hand, and justice claims on the other, is thus needed to make forceful political arguments for gender justice in the context of a global war economy. Drawing on feminist IPE, and especially the growing literature on gendered circuits of violence, the chapter traces back the entrenchment of socioeconomic and gender injustice to international interventions and especially economic reforms promoted in the aftermath of the Bosnian War. It provides an updated analysis of the rationale and gendered effects of economic reforms that reorganised welfare and jobs and promoted privatisations that accelerated deindustrialisation and continue to jeopardise livelihoods.

## Analysing international interventions through a "justice perspective"

International interventions in post-conflict economies have long addressed gendered inequalities and gendered harms in superficial or palliative ways that have entrenched, rather than challenged, injustice – for the purpose of this chapter, gendered forms of socioeconomic injustice in particular. There are three ways in which these interventions have foreshadowed tendencies we can now observe in the rise of a war economy where justice becomes once again subordinated and marginalised. First, in post-conflict contexts from the 1990s onwards and later with the rise of the war on terror, security matters have been removed from public scrutiny and systems of accountability, reinforcing gendered inequalities and a lack of meaningful participation. Feminist IPE and Security Studies scholars over the past decade (Elias 2015; Sjoberg 2015; Chisholm and Stachowitsch 2017; Martín de Almagro and Ryan 2020) have consistently warned against the risk of securitising political economy, where neoliberal economic reforms promoted by external actors, alongside other political interventions, must align or "converge" (Martín de Almagro and Ryan 2019:1061) with security interests. This process has in turn facilitated the inclusion of women and other marginalised groups into post-conflict economies in instrumental terms only: inclusion is seen as useful to the extent that it presents a relapse into violence, and only insofar as it supports the position and interests of international institutions and global powers operating in these contexts. This conditional inclusion, where questions of justice are subordinated to military and economic interest, makes any progress on women's economic empowerment or socioeconomic injustice shallow and precarious, and easy to roll back under circumstances declared to be crises or emergencies.

Second, the issue of reconstruction, relief and recovery has commonly been understood through frames borrowed from mainstream economics, informed by individualistic assumptions, positive views of the market and of marketised social relations, and reflects a view of the world that is imbued with gendered stereotypes that have led to addressing gendered inequalities in superficial or palliative ways. This clashes with women's lived realities of post-conflict economies that are shaped by power relations set by conflict itself, and where markets can be spaces of violence as well as sources of subsistence. Macroeconomic policies adopted by countries in the global south under the influence of the international actors have generally included a reduced role for the state in the economy, austerity, and liberalisation (see Cohn and Duncanson, this volume). The design of these policies has been commonly gender-blind (Berik et al. 2009), while women's "economic empowerment" programmes have been imbued with a neoliberal logic that entrenches a gendered separation between formal and informal labour, and privileges individualist forms of agency that cast women's economic participation as supportive of a primary wage earner (Martín de Almagro and Ryan 2019). Fairness and equality gains tend to be "postponed" until a later date when economic interventions will bear fruit. This approach not only subordinates gender-just outcomes to other kinds of economic goals that are prioritised in the short term, but it also hinders the implementation of transformative policies that could shake the foundations of unjust systems. Cohn and Duncanson (this volume) argue that when IFIs intervene in post-conflict contexts, what they have in mind is the *recovery of the economic system* and not a "real" recovery that encompasses social infrastructure and is supportive of care, social reproduction, and other non-market activities. Rather, progress on gender equality is assumed to emerge as a natural byproduct of the recovery of the economic system. So even where international institutions have, on the surface, committed to reducing gender inequality, they have often failed to make substantial progress as their economic policies inevitably fail to realise their professed social goals (see Schech and Vas Dev 2007 on the World Bank's attempts at gender mainstreaming).

Third, international interventions have evolved since the 1990s, but the policy prescriptions of organisations such as IFIs continue to be insensitive to the gendered harms produced by conflict. Already from the early 1990s, post-war economic reforms sustained by IFIs were largely inspired by neoliberal principles (Pugh 2005), and often oblivious to individual countries' histories and circumstances (on the Bosnian case, see Pugh and Cooper 2004; Donais 2005). As IFIs started opening up to gender concerns while at the same time sticking to neoliberal prescriptions (on the World Bank see for instance Prügl 2017), there is still a disconnect between international agendas such as Women, Peace, and Security and the work of these institutions in post-conflict contexts, despite stated commitments to gender equality and women's economic empowerment (True and Svedberg 2019). The conflict in Ukraine (starting from the invasion of Crimea and war in Donbas, before the full-scale Russian invasion of 2022), has demonstrated that IFIs involvement in conflict and post-conflict contexts is both growing in intensity and scale (see Dolan-Evans 2022 on the World Bank), and also continuing on a path of policy prescriptions that tends to be insensitive to the gendered harms produced by conflicts. IFI-sponsored rounds of energy reform in Ukraine after the Global Financial Crisis, for example, severely impacted not only the economic security of the most vulnerable households but also women's physical security, forcing them to venture into dangerous rural areas close to active fighting to secure alternative sources of fuel (Dolan-Evans 2023). Mathers (this volume) puts these interventions in the context of a developing war economy, one that depends on women's labour while simultaneously making them increasingly vulnerable due to the erosion of social safety nets. With the spread of armed conflict and of a war logic spanning across active zones of war and so-called peace, an increased attention to the question of justice is not only called for, but urgent.

In this chapter, I shift the focus away from the "transitional justice" paradigm that has predominantly interpreted BiH's justice struggles over the past 30 years through the lenses of the Bosnian War and marginalised socioeconomic and gender violence. It is only recently that socioeconomic issues have become more central to debates on transitional justice, especially thanks to feminist contributions (Ní Aoláin 2012; O'Reilly 2016; O'Rourke 2009). Crucially, scholarship on justice issues in post-conflict contexts is increasingly less tied to paradigmatic "transitional justice," and has embraced more "transformative" conceptions of justice that are more responsive to calls for systemic transformation, not only in response to war but also other forms of social struggles from racial and gender justice, to abolition (Cullors 2018; Gready and Robins 2014; Lambourne 2009). Through its attempts to better account for gendered harms, transformative gender justice is thus seen as a way to move past an artificial separation of conflict/post-conflict zones and times, and imagine alternative forms of justice that embed a range of issues and remedies (Martín de Almagro and Shulz 2022). We thus shift towards gender justice as a concept and tool through which we can challenge the compartmentalisation of justice interventions substantially and temporally.

Gender justice thus becomes a way to map how justice claims emerge not only in response to the legacies of wartime harms that are overlooked in post-conflict economies, but as a result of a similarly flawed management of subsequent crises. Centring gender justice also calls for deeper forms of engagement with the past, to trace back ongoing forms of injustice through their complex histories – in Bosnia's case from socialism to the war and the post-war transition, and subsequent crises. Political-economic reforms in Bosnia actively "bracketed" the past by excluding any alternatives to neoliberal economic restructuring that were reminiscent of "socialist era values, narratives, and cultural perspectives" (Gilbert 2008:168), preventing adequate consideration of how the condition of women had evolved from the socialist period through the war. The "bracketing" of the past contributed to entrenching the economic exclusion of women and ended up redesigning post-war societies based on the (re)establishment of traditional and gendered forms of labour (at home and outside), and where "female subjects are depoliticized by being reduced to simplified archetypes devoid of complexity so as to reproduce dominant patriarchal regimes and norms" (Husanović 2009:106). Paying attention to the notion of gender justice highlights how international actors tend to work with a kind of limited temporality and a restrictive notion of distributive justice.

Much of my past research on gendered circuits of violence in Bosnia and Herzegovina focused on the cities of Prijedor and Zenica to illustrate the connections between wartime socioeconomic violence and its legacies and the gendered reproduction of socioeconomic injustice through post-war economic reforms analysed in the following section. These cases highlighted the country-wide destruction or appropriation of socially owned industries that destroyed workers' communities while "ethnic" ones were being fostered and isolated from one another. Prijedor was subject to systematic ethnic cleansing targeting the non-Serb population, culminating in the transfer of civilians into mines and factories turned into camps, and killings and torture that ultimately drove away almost all of the city's Muslim population (Grève 1994). In Prijedor, violence perpetrated on an interethnic basis had a clear socioeconomic dimension – with people losing their jobs and livelihoods as the first step towards genocidal violence – that came to profoundly affect and define people's experiences of the conflict and continued to be felt in its aftermath. Even in Zenica, where interethnic violence was less prominent, civilians survived extreme deprivation, exploitation, and social marginalisation. Most of the employees of the Zenica steel mill, which had around 20,000 workers in the late 1980s, were fired or put on waiting lists during the war (UK DfID 2002a, 2002b), often for failing to report to the factory while displaced due to the conflict. Being enlisted in the army entailed physical risks in combat, but also granted steadier access to food supplies that were not available to civilian women, many of whom had lost their jobs in the factories. After the war, ArcelorMittal later bought the Zenica steel mill as well as part of the Prijedor mines, but – as Vučkovac (2016:2) argues – the company's presence legitimised the "smooth cooperation of global capital and local nationalism" in the process of privatisation that occurred through war and ethnic cleansing. This chapter assesses the impact of deindustrialisation and the entrenchment of injustice not only as an outcome of post-war international interventions but also as the basis for continued, more recent interventions that have laid the basis for the onset of a war economy whose localised effects are deeply felt in BiH, but which is global in scope.

## A war on gender justice? From post-conflict interventions to crisis management in a war economy

Bosnia and Herzegovina's post-war economy was deeply shaped by the intervention of international organisations against the background of a global push towards integrating former socialist countries into the global market economy. The IMF, for instance, had direct influence over the setting up of Bosnia's new Central Bank, underpinning many fundamental economic choices that would shape the country's transition, such as the establishment of the new currency and currency board arrangement (Tesche 2000; Coats 2003). Both the IMF and World Bank worked alongside other institutions such as the European Bank for Reconstruction and Development (EBRD), US Agency for International Development, UN Development Programme, European Union (EU), and the Office of the High Representative (OHR) to promote changes to welfare and labour laws, liberalisation, and privatisation. Thirty years after the end of the Bosnian War, these actors continue to shape Bosnia's political and economic life, intervening in the management of the pandemic, the migrant crisis, and struggles on the management of the country's ecosystems. This section thus looks at how the impact of these interventions underpins the gendered reproduction of socioeconomic injustice in BiH up until today.

### *Reorganising welfare and jobs*

Labour and welfare reforms in Bosnia's transition from a socialist to a market economy overlooked women's complex experiences of socioeconomic violence and contributed to entrenching gendered forms of injustice. The IMF and World Bank were both concerned with reducing the role of the state in the economy and liberalising the labour market. Reform agendas from the early transition years, such as the OHR-sponsored "Jobs and Justice" programme, clearly stated that "government cannot create jobs" and that it would be necessary to transform the economy so that it becomes capable of creating jobs, by "allowing the free market to flourish" (OHR 2004:4–5). The reforms also had to deal with workers who had been put on "waiting lists" during the war, while their socially owned firms were not operating. Many of these factories had ceased production: almost half of industrial facilities had been destroyed during the war, and by 1998 the productive sector employed only 53% of the workers it did in 1991 (Jahović 1999; World Bank 2014). While workers on waiting lists were still entitled to receive healthcare and pension contributions, firms often did not keep up with payments (European Training Foundation 2006:38). Moreover, many Bosnians had been unjustly dismissed during the war due to ethnic discrimination or other personal and political reasons.

The legitimate claims of workers to their rights to work and social services came to be seen by the international community as a legacy of socialism in need of permanent dismantling or reform, and this perception continued to inform policy even in the face of significant social mobilisation against it, as in 2014 (Lai 2020b). Labour Laws approved to comply with IFIs conditions in 1999 (FBiH) and 2000 (RS) and then again in 2015 (FBiH) and 2016 (RS) set time limits for the extinguishment of waiting lists while providing for very limited rights to compensation for those unjustly dismissed during the war, and also facilitated part-time and temporary employment, reduced severance compensation, and established easier procedures for the dismissal of employees (IMF 1998, 2016; World Bank 2000). OHR interventions into pension laws prevented Bosnian authorities from easing the pressure on the labour market through early retirement, and social services were also increasingly privatised and decentralised, with non-governmental actors receiving funds to provide social services (Deacon and Stubbs 1998:110). As Deacon et al. (2007) note, the ability of former Yugoslav states to develop social policies was limited by the constrains placed by IFIs conditionality on Ministries of Finance. The decentralisation of healthcare, now managed by entity- and cantonal-level health funds, resulted in great inequality of access to good-level health care within the country, and in high costs due to the funds' weakness in negotiating pharmaceutical provisions. Shrinking social services ultimately aggravated the situation of vulnerable citizens, whose rights to pensions, maternity leave, and healthcare were not adequately protected (Vaša Prava 2016:40).

Labour and social sector reforms were planned without accounting for the legacies of socioeconomic violence stemming from the war and contributed to entrenching heavily gendered forms of socioeconomic injustice both within households and whole communities in Prijedor and Zenica. Women, who were not drafted for combat, often bore the consequences of unjust dismissal from work during the war. In Zenica, for instance, women put in charge of carrying children to safer cities in Croatia were fired from the steel mill for failing to report back at work after a period of leave, when travelling back to Bosnia became too dangerous. Dismissals, forced unpaid leave, and lack of food supplies made women dependent on army packages and humanitarian aid. During the worst phase of the conflict, the situation of one interviewee in Zenica became so dramatic that her body weight shrank to 38 kilograms. As her husband did not come home after the end of the war and she was left alone with two young children, the legacy of wartime deprivation was entrenched in its aftermath, when food reappeared in the shops, but she had no money to buy it, as she had been dismissed from her steel mill job after a light back injury. In Prijedor, the dismissal of non-Serbs was the first step towards the ethnic cleansing of the city. In some strategic sectors like healthcare, female workers were often kept at work for longer than other non-Serbs in the city, only to risk deportation to the infamous Prijedor prison camps once the authorities demanded it.

Post-industrial cities like Zenica and Prijedor continued to suffer dramatically from low formal employment levels, low activity rates for women and, often as a result of this, emigration. The lack of active employment policies made it particularly hard for returnees in places like Prijedor to reintegrate into the socioeconomic life of their community. In both cities, the relief for the end of the conflict was compromised by unemployment and lack of social services. While Yugoslav citizens had enjoyed a relatively good standard of life (Grandits and Taylor 2010), especially if compared to most countries of the communist bloc, at the end of the war people struggled to make sense of the institutions' lack of care for the widespread deprivation they faced. Looking at the micro-cases of Zenica and Prijedor, and the position of women in these communities, highlights the international organisations' inability to understand socioeconomic violence as a constitutive part of women's experiences of wartime violence. Because they did not engage with this gendered dimension of wartime violence, internationally sponsored reforms were not able to prevent injustice from becoming entrenched in Bosnian communities and contributing to forms of depletion stemming from social exclusion. Chiefly, among these, emigration has taken a toll on Bosnian households (most interviewees in Prijedor and Zenica had close family members living abroad), and is a gendered phenomenon, as more women than men cancel their residence in BiH each year (55% compared to 45%; BiH Ministry of Security 2016:54).

In BiH as a whole, women continue to comprise a much larger share of the inactive population and a higher percentage of those unemployed (IMF 2024a, 24). At the end of 2023, women's participation (37%) and employment (31%) rates were significantly lower than men's rates (60.7% and 54%, respectively). Women's and youth unemployment in BiH continues to be among the highest in the Western Balkan region (IMF 2024b, 14–15). In this context, the onset of the COVID-19 pandemic gave another example of inadequate reaction to a crisis that had profoundly gendered effects. A UNDP and UNICEF report on the social effects of the pandemic in BiH highlighted the impact on women as they experienced heavier job losses as well as increased childcare and domestic work burdens (UNDP and UNICEF 2021:9). Gender also intersected with specific conditions of vulnerability such as being single parents, being disabled, or being part of an ethnic minority in one's community. These groups were more likely to have difficulty accessing healthcare and food insecurity, or have to rely on coping mechanisms such as subsistence farming and remittances in order to get by (UNDP and UNICEF 2021:23–25). Even at times of high inflation and cost of living crisis, IMF recommendations continue to advise limiting minimum wage increases (IMF 2024b:14–15), delinking social benefits from such increases, and focusing instead on reforms that encourage labour market participation and discourage emigration.

The COVID-19 pandemic occurred in the context of a worrying trend of emigration on the part of Bosnian doctors and nurses, with Germany attracting a growing number of healthcare professionals – a majority of whom are women. While statistically this emigration does not appear to have significantly reduced the number of healthcare professional in the country, the emigration of doctors from the main cities for example triggered internal migration of professionals away from rural areas, which would lead to specific services no longer being available in certain regions (IOM 2021:67–68). Faced with the loss of specialised doctors and nurses, institutions during the pandemic Bosnian tried to cope by hiring new graduates and retraining personnel in new roles, and struggled under preexisting financial pressures that were exacerbated by the emergency (WHO 2022:14). One of the consequences is that a growing number of patients then need to be referred for health treatment abroad, which puts a heavy burden on carers who are also predominantly women (IOM 2021:68).

From the perspective of gender justice, international recommendations have continued falling short of accounting for the gendered harms generated by war, cemented by the transition, and further exacerbated by the pandemic. Interventions performed in the post-war period set the groundwork for a progressive erosion and dismantling of welfare, paving the way for an ongoing, deeply gendered social crisis and care crisis.

### *The gendered dimension of privatisations*

Privatisations were another crucial component of IFIs efforts in Bosnia, and – coupled with the support for microcredit programmes – constituted a second element in the process of entrenching social injustice after the war. While reforms linked to IMF conditionality in the 1980s had already pushed the Yugoslav market to open up, it was after the war that most privatisations got under way under international pressure (IMF 1998; for a comprehensive discussion of the IFIs role in Bosnian privatisations see Donais 2005). Domestic elites also had strong incentives to stir the privatisation process to benefit from it, by creating strong patronage networks that would support ethnonationalist parties in power. The privatisation process, more so than labour reforms, depended on IFIs initiative combined with Bosnian elites' need for external validation (from international actors) and ethnonationalist control over the political and economic system.

At first, similarly to other Eastern European countries, a voucher model was set up, where citizens would be eligible for titles corresponding to lost foreign currency savings, unpaid salaries for soldiers, and as compensation for nationalised property (Jahović 1999; Tesche 2000). In practice, Privatisation Investment Funds (PIFs) were often created to acquire privatised property, but these operations largely led to asset-stripping (OHR 2004). This was due, at least in part, to IFIs requirement that enterprises be sold before being internally restructured, despite their generally poor state at the end of the war (Stojanov 2001). On the other hand, as the international community recognised the shortcomings of this approach, IFIs increasingly sought FDI for large strategic firms yet to be sold (Donais 2005:143), while giving little financial support to the modernisation of the industrial sector in Bosnia. Reforms of the ownership structure were carried out in a context of destruction of industrial facilities (Bojičić and Kaldor 1999:94), deindustrialisation and dispossession, with new internal borders separating different parts of the extractive and production sites (Steblez 1998). Those who had accumulated wealth during the war, often through black markets and war profiteering, and had developed connections with ethnonationalist elites, were often best placed to take advantage of the privatisation process. The political economy of the war effectively played a crucial role in determining the reorganisation of property ownership in post-war Bosnia.

Yet, against this background the acquisition of the Zenica Steelworks by ArcelorMittal (and its subsequent investment in the Prijedor iron ore mines) was considered a privatisation success story. At the time, this was Bosnia's largest foreign investment since the end of the war, supported by an EBRD contribution of €25 million in the hope of stimulating further FDI. A closer look at the post-war communities of Prijedor and Zenica, however, shows the contradictory outcomes of "successful" privatisations carried out with no regard for socioeconomic justice. In Zenica, the steel mill now employs one tenth of the approximately 20,000 workers it had before the war, which is half what the privatisation contract required Mittal to keep (Slavnić et al. 2013:43). The number of workers has been gradually reducing, and the future of the steelworks is even more in question now that ArcelorMittal has decided to shut down its coke oven and rely on imported coke for the site instead (Kolisnichenko 2024). The Prijedor site is likely to face similar challenges to its viability in the future due to the decreasing concentration of metal in the iron ore that is mined there (Reuters 2023).

The long-term impact of privatisation and deindustrialisation has been dramatic and disproportionately felt by women and more vulnerable groups. In addition to the frustration for not being involved in the privatisation process, the citizens of Zenica after the war have had to cope with staggeringly high air pollution levels, which studies have shown to have gendered effects on household care responsibilities and consequently the labour market (Montt 2018). In fact, the installation of filters for the plant was envisaged by the EBRD project, but there was a subsequent lack of monitoring and engagement with the issue of air pollution, on the part of the Bank and other international organisations alike. Additionally, in both cities the fall of socialist industries deprived people of a working-class identity that entailed positive values, especially if contrasted with the exclusive ethnonational identity promoted by Bosnian politicians. Despite the shortcomings of the socialist system on gender disparities, privatisations also pushed women out of workplaces where they had been guaranteed some forms of social and economic equality and participation. This had implications not only for individual women, but also for households and whole communities, through the removal of a series of services – such as canteens, holiday resorts for workers and their children, and care services – which had previously provided support social reproductive work that traditionally fell onto women. Thus, exclusion from the workplace gave rise to a particular form of depletion stretching from the household as a site of social reproduction to the workplace as a site of socialisation and community building.

Post-war interventions set the stage for continued privatisations, and for the promotion of the private sector and individual entrepreneurship as the desirable sources of employment and growth. This is despite the limited success of programmes such as microcredit schemes and employment projects, which have often been planned without taking into account the education level, skills, or aspirations of Bosnian women, and have been critiqued for depoliticising and atomising women's agency (Stavrevska 2018), and generated informal debt used as a coping mechanism, alongside formal loan repayments (Jašarević 2014). International institutions have continued in recent years to advocate for reforming public owned enterprises. Public enterprises account for 11% of total employment and the Fund argues they distort labour markets as they are thought to have excess staff and higher than average salaries, as well as being either barely profitable or operating at a loss (IMF 2021:24, 66). The IMF has argued that many of these do not serve public policy objectives (IMF 2021:21) and should be opened to private capital. The energy sector has been recently singled out for reform as it is still dominated by two entity-based state-owned enterprises. The IMF calls for price liberalisation as part of a push towards reducing consumption and meeting carbon emission targets, as well as making the Bosnian market compatible with the upcoming EU Carbon Border Adjustment Mechanism (CBAM). The Fund argues that price liberalisation, accompanied by the institution of an Emission Trading System or carbon pricing and transitional measures like excises on fuel and coal use, would pass onto the consumer the increased cost of energy and thus reduce emissions (IMF 2024b:26–29). While the IMF report only provides a short paragraph on the distributional impact of these measures (and no gender analysis), stating they would affect the lower four deciles of the income distribution the most (IMF 2024b:34), Dolan-Evans' (2023) work on Ukraine shows the unjust and even violent consequences of energy reform if carried out without gender justice considerations in mind.

## Conclusion

This chapter has shown that war economies are made possible, and in fact underpinned, by the long-term involvement of international actors that promote policies that are insensitive to gendered harms and forms of injustice. Far from addressing or transforming the legacies of the war, internationally sponsored reforms in Bosnia and Herzegovina entrenched injustice and paved the way for the subordination of a growing number of issues to war and security needs in response to continued crises. What my previous research identified as the intersections of gendered circuits of violence and unheeded justice claims in BiH are now extending into a post-pandemic gendered crisis of care and livelihoods that is compounded by the geopolitical and ecological crises, both at global and local level. While energy reform might be justified through the need for a "green transition," and welfare reform as a way of stabilising the country's finances, in practice, this continuation of gender-blind policy prescriptions constitutes an ongoing source of insecurity and injustice in countries like Bosnia and Herzegovina. The chapter thus also echoes Bojicic-Dzelilovic, Kostovicova and Henry (this volume) conclusion that the cumulative dynamics that characterise the operation of gender-based violence along multiple continuums generate escalating effects in a context of chronic economic crisis.

An understanding of the long-term trajectory of international involvement in reforming BiH's economy is essential to appreciate the country's current trajectory. The political economy of the war partly based on destruction, dispossession, and trafficking, as well as on the dismantling of workers' communities, turned into a peacetime intervention that responded to IFIs economic agendas while discounting the gendered consequences of wartime violence. In fact, one of the main aims of the chapter has been to show that changes to labour legislation and industrial policies intervened onto preexisting situations of socioeconomic injustice that were not only left unaddressed but were even aggravated by the international efforts at economic reform. Rather than intentionality on the part of IFIs and their international partners (which the chapter does not attempt to prove), the discussion of reforms shows that this lack of consideration for justice issues reflects a narrow understanding of post-war processes of dealing with the past, which is further reinforced by the unhelpful separation between transitional justice and political economy. The chapter has also highlighted how the management of subsequent crises, such as the COVID-19 pandemic, has shown a similar insensitivity towards gendered harms that risk perpetuating similar problems in the future. The reorganisation of welfare and jobs was blind to the ways in which women had borne the brunt of socioeconomic violence in war and were being once again excluded from a fair reintegration in social and economic life by neoliberal reforms. Jasmina Husanović (2009) suggests that the importance of adopting "Bosnian lenses" when making sense of gender politics resides in the power of witnessing, which constitutes a way of continuously reshaping and questioning established identities and affiliations.

Witnessing to the "twin crises" of "(post)-war trauma" and "(post)-socialist losses," or destitution (Husanović 2009:100) represents a way, for Bosnian feminists, to escape a political order that ties post-war stability to subordination and violence. It is through these lenses that the chapter tries to show the continued importance of the Bosnian experience for demonstrating how international interventions meant to support post-war economic reform do so at the expense of gender justice.

## References

Andreas P (2009) 'Symbiosis Between Peace Operations and Illicit Business in Bosnia', *International Peacekeeping*, 16(1):33–46.

Berik G, van der Meulen Rodgers Y and Seguino S (2009) 'Feminist Economics of Inequality, Development, and Growth', *Feminist Economics,* 15(3):1–33.

Bojičić V and M Kaldor (1999) 'The "Abnormal" Economy of Bosnia-Herzegovina', in Schierup C (ed) *Scramble for the Balkans: Nationalism, Globalism and the Political Economy of Reconstruction,* Palgrave Macmillan, Basingstoke.

Brezar A (7 October 2022) *Bosnia's Peace Envoy Changed Laws Mid-Election. But What Does It Mean?* Euronews. https://www.euronews.com/my-europe/2022/10/07/bosnias-peace-envoy-changed-laws-mid-election-but-what-does-it-mean

Chisholm A and Stachowitsch S (2017) 'Reintegrating Feminist Security Studies and Feminist Global Political Economy: Continuing the Conversation', *Politics and Gender* 13(4):710–15.

Coats W (2003) *The Early History of the Central Bank of Bosnia and Herzegovina*, accessed 15 July 2019. https://works.bepress.com/warren_coats/12/download/

Cullors P (2018) 'Abolition and Reparations: Histories of Resistance, Transformative Justice, and Accountability', *Harvard Law Review*, 132:1684.

Deacon B and Stubbs P (1998) 'International Actors and Social Policy Development in Bosnia-Herzegovina: Globalism and the 'New Feudalism'', *Journal of European Social Policy*, 8(2):99–115.

Deacon B, Lendvai N and Stubbs P (2007) 'Conclusions', in Deacon B, Lendvai N and Stubbs P (eds) *Social Policy and International Interventions in South East Europe,* Edward Elgar, Cheltenham:221–42.

Djugum A, Bajrović E and Heil A (5 May 2020) *How Did a Bosnian Raspberry Farm Get a State Contract to Acquire 100 Ventilators?* RFE/RL. https://www.rferl.org/a/bosnia-ventilators-scandal-covid-19-raspberry-farm-multimillion-deal-procurement/30594315.html

Dolan-Evans E (2022) 'Making War Safe for Capitalism: The World Bank and Its Evolving Interventions in Conflict', *Security Dialogue,* 53(6):531–49.

Dolan-Evans E (2023) 'Pipes, Profits and Peace: Toward a Feminist Political Economy of Gas during War', *Review of International Political Economy,* 30(2):437–62.

Donais T (2005) *The Political Economy of Peacebuilding in Post-Dayton Bosnia*, Routledge, London, NY.

EBRD (European Bank for Reconstruction and Development), (2015–16) *Transition Report 2015–16*, Rebalancing Finance.

Ejdus F, Rečević T and Kovačević M (2023) 'Military Dynamics, Conventional Arms Control, and Regional Security in the Western Balkans', in Džuverović N and Stojarová V (eds), *Peace and Security in the Western Balkans: A local perspective,* Routledge: 129–155.

Elias, J. (2015). Introduction: Feminist security studies and feminist political economy: Crossing divides and rebuilding bridges. *Politics & Gender, 11*(2), 406–8.

European Training Foundation (2006) *Labour Market Review of Bosnia and Herzegovina*, Report Prepared for the European Commission, accessed 30 July 2018. https://www.etf.europa.eu/pubmgmt.nsf/(getAttachment)/386360B8F2B2F27DC12572CF0059128E/$File/NOTE72TLZT.pdf

Gilbert A (2008) *Foreign Authority and the Politics of Impartiality in Postwar Bosnia-Herzegovina*, PhD dissertation, Department of Anthropology, University of Chicago.

Grandits H and Taylor K (2010) *Yugoslavia's Sunny Side: A History of Tourism in Socialism (1950s-1980s)*, CEU Press, Budapest.

Gready P and Robins S (2014) 'From Transitional to Transformative Justice: A New Agenda for Practice', *International Journal of Transitional Justice*, 8(3):339–361.

Grève HS (1994) *The Prijedor Report*, Annex V to the Final report of the United Nations Commission of Experts established pursuant to UNSC Resolution 780 (1992), S/1994/674/Add.2, (1).

Hozić AA (15 May 2024) *Insecurity and Economies of Care*, New Lines Institute. https://newlinesinstitute.org/political-systems/insecurity-and-economies-of-care/

Hozić AA and True J (2017) 'Brexit as a Scandal: Gender and Global Trumpism', *Review of International Political Economy*, 24(2):270–287.

Husanović J (2009) 'The Politics of Gender, Witnessing, Postcoloniality and Trauma: Bosnian Feminist Trajectories', *Feminist Theory*, 10(1):99–119.

IMF (International Monetary Fund) (29 May 1998) *Press Release No. 98/19*, IMF Approves Stand-by for Bosnia and Herzegovina.

IMF (International Monetary Fund) (7 September 2016) *Press Release No. 16/396*, IMF Executive Board Approves Three-Year €553.3 Million Extended Arrangement under EFF for Bosnia and Herzegovina.

IMF (International Monetary Fund) (2018) *Bosnia and Herzegovina IMF Country Report 18/3.*

IMF (International Monetary Fund) (2021) *Bosnia and Herzegovina: 2020 Article IV Consultation Report,* IMF Country Report 21/43.

IMF (International Monetary Fund) (2024a) *Bosnia and Herzegovina: 2024 Article IV Consultation Report*, IMF Country Report 24/175.

IMF (International Monetary Fund) (2024b) *Bosnia and Herzegovina: Selected Issues,* IMF Country Report 24/176.

IOM (2021) *Emigration of Health and Information and Communication Technology Professionals from Bosnia and Herzegovina: Challenges and Opportunities*, IOM, Sarajevo.

Jahović N (1999) 'The State of the Economy in Bosnia and Herzegovina and its Consequences for Social Problems in the Country', *SEER: Journal for Labour and Social Affairs in Eastern Europe*, 2(1):87–98.

Kolisnichenko V (29 April 2024) *ArcelorMittal Zenica Has Finally Stopped Coke Production*. GMK Center. https://gmk.center/en/news/arcelormittal-zenica-has-finally-stopped-coke-production/

Kurtić A (29 November 2024) *Bosnia Federation's Jailed PM to Take 'Respirators Case' Conviction to Strasbourg*, Balkan Insight. https://balkaninsight.com/2024/11/29/bosnia-federations-jailed-pm-to-take-respirators-case-conviction-to-strasbourg/

Kurtović L (2018) 'Conjuring "The People": The 2013 Babylution Protests and Desire for Political Transformation in Postwar Bosnia-Herzegovina', *Focaal*, 80:43–62.

Lai D (2020a) 'What Has Justice Got To Do With It? Gender and the Political Economy of Post-War Bosnia and Herzegovina', *Review of International Political Economy*, 27(6):1257–1279.

Lai D (2020b) *Socioeconomic Justice: International Intervention and Transition in Post-War Bosnia and Herzegovina,* Cambridge University Press, Cambridge.

Lambourne W (2009) 'Transitional Justice and Peacebuilding after Mass Violence', *International Journal of Transitional Justice,* 3(1):28–48.

Majstorović D (2021) *Discourse and Affect in Postsocialist Bosnia and Herzegovina. Peripheral Selves,* Palgrave Macmillan.

Martín De Almagro M and Ryan C (2019) 'Subverting Economic Empowerment: Towards a Postcolonial-Feminist Framework on Gender (in) Securities in Post-War Settings', *European Journal of International Relations,* 25(4):1059–79.

Martín de Almagro M and Ryan C (2020) 'Introduction: (Re)Integrating Feminist Security Studies and Global Political Economy: Continuing the Conversation through Empirical Perspectives,' *Politics & Gender* 16(3):1–6.

Martín De Almagro M and Schulz P (2022) 'Gender and Transitional Justice', in *Oxford Research Encyclopedia of International Studies,* Oxford University Press, doi:10.1093/acrefore/9780190846626.013.669

Montt G (2018) *The Gendered Effects of Air Pollution on Labour Supply*, International Labour Organization, Research Department, Working Paper No. 27.

Ní Aoláin F (2012) 'Advancing Feminist Positioning in the Field of Transitional Justice', *International Journal of Transitional Justice*, 6(2):205–228.

OHR (Office of the High Representative) (2004) *Newsletter: Economic Reform and Reconstruction Bosnia and Herzegovina*, 7(1), accessed 19 September 2016. https://www.ohr.int/ohr-dept/econ/newsletter/pdf/7.1-econ-eng.pdf

O'Reilly M (2016) 'Peace and Justice Through a Feminist Lens: Gender Justice and the Women's Court for the Former Yugoslavia', *Journal of Intervention and Statebuilding,* 10(3):419–445.

O'Rourke C (2009) *Gender Politics in Transitional Justice*, Routledge, New York.

OSCE (4 January 2024) *OSCE Mission to Bosnia and Herzegovina statement ahead of 9 January*. https://www.osce.org/mission-to-bosnia-and-herzegovina/561445

Prügl E (2 January 2017) 'Neoliberalism with a Feminist Face: Crafting a New Hegemony at the World Bank', *Feminist Economics,* 23(1):30–53. doi:10.1080/13545701.2016.1198043

Pugh M (2005) 'The Political Economy of Peacebuilding: A Critical Theory Perspective', *International Journal of Peace Studies,* 10(2):23–42.

Pugh M and Cooper N (2004) *War Economies in a Regional Context: Challenges of Transformation,* Lynne Rienner Publishers, Boulder, London.

Reuters (17 November 2023) *ArcelorMittal Suspends Output in Bosnia as Steel Demand Drops*. https://www.reuters.com/markets/commodities/arcelormittal-suspends-output-bosnia-steel-demand-drops-2023-11-17/.

RFE/RL (Radio Free Europe/Radio Liberty) (24 May 2024) *Bosnian Serbs' Move Towards Secession 'Dangerous, Irresponsible', U.S. Envoy Warns*. https://www.rferl.org/a/dodik-secession-resolution-murphy-dayton-srebrenica/32962229.html

Schech S and Vas Dev S (2007) '"Gender Justice: The World Bank's New Approach to the Poor?"', *Development in Practice,* 17(1):14–26.

Sjoberg L (2015) 'From Unity to Divergence and Back Again: Security and Economy in Feminist International Relations', *Politics and Gender,* 11(2):408–13.

Slavnić Z, Likić-Brborić B, Nadin, S and Williams CC (2013) 'From Workers' Self-management in Socialism to Trade Unions Marginalisation in" Wild Capitalism": A Case Study of ArcelorMittal in Bosnia and Herzegovina', *Revija za sociologiju*, 43(1):31–55.

Stavrevska E (2018) 'The Mother, the Wife, the Entrepreneur? Women's Agency and Microfinance in a Disappearing Post-Conflict Welfare State Context', *Civil Wars*, 20(2): 193–216.
Steblez WG (1998) *The Mineral Industries of Bosnia and Herzegovina*, US Geological Survey Minerals Yearbook:8–1.
Stojanov D (2001) 'Bosnia-Herzegovina since 1995: Transition and Reconstruction of the Economy', in Papić Z (ed), *International Support Policies to SEE Countries – Lessons (Not) Learned in Bosnia-Herzegovina*, Open Society Fund Bosnia-Herzegovina/Soros Foundations, Sarajevo.
Tesche J (2000) 'Banking in Bosnia and Herzegovina. Bosnia and Herzegovina: The Post-Dayton Economy and Financial System', *MOCT-MOST* 3–4:311–324.
True J and Svedberg B (2019) 'WPS and International Financial Institutions', in Davies SE and True J (eds) *The Oxford Handbook of Women, Peace, and Security.* Oxford University Press, Oxford:336–50.
UK DfID (Department for International Development) (2002a) Annex D – *The Local Economies of Travnik, Trebinje and Zenica, Employment and Labour Market Status and Potential for Policy Development in Bosnia and Herzegovina* (Draft for Discussion), Output of the UK DfID Project 'Labour and Social Policy in Bosnia and Herzegovina: The Development of Policies and Measures for Social Mitigation'.
UK DfID (Department for International Development) (2002b) Annex G – *Report on the Local Study for Zenica, Employment and Labour Market Status and Potential for Policy Development in Bosnia and Herzegovina* (Draft for Discussion), Output of the UK DfID Project 'Labour and Social Policy in Bosnia and Herzegovina: The Development of Policies and Measures for Social Mitigation'.
UNDP and UNICEF (2021) *Social Impacts of COVID-19 in Bosnia and Herzegovina. Second Household Survey. https://www.undp.org/bosnia-herzegovina/publications/social-impacts-covid-19-bosnia-and-herzegovina-second-household-survey.*
Vaša Prava (2016) *Final Report. Analysis of Labour Legislation in Bosnia and Herzegovina*, Vaša Prava Legal Aid Network, Sarajevo.
Veličković M (6 May 2020) *Crisis and Resistance at the Periphery: Bosnian Responses to Covid-19*, Critical Legal Thinking. https://criticallegalthinking.com/2020/05/06/crisis-and-resistance-at-the-periphery-bosnian-responses-to-covid-19/
Vučkovac Z (20 April 2016) *The Political Life of Exported Steel*, Paper presented at the Center for European Studies at the University of Florida.
WHO (2022) *Health Systems in Action: Bosnia and Herzegovina.* https://eurohealthobservatory.who.int/publications/i/health-systems-in-action-bosnia-and-herzegovina-2022
WHO (2023) *Bosnia and Herzegovina: The Current COVID-19 Situation.* https://www.who.int/countries/bih
World Bank (2000) *Country Assistance Strategy FY00–02*, Report No. 20301 – BiH, April 2000, accessed 11 July 2019. https://documents.worldbank.org/curated/en/610431468198559158/pdf/multi-page.pdf
World Bank (May 2014) *Bosnia and Herzegovina Public Expenditure and Financial Accountability Assessment (PEFA)*, accessed 1 October 2025. https://www.pefa.org/sites/default/files/2020-10/BA-May14-PFMPR-Public.pdf

# 10

# CONFLICT FOR FUEL OR FUELLING CONFLICT DURING WAR IN GAZA AND UKRAINE

*Elliot Dolan-Evans*

The devastation wrought across Gaza and Eastern Ukraine is evident in the thousands of lives lost, flattening of urban centres, gratuitous violence against civilians, and mass, enforced displacement. What is more hidden in these theatres of war, though constituting an inherent logic to the aims of the Israeli and Russian aggressors, is the purposeful depletion of life- and survival-making processes in the conflict-affected populations. Israel and Russia's respective campaigns utilise well-used levers of their war economies, where entire economic sectors are subordinated to logics of annihilatory violence, which have been practised and honed for decades, even during so-called "peace times." Particularly, Israel and Russia have brazenly weaponised *energy* against Palestinians and Ukrainians, respectively, with their routine and methodological manipulations of this life-source at the "national level" that then transcends spatial boundaries to devastate everyday communities, households, and people.

Energy within these war economies is both utilised for state-driven "emergency" measures that strangle, at politically opportune times, entire populations of the dehumanised "Other," and serves as a source of capital accumulation. The levers of the "energy weapon" have been deployed for decades by Israel and Russia to control, contain, and punish "Enemy" populations, while equally earning the state windfall returns on global and regional markets – an interlinked circuit of violence and capital. In the most recent Israeli and Russian invasions, energy has again been weaponised within their war economies to fulfil a key war aim: to constrict the possibility of life-making and social reproduction within Palestinian and Ukrainian populations, respectively. Interestingly, the political economic transformations in the Ukrainian state since the 2014 War in Donbas, influenced by Western international financial institutions, have also catalysed a dynamic war economy. The Ukrainian war economy has similarly centred on its control and

DOI: 10.4324/9781003571667-13

capitalisation of energy assets, privileging capital accumulation for the state and investors through the privatisation and deregulation of the means of social reproduction, such as energy, while boosting military spending.

Despite the disparate geography, history, and circumstances separating these carnages, Israel's aggression on Gaza and Russia's invasion into Ukraine are both campaigns against the very life-making, social reproduction processes that Palestinian and Ukrainian women primarily undertake. Palestinian and Ukrainian women bear the brunt of not only every imaginable and unimaginable corporeal brutality in these ruthless campaigns, but equally suffer disproportionately from the unbridled, mobilised war economies that are centred on the energy sector. This chapter argues that the control and curtailment of energy within state-level war economies is key to the calculated obliteration of Palestinian and Ukrainian everyday social reproduction, building on recent feminist work (e.g. Lingham and Johnston 2024). The gendered violence painfully seen throughout Gaza and Eastern Ukraine is built on the degradation of women's life-making abilities through restricting the energy necessary for such social reproduction. In both warzones, it is the curtailment of energy that centrally animates the war economies fuelling these "death worlds" (Mbembe 2019).

This chapter deploys a critical, everyday feminist political economy centred on social reproduction to bring a further dynamism to understanding war economies of the contemporary "new-new wars." War economies are multifactorial and complex, which extend from Agamben's state-of-exception emergency measures at the state-level to mobilise resources for war, all the way down to the war economies of subsistence that conflict-affected people navigate to survive. This is broader than the war economy classically equated with John Keynes' concern of paying for warfare, for example, and engages with the plural and diverse war econom*ies* that are the basis of everyday survival. To do so, social reproduction is utilised here as an inter-scalar framework to conceptualise the gendered violence of war economies (Bhattacharya 2017:2). This approach analyses processes of reproduction across spaces, from state-level transformations down to gendered household dynamics, which allows us to understand the circuits of violence that radiate throughout such spaces and how they develop. It connects the seemingly disparate state-level processes of Israel's siege on Gaza, Russian attacks on energy infrastructure, and gas privatisation by the Ukrainian government, with the possibilities for daily social reproduction and survival for conflict-affected people within such "coping economies" (Peterson 2016).

This chapter builds on Henry Lefebvre's understanding of everyday life as a reflection of capitalist imperatives (Lefebvre 1968; Davies 2006), with an analytical focus on the social reproduction crucial to these quotidian tasks. In this understanding, everyday actions are regular, routine "politico-economic practices" that make existence possible and have a historical basis (Elias and Roberts 2016:788). These activities span intertwined production and reproduction processes from the household all the way "up" to global and transnational phenomena, which are also dynamic across time (Elias and Rai 2019:202). Understanding everyday social reproduction processes in this *relational* manner, through historically given contexts, helps to reveal the underlying logic of fluid, interrelated social structures across time that determine the social relations that make such life-making work possible (True and Hozić 2020:8). As demonstrated below, an everyday feminist political economy of life-making for Ukrainians and Palestinians reveals that an energy-centred war economy was not only present far before Russia's 2022 Invasion or Israel's 2023 War on Gaza, respectively, but a direct antecedent for the unprecedented and gendered depths of violence wrought in these theatres. This framework brings into perspective circuits of violence within social spaces that may be imperceptible during "peace time," or even war, which are revealed by closely studying how people survive and struggle to fulfil social reproduction practices of everyday life throughout the continuum between war and peace.

## Outline

This chapter investigates the centrality of energy in the violent, gendered destruction of wars in Gaza and Ukraine. It highlights that the control of energy is a main pillar of war economies that determines the survival of conflict-affected peoples in two devastatingly brutal wars of the 21st century. The chapter begins in Eastern Ukraine and reviews the geopolitical position of Ukraine between, and within, circuits of violence and capital constituted by Russia and the European Union. Ukraine's early independent history was dominated by Russia's energy-based war economy in "peace time" that manipulated gas to discipline its neighbour. Then, the ruptures of the War in Donbas provided the conditions for energy restructuring influenced by the International Monetary Fund in Ukraine, mobilising the sector into Ukraine's own war economy for state- and private-accumulation, which bled into dramatic and gendered impacts for the everyday survival of conflict-affected people on the frontlines. Finally, Russia's 2022 invasion sparked a redeployment of energy as a key weapon of the Russian and Ukrainian war economies, as both physical destruction and capitalisation, respectively, further eroded life-making and social reproduction. The next section takes us to Gaza. Israel has methodologically manipulated the entry of energy into the enclave since at least 2005, effectively honing energy as a brutal, non-discriminatory weapon in their arsenal against an entire population. The political and economic suffocation of Gaza by Israel's weaponisation of energy equally ensured their control over this resource for future capital accumulation. With Israel's ongoing (at the time of writing) aggression against Gaza since October 2023, this well-honed tool of their war economy is deployed to restrict Palestinian quotidian life-making and survival, rendering the Gaza Strip totally uninhabitable, constituting arguably the worst crimes of this era.

## Gas, geopolitics, growth, and gender in Ukraine

The post-independence Ukrainian population has been captive to concurrent, spatial circuits of violence and capital. On the one hand, Russia has manipulated their supply of gas to Ukraine, a structural legacy of the Soviet Union, to extract political and economic concessions and, more recently, to erode the bases of Ukrainian communal social reproduction. On the other hand, Ukraine has been subject to an extreme energy restructuring programme by the International Monetary Fund (IMF) since the 2007–2008 Global Financial Crisis, which has made Ukraine's energy infrastructure desirable for investment while ensuring everyday life-making of the population is more difficult. Following the 2014 War in Donbas, energy equally became a key factor of Ukraine's own war economy as IMF restructuring dominated after Russia ceased its gas supply to Ukraine. This section tracks the spatial circuits of energy-based violence and capital accumulation radiating across Ukraine from Russia to Europe, before the War in Donbas sparked the emergence of Ukraine's own gas-based war economy for state- and private-accumulation, fuelled by the IMF. Then, the analysis investigates how Ukraine's state-level transformation radiated down to the war economies on the frontlines amid Russia's deployment of energy as a weapon during the 2022 invasion, determining the everyday survival of the conflict-affected population.

Ukraine's geographical position between Russian gas production and European consumers has made the country a primary interest for energy security studies that focus on securing European Union (EU) supplies (Yergin 2006). In the 1990s, the relationship between Russia and Ukraine in terms of gas transit was relatively non-confrontational (except in 1992), as *nouveau* oligarchs from both countries accumulated "rents" from the gas trade; whether through barter trade or directly siphoning gas from pipelines. This changed by the early 2000s as the Ukrainian Orange Revolution brought a "pro-Western" government to power (Wolczuk 2016). The 2006 Gas Crisis was Russia's response to Ukrainian political intransigence and inability to pay new, unaffordable gas prices, as Moscow limited gas flows to Ukraine and downstream European countries during winter (Pirani 2007). The 2006 episode ended after Russian and Ukrainian elites negotiated a new deal that fostered the rent seeking of each (Balmaceda 2013).

Russian gas was then suddenly not as cheap for Ukraine as previously and this, coupled with the severe impacts of the Global Financial Crisis, catalysed an unprecedented economic crisis. The Ukrainian government had to approach the IMF for desperately needed capital, and the Fund demanded the sudden increase of gas prices for households in exchange. These reforms, amid a deep winter and collapsing economy, impoverished substantial segments of the population (Rozwalka and Tordengren 2016). Turning the screws a year out from Ukraine's Presidential election, Russia again cut gas supplies in early 2009, plunging the "pro-Western" government and the populace into deeper crisis (Balmaceda 2013:131); arguably contributing to Viktor Yanukovych's subsequent electoral success. Even in so-called "peace" time, Russia weaponised gas as an economic "sword" to discipline Ukrainian national politics, though the full, gendered impact on the population was relatively underexplored in the literature at the time. However, the everyday, gendered effects of gas production, circulation, and consumption within the war economy would be thrown into stark relief as the twin circuits of Russian violence and IMF-led capital accumulation converged upon Ukraine during the War in Donbas.

## Gas leaks in Donbas

The typical origin narrative of the War in Donbas is that Ukrainians rallied against President Yanukovych when he withdrew from the EU-Ukraine Association Agreement in favour of Russian integration, sparking the 2013–2014 Revolution of Dignity (Euromaidan in Western press). The protests eventually overthrew the government and destabilised Eastern Ukraine, allowing for the emergence of "pro-Russian" separatists, supported by the Russian state, to seize parts of Donetsk and Luhansk (Fischer 2019). What is often missed here, however, is the pivotal role of gas in the eruption of the conflict and then its use as both a weapon by Russia and as a tool for capital accumulation by the IMF, fuelling gendered circuits of violence that were embedded into Ukrainian war economies.

Behind the public interests of Ukraine, EU and Russia during these historical events, the gigantic gas reserves in the Donbas (the "Jewel of the Steppes") and surrounding Crimea (KPMG 2017) were a hidden consideration. These reserves, amounting to 1.2 trillion cubic metres, had reportedly been behind EU-Russian struggles for decades (Balmaceda 1998), and their relevance came to a head in 2013 as a coterie of Western companies began to develop them (Balmaceda 2013:149; Pirani 2017:7). Their size could make Ukraine a net gas exporter and perhaps solve the EU's energy problem, but they deeply threaten Russia's monopoly. The seizure of Crimea and crucial segments of Eastern Ukraine by Russia and "pro-Russian" separatists in 2014, therefore, could be read as a violent disruption of the efforts by the EU to secure Ukraine's energy production potential for European energy security. The struggle for of gas across the European continent during so-called "peace" times, eventually catalysed a hot war in Donbas.

## Fuelling the war economy

Although Ukraine's large eastern gas fields were disrupted or taken by Russian interests, the IMF resumed its agenda of "opening up" Ukraine's energy sector for private profit. The Fund pursued this objective unperturbed by, and perhaps because of, humanitarian crisis, economic collapse, and the increasingly violent War in Donbas. Alongside the visible violence of the war, where over 3,000 civilians were killed and over one-and-a-half million people were internally displaced (UNOCHA 2021), the relatively hidden and unproblematised economic restructuring also promoted a vicious war economy that further catalysed displacement, poverty, and insecurity for Ukraine's conflict-affected populace (Dolan-Evans 2021). The IMF was a major actor in instigating an energy reform programme in Ukraine that engendered a gas-fuelled war economy at the national level for state- and private-accumulation, which was characterised by the unbundling of energy assets for privatisation and the acceleration of household energy costs (Pirani 2020). Indeed, household gas prices increased approximately 650% under IMF-backed economic restructuring during the war to be some of the highest in Europe (Dolan-Evans 2021; Pysar and Dergacheva 2018:343).

The centrality of gas to social reproduction in Ukraine cannot be overstated, with the commodity piped into most households and used for heating, boiling, and cooking; tasks primarily completed by women to ensure their own, and their families and/or dependents, daily life-making. As the War in Donbas progressed, gas rapidly became more expensive while women's burden of everyday social reproduction deepened, as the neoliberal state retreated from the provision of social services (Women's International League for Peace and Freedom 2017). Women were tasked to care for injured veterans (Mathers 2020), and households near the contact line burgeoned as internally displaced persons, mostly pensioners, women, and children, fled the Donbas into Ukrainian-controlled territory. The contradiction between women's increased burden of daily care work, and the extreme unaffordability of gas that mediated this labour, percolated a viciously gendered war economy.

Along the contact line, situated in rural regions of Donetsk and Luhansk, this contradiction was most forcefully felt in areas already experiencing profound economic depression and violence. Exploding gas bills were the primary factor in crippling the everyday ability of conflict-affected Ukrainians to survive, with many experiencing steeply increasing material deprivation as violent war and structural adjustment jointly hit (Dolan-Evans 2021; Goncharuk and Cirella 2020). The necessity to cook food, boil water, and heat the home on the frontlines, especially during freezing winters, as households were packed with dependents who were sick, injured, and/or elderly, forced Ukrainian women to undertake dangerous mitigation strategies.

A prominent, forced adaptation in performing everyday survival tasks while war raged was an unprecedented reversal on the energy ladder, as frontline households transitioned from modern to simple fuels. Previously unimaginable gas costs sent conflict-affected households tumbling down the energy ladder – from using gas piped directly into the home, to relying on locally sourced biomass, such as foraged wood, paper, or plastics. Women and children predominantly ventured outside to collect such biomass fuels, and were exposed to heightened, gendered insecurity through the dangers of encountering military personnel or stumbling upon landmines or unexploded ordnances – the third most dangerous area in the world for landmine casualties (UNOCHA 2018). If wood, paper, and/or plastics were successfully collected, these basic fuels were typically burned inside for household quotidian tasks, which presented significant health risks to the women who predominantly did this work, as burning such biomass releases black carbon and particulate matter (Kusumawardhani et al. 2017).

Further, the deployment of energy in Ukraine's war economy impacted water consumption for conflict-affected households on the frontlines of the Donbas war. Water in Ukraine is purified via gas-fuelled sources and as such, the cost of water skyrocketed alongside gas. My fieldwork suggested that water costs doubled between 2014 and 2017 (Dolan-Evans 2021), which pushed frontline households to use water from dug wells due to the prohibitive cost of piped, purified water (REACH 2017:34). However, the ground water quality was very poor in the warzone, due to contamination from agricultural run-off, spilled oil, and other military waste, and was a breeding ground for communicable disease (UNOCHA 2018:5). Together, the inhalation of black carbon and particulate matter alongside the spread of contaminants and contagious disease via groundwater, which accompanied the regular tasks of everyday social reproduction work, deepened the health crises facing conflict-affected households in the Donbas.

## Russian invasion and capital accumulation

These dynamics of the gas-fuelled war economy in Ukraine dramatically deepened with Russia's invasion in 2022, which also meant the violent reimposition of Russia's own energy-based war economy. Russia previously cut off gas supplies to Ukraine in 2014, and the latter subsequently relied on reverse-flows of gas from Europe (Wolczuk 2016:130). With the 2022 invasion, Russia began a systematic campaign of actively destroying energy infrastructure in Ukraine. These attacks cynically escalated during winter, the exact moments when Ukraine's conflict-affected population rely most on gas to heat their homes and cook food, amongst other social reproduction tasks. As a result, Ukraine had to import unprecedented amounts of energy to keep the lights on (Matuszak 2024). However, at the same time Russia escalated its violent destruction of Ukraine's energy infrastructure, the Ukrainian government moved to make the sector more attractive to foreign investors, at the behest of both the IMF and World Bank.

As war-related violence escalated, the Ukrainian government continued unaffordable gas prices for Ukrainians and spent big on subsidising private energy companies. First, to mitigate the business impacts of a gas export ban, the government purchased gas from private owners to the tune of between 35 and 48% above their breakeven price, ensuring handsome profits (Afanasiev 2024). Second, the Zelensky administration pledged to fully reimburse private gas suppliers for any payment shortfalls from Ukrainian households (Revutska 2023:6, 10). Third, the government eagerly adopted demands from the World Bank to "pull in significant private investment" and build a framework that "protects…private investors" as violence spiralled out of control (Government of Ukraine 2022:929; World Bank 2022:16). Despite the severe economic crisis that engulfed Ukraine

(Heinonen & Korhonen 2023), the administration found public money to protect, and ensure the profitability of, private capital while fastidiously levying extortionate gas rates for the conflict-affected populace (Dolan-Evans 2022).

The gas-based war economies centred on the Donbas are constituted by these several interrelated, gendered circuits of violence and capital that cuts across temporality, spatiality, and scale. Gas is wielded as a weapon not only by Russia, who purposely restricts and destroys energy infrastructure amid freezing temperatures, but also by international financial institutions alongside the Ukrainian government to ensure the profitability of gas companies. At the time of writing, this latter dynamic may potentially intensify after US President Trump demanded control of Ukraine's gas pipelines as "payback" for prior weapon deliveries (Harding 2025), which will inevitably further capitalise Ukrainian gas for foreign, private interests. While Russia aims missiles and drones at power plants, dams, and other means of energy production that immediately impacts households, seemingly technical, apolitical reforms at the national level cascade "down" to conflict-affected Ukrainians in their everyday social reproduction practices – both with immediate and slow-burning consequences. These circuits of violence, whether underscored by physical brutality or capital accumulation during war, have devastating, gendered impacts. The cumulative impacts deepened the feminisation of poverty, sent conflict-affected families down the energy ladder, increased gendered insecurity on the frontlines, and negatively affected the health and wellbeing of conflict-affected Ukrainians.

## The gendered war on Gaza: what is worth living for

Israel's war on Gaza from 2023 to the time of writing (April 2025) is paradigmatic of the 21st century's "new wars" on women (UN Women 2024a). At least 12,000 women (Bernama 2025) and 18,000 children been murdered by indiscriminate Israeli bombardment on the Gaza Strip (Oxfam 2024; Rosen and Moghli 2025),[1] illustrating a direct physical war on women and their dependents. Alongside this direct violence, Israel equally and industrially produces death worlds across the tiny enclave that are centrally constituted by the calculated obliteration of women's daily life-making. This is not simply the depletion that Rai et al. (2013) theorise, but the wholesale, specific and targeted *destruction* of social reproduction (Dieng 2023). This stratagem by the Israeli military did not suddenly begin in October 2023, but was developed, refined, and honed through the practices of Israel's persistent war economies throughout its long war on Palestine (Dana 2024), and has reached its apocalyptic apogee in this particularly brutal phase. Indeed, these "indignities of the everyday" are part of the broader containment of Palestinian social reproduction across the Occupied Palestinian Territories that is "integral to the Israeli settler colonial project" (Chilmeran and Pratt 2019:595), and noted within the International Court of Justice's (2024) recent opinion that found Israel's implementation of a racially-segregated or apartheid system. As demonstrated below, the restriction, manipulation, and annihilation of energy have been the foundational plank of Israel's war economies' cyclonic destruction, which has deliberately targeted Palestinian women's quotidian social reproduction in Gaza.

## Energising de-development

As background, it is important to conceptualise the complex structure of power supply into Gaza that made the enclave reliant on external, and primarily Israeli, sources of energy.[2] Regarding electricity, there were ten connection points from Israel that potentially provided 120MW of capacity (when not restricted), and three connections from Egypt that theoretically supplied 30MW (World Bank & ESMAP 2016).[3] The Egyptian connection had historically been highly unreliable and frequently interrupted due to a lack of maintenance and poor-quality supply. The only indigenous electricity supply was from the Gaza Power Plant (GPP) that entered operation in early 2004 and required diesel fuel to run (planned to be replaced by natural gas), which hypothetically could produce 140MW of power. However, the fragile Gaza electricity grid and lack of diesel due to Israeli restrictions on imports of fuel, equipment and technicians/engineers meant the GPP did not operate beyond 70MW output (Nashashibi and Gal 2019:17). At best, this combined electrical generation of 220MW did not meet anywhere near the needs of the Gazan population of approximately 450MW (Euromed and Middle East Unit 2016:5). Because of such deficits in imported energy, approximately 56% of households owned solar heaters (Ismail et al. 2013:121) and 30% had private generators (Nashashibi and Gal 2019:21). While gas is the main source of cooking and heating for Palestinians in Gaza (Palestinian Central Bureau of Statistics 2013:41).

Despite Gaza's reliance on external energy sources, it has long had the potential to be self-sufficient and provide the energy required for social reproduction on a population-wide scale across the Occupied Territories (Power 2015:24). Two huge gas fields were discovered off Gaza's coast in 2000 with a total capacity of approximately 30bn cubic metres: the Gaza Marine and the Border field (Ismail et al. 2013:127). The gigantic Gaza Marine is located 17–21 nautical miles off the Gaza coast and is entirely within Palestinian territorial waters, while the Border field adjoins Israel's Noa south field and is contiguous with the agreed maritime border (Antreasyan 2013). However, Israel decreed a naval closure over Gaza the same year these gas fields were discovered, prohibiting any activity five nautical miles from the shoreline, which clearly violated the Oslo Accords, while it also stipulated the Border field was within a "closed military area" (Power 2015:16, 35, 50). Subsequently, negotiations to develop the Gaza Marine broke down by 2007 (Antreasyan 2013:33).[4]

The relationship between Israel and Gaza was famously coined "de-development" by Sara Roy (2016:4), a "deliberate, systematic deconstruction of an indigenous economy by a dominant power." This process intensified after 2005, when Israel disengaged from the Gaza Strip and turned it into "the biggest prison on Earth," quoting Israeli historian Ilan Pappé. Not only did Israel's dominance of Gaza change from direct settlement to overseeing an "imprisoned and diminished canton," which the Israeli military would regularly and callously bomb (euphemistically "mowing the grass"), but the disengagement purposely froze the political peace process (Roy 2016:xxiii–xxiv). Then, after Hamas won the 2006 Palestinian legislative elections and took over Gaza in 2007, Israel implemented a suffocating blockade on the Strip, deploying technologies of control through its war economies within a spatial "zone of exception," which explicitly curtailed the ability of Palestinians in Gaza to carry out activities of everyday social reproduction. The Israeli Ministry of Health scientifically determined the "minimal subsistence basket" to keep Gaza just shy of widespread malnutrition, establishing a restricted supply of fuel and foodstuff to barely sustain a caloric minimum that deliberately kept the "Gazan economy on the brink of collapse" (Roy 2016:xxviii; Winter 2015:315). Central to Israel's besiegement was the weaponisation of energy, expressed as restrictions on both fuel and electricity to Gaza, sanctioned by the Israeli Supreme Court (Roy 2016:xxix).[5]

Outside of the suffocating blockade, Israel sought to specifically destroy Palestinian energy infrastructure throughout every single military attack on Gaza. For example, during "Operation Summer Rains" in 2006, Israel attacked the GPP and closed a crucial energy pipeline into the enclave; in 2008–2009's "Operation Cast Lead," Israel targeted and damaged power lines connecting Gaza to Israel and Egypt while it destroyed an electricity factory; and in "Operation Protective Edge" in 2014, Israel consistently attacked the GPP, causing irrevocable damage that permanently reduced its capacity (Japan International Cooperation Agency 2017:10; Power 2015:60–62).

Israeli restrictions to, and destruction of, energy infrastructure prior to the 2023 aggression had already pushed Palestinians in Gaza to a dire humanitarian crisis (Japan International Cooperation Agency 2017:4). Most households in Gaza experienced power blackouts that reached 20 hours per day (Association of International Development Agencies 2017:22), and because water delivery and desalination relied on electricity, households received only 6–8 hours of piped water every two to four days, invariably contaminated (ACAPS 2023:3, Euromed and Middle East Unit 2016:5,13). This prolonged, direct weaponisation of energy by the Israeli war economy meant that Gaza became practically "unliveable" by 2020, as decried by the United Nations (2017). Palestinian women bore the brunt of the enforced depletion of communal social reproduction (Bargawi et al. 2022), typically performing such labour for households with seven or more members (Pettit et al. 2017:5), necessitating increased hours in household work and negative coping mechanisms to handle spoiling food, heightened financial burdens, and deepened stress and anxiety (Abu Mezied 2023:6).

And so, prior to October 2023, the ability of Palestinians in Gaza to engage in everyday life-making was incredibly constrained, difficult, and depleting, especially for Palestinian women who performed the bulk of social reproduction work.

Following the October 7 attacks on Israeli military installations and settlements by Palestinian militant groups that led to the death of 1,200 Israeli soldiers and civilians, alongside the capture of 250 others, Israel launched a ferocious aggression on Gaza. Israel's assault has been incomprehensible in its destructiveness, unbearable to witness, brutal in its targeting of civilians and cultural, educational, and religious institutions, and calculated to tear apart the very social fabric of Palestinian life in the Gaza Strip. It has also been a war on women by not only unbelievably brutal and direct physical violence, but in the weaponisation of energy through Israel's war economy to enact a very purposive destruction of the capacity for Palestinian everyday social reproduction.

## If I must die: Israel's fuel for its war economies

Israel has honed its technique of energy manipulation within its war economy against Gaza to cataclysmic proportions, which is now, this section argues, a central plank in Israel's deliberate, gendered obliteration of Palestinian quotidian life-making. A total siege on Gaza was declared by Israeli authorities on October 9, 2023, with the enclave totally and suddenly cut off from fuel imports and electricity (ACAPS 2023:4).[6] By mid-November, Israel committed to allowing 140,000 litres of fuel to enter Gaza every two days (UNESCWA 2023:8), then 120,000 litres of fuel daily on December 6, 2023 (International Crisis Group 2024). However, this, firstly, did not eventuate, with only approximately 35,000 litres on average entering Gaza daily as demonstrated by UNRWA data;[7] and, secondly, been wildly insufficient, as basic humanitarian operations require 160,000 litres of fuel a day (International Crisis Group 2024). Additionally, Israel has methodically destroyed solar energy stations across Gaza, especially those supplying institutions of communal social reproduction such as hospitals, schools, and factories (UNESCWA 2023:8). By the end of 2023, Israel already destroyed more than 70% of Gaza's energy infrastructure (Hammouda 2023:4). By early 2025, it was estimated that Israel's aggression already resulted in $450 million worth of damages to an already depleted system (Middle East Monitor 2025).

The broad manner by which Israel's energy-based war economy decimated Palestinian women's ability to perform social reproduction is similar to that analysed in Ukraine above. However, the severity of this annihilation in Gaza is even more dire than Eastern Ukraine, as life-making has been shattered in an already impoverished population, living in one of the densest areas in the world, and who have all become internally displaced. The explosive intensification of the war economy against Palestinians in Gaza by Israel following October 2023 is constituted by several interconnecting gendered circuits of violence, which are centred on Israel's total deprivation of energy for Palestinians in Gaza: the transition to even more dangerous biofuels than the Ukrainian case and the health impacts this entails; the inability to cook due to the lack of fuel and subsequent starvation; and the total spoiling of water that has produced inhospitably unsanitary conditions, especially for women.

The purposefully energy-starved war economy has not simply sent Palestinians falling down the energy ladder but kicked out the ladder from under them. After Israeli severely restricted the entry of any fuel into Gaza, regular Palestinians were unable to afford the miniscule amounts that remained – with cooking gas 4,000% more expensive in early 2025 compared to mid-2023 (World Food Programme 2025). The lack of cooking gas, the primary cooking fuel prior to the war, meant that Palestinians initially burned firewood and wood residues; however, when these sources were extinguished, waste products were used, with over 25% of households in the Northern governorates burning waste already by end 2023 (World Food Programme 2023b:7), and 15% in the Southern governorates not even having access to waste fuel (World Food Programme 2023a:5). There were widespread reports that already within two months of Israel's calamitous aggression on Gaza, Palestinians resorted to burning cardboard, plastic, clothes, and books for cooking fuel (Arab News 2023). By early 2025, between 29% and 35% of Palestinians resorted to burning waste for fuel across the Strip (World Food Programme 2025). The health impacts were similar to those in the Donbas noted above, with particulate matter from burning dangerous fuels severely impacting respiratory health for women and children primarily tasked with cooking, but these impacts were magnified by the cramped and devastated environment (New Arab Staff 2024; UNESCWA 2023).

The lack of fuel to cook food has been a major determinant of enforced famine across Gaza by early 2024. The unavailability of cooking gas and water was cited by Palestinians as a crucial component of the pervasive food insecurity on the Strip, with 95% of surveyed households limiting the number of meals consumed (Insecurity Insight 2024:2, 9). By March 2024, about 2.13 million people in Gaza faced high levels of food insecurity, with 677,000 Palestinians experiencing "catastrophic food insecurity," characterised by "lack of food, starvation, and exhaustion of coping capacities" (World Bank et al. 2024:3). This particularly hit Palestinian women hard who are often tasked with sourcing and cooking food, though often eating last and less than other family members. Further, the conditions of man-made starvation are catastrophic for pregnant and breastfeeding women, who are at extreme risk of insufficient micronutrient intake (IPC 2024:15, 17). The gendered circuits of fuel and famine overlap to entirely undercut quotidian life-making within the vortex of Israel's war economy, which emaciate the bodies of Palestinians and endanger the biological survival of Palestinians unborn.

Foundational to Israel's curation of death worlds upon the Palestinian population in Gaza, operationalised through an energy-centred war economy, is the depravation of water consumption, a foundational life-making resource. By February 2024, nearly 60% of water, sanitation and hygiene facilities were damaged or destroyed by Israel, with the remaining lacking the fuel needed to operate them (World Bank 2024:5). The fuel-centred war economy ensured that no energy was available to pump life-necessitating water from wells in Gaza or run crucial desalination plants (ACAPS 2023:5). As early as November 2023, only between 60 and 120 wells were available to supply the water network (down from 282 to 307), with water not to drinking standards (State of Palestine WASH Cluster 2023). This meant the daily supply of water to Palestinians was 1.5 litres per day, far below the minimum recommendation of 15 litres per day. This is particularly disastrous for pregnant and lactating women, who need at least 7.5 litres of water a day to keep themselves and their babies hydrated (UN Women 2024, p. 7).

Relatedly, another catastrophe emitting from Israel's fuel-focused war economy centred on the Strip is the interlinked tsunami of wastewater that spatially engulfs the entire enclave. Wastewater treatment in Gaza is energy intensive (UNESCWA 2023:9), and the lack of fuel has resulted in untreated sewage water spilling out onto the streets, creating substantial health hazards (State of Palestine WASH Cluster 2023). This has contaminated the little water sources available, catalysing hepatitis A, diarrhoea, meningitis, and other communicable disease outbreaks across the embattled enclave (ACAPS 2023:5). As UN Women finds, this has put women and girls at a heightened risk of exposure, due to their traditional domestic responsibilities and role in caring, social reproduction work (UN Women 2024b:8).

The extent of death and destruction in Gaza from the unmitigated brutalities of the Israeli military is unprecedented in this era. The human, economic, cultural, political, and institutional costs of this unrepentant and unconstrained aggression by Israel on Gaza is unparalleled. This analysis has emphasised that Israel has violently progressed its long-standing project of constraining the life-making possibilities of the Palestinian populace by not only brutal, physical violence, but through an energy-focused war economy that destroys the bases of everyday social reproduction, which has fuelled and propelled concomitant and constitutive circuits of gendered violence in food, water, and sanitation.

## Conclusion

V. Spike Peterson (2016) theorised the coping economies of conflict-affected people within broader war economies, foregrounding the crises in social reproduction. However, what we are seeing in the "new-new wars" in Gaza and Eastern Ukraine is that social reproduction within these war economies is not just in crisis but purposefully maintained in a permanent state of *catastrophe* that is fuelled by the restriction, manipulation, capitalisation, and destruction of energy (Lingham and Johnston 2024). The methodological and calculated nature of the gendered decimation of quotidian life-making through the obliteration of energy required to perform these tasks has catalysed what Mbembe calls "death worlds" across Gaza and Eastern Ukraine (Mbembe 2019). Both Russian and Israeli belligerents have practised and honed these techniques over time that are characteristic of the "new wars" of 21st-century neoliberal cosmopolitanism. The link between the war economies of these warring powers and the attempts by the Ukrainian government and international financial institutions to make the Ukrainian conflict environment safe for business is, paraphrasing Silvia Federici (2024), the common ramifications for conflict-affected people – that of displacement, the transfer of land to new masters, deeper burdens to survive, and protecting the interests of capital.

For Israel's rampage in Gaza, the targeted and purposeful destruction of everyday social reproduction of Palestinian women through the eradication of energy sources required for this work, centrally animates accusations of genocide. The first element of the crime of genocide under Article II of the *Genocide Convention* includes "deliberately inflicting on the group conditions of life calculated to bring about its physical destruction in whole or in part," which means that it is a crime of "reproductive violence" (Von Joeden-Forgey 2017:73). The UN Special Rapporteur, Francesca Albanese (2024:9), has noted that the asphyxiation of energy to the Gaza Strip falls distinctively within this element. Indeed, Nina Tzouvala (2024) argued that South Africa's genocide case against Israel at the International Court of Justice hinges on this central element of destroying the "conditions of life" necessary to sustain a political community, which the Court has found reasonably likely (*South Africa v Israel* (2024)). The International Criminal Court (2024) has also issued arrest warrants against Israeli leaders based on cutting of fuel and electricity to the entire Palestinian population in Gaza. This is a form of destruction that does not exactly resemble the archetypal model of industrial death camps in the Holocaust, but rather the precedents of colonial and settler-colonial genocides that were deployed to depopulate areas of indigenous peoples (Whyte 2024:12).

The use of an everyday feminist political economy to understand the war economies of contemporary wars, curated by both Israeli and Russian belligerents but also by the capital-accumulating imperatives of the Ukrainian state, yields new insights. This perspective, first, helps to discern the gradual, accumulating violence over time and space against women's ability to reproduce themselves, their dependents, and their communities, which has occurred in these war economies during so-called "peace time." Secondly, this framework helps scholars engage with the "messiness" of war, paraphrasing Cynthia Enloe (2015:438). War physically attacks the social spaces and structures that are typically conceptually fixed, such as the "household" that is the centre of typical feminist theorisation – obliterated out of existence by the death worlds conjured up by the new-new wars of contemporaneous neoliberal cosmopolitanism. An everyday critical feminist political economy that holds a relational ontology can look deeper than set categories of thought that may reify analysis during unprecedented violence and recognise processes of life-making and survival as interconnected within and throughout a myriad of structures, people, temporalities, and social spaces. Finally, it also uncovers the techniques that Israel and Russia purposely deploy to prevent life-making in a manner that constitutes heinous crimes (Bhattacharya 2024).

However, simply turning the gas "back on" will not solve these theatres of catastrophic violence – the very everyday politics and economic conditions that have allowed such war economies to be permissible domestically and internationally must be completely broken down and reconstituted. Part of this task must fall to feminists and academics across the globe. The universities in which we work often invest in companies and weapons manufacturers with ties to the Israeli or global military complexes and suppress pro-Palestinian activism under their *cause célèbre* of "academic neutrality" (Shoman et al. 2025). A feminist ethics of care, and academic integrity, demands that we actively oppose war crimes, whether committed by Israel, Russia, or other (or our own) militaries (Kynsilehto 2024), to promote meaningful solidarity and aim to transform the world so that war economies asphyxiating social reproduction cannot ever exist.

## Notes

1 These are *identified* casualties as of March 8, 2025 (women) and January 15, 2025 (children), which most analysts consider a gross underestimate. See Khatib et al. (2024).
2 For an excellent, concise history, see Cuyler (2024).
3 Disconnected in 2018 (IMF 2023, p. 8).
4 Interestingly, these negotiations were revived in 2021, and the Israeli government approved the development of the Gaza Marine by a Palestinian Egyptian consortium in June 2023 (Youssef 2023). Then in late October 2023, Israel awarded gas exploration licences to several companies off Gaza's coast in Palestinian maritime waters (Adalah 2024).
5 The only relief were fuel imports via the expansive Hamas-administered tunnel trade (Haddad 2019).
6 On 14 November 2024, the South Sea desalination plant was the only facility in Gaza reconnected to Israel's electricity grid but was disconnected again in early March 2025 (Amnesty International 2025).
7 See www.unrwa.org/what-we-do/gaza-supplies-and-dispatch-tracking.

## References


Abu Mezied A (2023) *Confronting Energy Poverty in Gaza*, Al-Shabaka, accessed 9 April. https://al-shabaka.org/briefs/confronting-energy-poverty-in-gaza

ACAPS (2023) *Palestine: Water Crisis in the Gaza Strip*, ACAPS, accessed April 9, 2025. www.acaps.org/fileadmin/Data_Product/Main_media/20231213_ACAPS_briefing_note_Palestine_water_crisis_in_the_Gaza_Strip.pdf

Adalah (2024) *Israeli Gas Exploration Licenses in Palestine's Maritime Areas Are Illegal and Violate International Law,* Adalah, accessed April 9, 2025. www.adalah.org/en/content/view/11036

Afanasiev V (2024) *Ukraine's Gas Export Ban Hits Independent Producers Hard*, Upstream, accessed April 9, 2025. www.upstreamonline.com/production/ukraines-gas-export-ban-hits-independent-producers-hard/2-1-1602914

Albanese F (2024) *Anatomy of a Genocide: Report of the Special Rapporteur on the Situation of Human Rights in the Palestinian Territories Occupied Since 1967*, Human Rights Council, Geneva, 55th Session, 26 February–5 April.

Amnesty International (2025) *Israel's Decision to Cut off Electricity Supply to Gaza Desalination Plant Cruel and Unlawful,* Amnesty International, accessed April 9, 2025. www.amnesty.org/en/latest/news/2025/03/israels-decision-to-cut-off-electricity-supply-to-gaza-desalination-plant-cruel-and-unlawful/

Antreasyan A (2013)' Gas Finds in the Eastern Mediterranean', *Journal of Palestine Studies*, 42(3):29–47.

Arab News (2023) *Antique Atoves in Gaza the Only Way to Cook During War,* Arab News, accessed April 9, 2025. https://arab.news/zw4fs

Association of International Development Agencies (2017) *50 Weeks of Occupation: Dispossession, Deprivation and De-development,* Association of International Development Agencies, accessed April 9, 2025. https://ps.boell.org/en/2018/02/14/new-report-ngos-working-palestine-details-economic-humanitarian-impacts-50-years-israeli

Balmaceda M (1998) 'Gas, Oil and the Linkages between Domestic and Foreign Policies: The Case of Ukraine', *Europe-Asia Studies*, 50(2):257–286.

Balmaceda M (2013) *Politics of energy dependency: Ukraine, Belarus, and Lithuania between domestic oligarchs and Russian pressure*, University of Toronto Press, Toronto.

Bargawi H, Alami R and Ziada H (2022) 'Re-Negotiating Social Reproduction, Work and Gender Roles in Occupied Palestine', *Review of International Political Economy*, 29(6):1917–1944.

Bernama (2025) *Over 12,000 Women Killed by Israeli Aggression in Gaza – Ministry*, Bernama, accessed April 9, 2025. www.bernama.com/en/news.php?id=2400635

Bhattacharya T (2017) 'Introduction: Mapping Social Reproduction Theory', in Bhattacharya T (ed) *Social Reproduction Theory*, Pluto Press, London:1–20.

Bhattacharya T (2024) *I Forgot to Die*, Spectre Journal, accessed 9 April. https://spectrejournal.com/i-forgot-to-die/

Chilmeran Y and Pratt N (2019) 'The Geopolitics of Social Reproduction and Depletion: The Case of Iraq and Palestine', *Social politics*, 26(4):586–607.

Cuyler Z (2024) *Power Struggles—Energy as a Weapon of War, Domination and Resistance in Palestine,* Middle East Report, accessed 6 April. https://merip.org/2025/01/power-struggles-energy-as-a-weapon-of-war-domination-and-resistance-in-palestine/

Dana T (2024) *Merchants of Death: Israel's Permanent War Economy,* Security in Context, accessed April 9, 2025. www.securityincontext.org/posts/merchants-of-death-israels-permanent-war-economy

Davies M (2006) 'Everyday Life in the Global Political Economy', in de Goede M (ed) *International Political Economy of Poststructural Politics*, Palgrave, London:219–237.

Dieng R (2023) *Why Palestine is a Feminist and an Anti-Colonial Issue*, ROAPE, accessed April 9, 2025. https://roape.net/2023/11/21/why-palestine-is-a-feminist-and-an-anti-colonial-issue/

Dolan-Evans E (2021) 'Pipes, Profits and Peace: Toward a Feminist Political Economy of Gas during War', *Review of International Political Economy*, 30(2):437–462.

Dolan-Evans E (2022) 'Making War Safe for Capitalism: The World Bank and Its Evolving Interventions in Conflict', *Security Dialogue*, 53(6):531–549.

Elias J and Rai S (2019) 'Feminist Everyday Political Economy: Space, Time, and Violence', *Review of International Studies*, 45(2):201–220.

Elias J and Roberts A (2016) 'Feminist Global Political Economies of the Everyday: From Bananas to Bingo', *Globalizations*, 13(6):787–800.

Enloe C (2015) 'Closing Reflection: Militiamen Get Paid; Women Borrowers Get Beaten', *Politics & Gender*, 11(2):435–438.

Euromed and Middle East Unit (2016) *Background Note on Energy and Water Issues in Palestine*, European Parliament, accessed April 9, 2025. www.europarl.europa.eu/meetdocs/2014_2019/documents/dpal/dv/background_note_hala/background_note_halaen.pdf

Federici S (2024) *Palestine is the World (2002)*, Counterpunch, accessed April 9, 2025. www.counterpunch.org/2024/03/12/palestine-is-the-world-2002/

Fischer S (2019) *The Donbas Conflict: Opposing Interests and Narratives, Difficult Peace Process,* Stiftung Wissenschaft und Politik, accessed April 9, 2025. www.swp-berlin.org/publications/products/research_papers/2019RP05_fhs.pdf

Goncharuk A and Cirella G (2020) 'A Perspective on Household Natural Gas Consumption in Ukraine', *The Extractive Industries and Society*, 7(2):587–592.

Government of Ukraine (2022) *Ukraine's National Recovery Plan*, Government of Ukraine, Kyiv.

Haddad T (2019) 'From Singapore to the Stone Age: The Gaza Strip and the Political Economy of Crisis', in Turner M (ed) *From the River to the Sea*, Lexington Books, London:179–211.

Hammouda A (2023) *The Electricity Sector in Palestine: Towards Less Dependence on Israel*, Institute for Palestine Studies, accessed April 9, 2025. www.palestine-studies.org/en/node/1654826

Harding L (2025) *US 'Demands Control' from Ukraine of Key Pipeline Carrying Russian Gas*, The Guardian, accessed April 17, 2025. www.theguardian.com/world/2025/apr/12/us-demands-control-from-ukraine-of-key-pipeline-carrying-russian-gas

Heinonen L and Korhonen I (2023) *The Effects of the War on the Ukraine Economy: The Situation at the End of 2022*, Bank of Finland, Helsinki.

IMF (International Monetary Fund) (2023) *West Bank and Gaza: Selected Issues*, IMF, Washington.

Insecurity Insight (2024) *Flash Analysis Report: Over Five Months of Attacks on Food Security in Gaza, March 2024*, Insecurity Insight, accessed April 9, 2025. https://insecurityinsight.org/wp-content/uploads/2024/03/Flash-Analysis-Over-Five-Months-of-Attacks-on-Food-Security-in-Gaza.pdf

International Court of Justice (2024) *Declaration of Judge Charlesworth*, International Court of Justice, accessed April 9, 2025. www.icj-cij.org/sites/default/files/case-related/186/186-20240719-adv-01-10-en.pdf

International Criminal Court (2024) *Situation in the State of Palestine: ICC Pre-Trial Chamber I rejects the State of Israel's challenges to jurisdiction and issues warrants of arrest for Benjamin Netanyahu and Yoav Gallant,* International Criminal Court, accessed April 10, 2025. www.icc-cpi.int/news/situation-state-palestine-icc-pre-trial-chamber-i-rejects-state-israels-challenges

International Crisis Group (2024) *Stopping Famine in Gaza*, International Crisis Group, accessed April 9, 2025. www.crisisgroup.org/middle-east-north-africa/east-mediterranean-mena/israelpalestine/244-stopping-famine-gaza

IPC (2024) *IPC Global Initiative – Special Brief – Gaza Strip: Acute Food Insecurity Analysis 15 February 2024 – 15 July 2024*, IPC, accessed April 9, 2025. www.ipcinfo.org/fileadmin/user_upload/ipcinfo/docs/IPC_Gaza_Strip_Acute_Food_Insecurity_Feb_July2024_Special_Brief.pdf

Ismail M, Moghavvemi M and Mahlia T (2013) 'Energy Trends in Palestinian Territories of West Bank and Gaza Strip: Possibilities for Reducing the Reliance on External Energy Sources', *Renewable and Sustainable Energy Reviews*, 28:117–129.

Japan International Cooperation Agency (2017) *Data Collection Survey on Gaza Reconstruction in Water and Energy Sector in Palestine: Volume II Energy Sector*, Japan International Cooperation Agency, accessed April 9, 2025. https://openjicareport.jica.go.jp/pdf/12301578.pdf

Khatib R, McKee M and Yusuf S (2024) 'Counting the Dead in Gaza: Difficult but Essential', *The Lancet,* 404(10449):237–238, doi:10.1016/S0140–6736(24)01169-3

KPMG (2017) *Situation of the Ukrainian Natural Gas Market and Transit System: Market Study*, KPMG Advisory, Budapest.

Kusumawardhani N, Hilman R, Laan T, Warda N and Nurbani R (2017) *Gender and Fossil Fuel Subsidy Reform: An Audit of Data on Energy Subsidies, Energy Use and Gender in Indonesia,* International Institute for Sustainable Development, accessed April 10, 2025. https://www.jstor.org/stable/pdf/resrep14784.1.pdf

Kynsilehto A (2024) 'Feminist Silences and Silencing the Critique of Gaza genocide', *Gender, Place & Culture*, doi:10.1080/0966369X.2024.2409703

Lefebvre H (1968) *Everyday Life in the Modern World*, translated by Rabinovitch S, Harper & Row, London.

Lingham J and Johnston M (2024) 'Running on Empty: Depletion and Social Reproduction in Myanmar and Sri Lanka', *Antipode*, 57(2):494–514.

Mathers J (2020) 'Women, War and Austerity: IFIs and the Construction of Gendered Economic Insecurities in Ukraine', *Review of International Political Economy*, 27(6): 1235–1256.

Matuszak S (2024) *Ukraine: A Major Blow to the Energy Sector*, OSW, accessed April 10, 2025. www.osw.waw.pl/en/publikacje/analyses/2024-03-28/ukraine-a-major-blow-to-energy-sector

Mbembe A (2019) *Necropolitics*, translated by Corcoran S, Duke University Press, New York.

Middle East Monitor (2025) *Gaza Electricity Company Estimates War Losses at $450m*, Middle East Monitor, accessed April 6, 2025. www.middleeastmonitor.com/20250218-gaza-electricity-company-estimates-war-losses-at-450m/

Nashashibi K and Gal Y (2019) *Gaza Electricity Reform & Restoration,* Abu Tor Economic Research Collaborative, accessed April 10, 2025. www.kas.de/documents/268421/4261447/Gaza+Electricity+Reform+and+Restoration+-+Fast+Track+Approach+to+Economic+Revival.pdf

New Arab Staff (2024) *Gaza: Hundreds of Respiratory Illness Cases Reported Amid Cooking Gas Shortages*, The New Arab, accessed April 10, 2025. www.newarab.com/news/gaza-scores-respiratory-illness-cases-amid-gas-shortages

Oxfam (2024) *More Women and Children Killed in Gaza by Israeli Military Than Any Other Recent Conflict in a Single Year,* Oxfam, accessed April 10, 2025. https://media.oxfam.org.au/2024/10/more-women-and-children-killed-in-gaza-by-israeli-military-than-any-other-recent-conflict-in-a-single-year-oxfam/

Palestinian Central Bureau of Statistics (2013) *Household Energy Survey*, State of Palestine, Ramallah.

Peterson V (2016) 'Gendering Insecurities, Informalization and "War Economies"', in: Harcourt W (ed) *The Palgrave Handbook of Gender and Development*, Palgrave, London: 441–462.

Pettit J, Presler-Marshall E and Abu Hamad B (2017) *Adolescent Girls in Gaza*, UK Aid, London.

Pirani S (2007) *Ukraine's Gas Sector*, Oxford Institute for Energy Studies, accessed April 10, 2025. www.oxfordenergy.org/publications/ukraines-gas-sector/?v=6cc98ba2045f

Pirani S (2017) *Adversity and Reform: Ukrainian Gas Market Prospects*, Oxford Institute for Energy Studies, accessed April 10, 2025. www.oxfordenergy.org/publications/adversity-reform-ukrainian-gas-market-prospects/

Pirani S (2020) *The Market Takes Shape: The Ukrainian Gas Sector to 2030*, Oxford Institute for Energy Studies, accessed April 10, 2025. www.oxfordenergy.org/publications/the-market-takes-shape-the-ukrainian-gas-sector-to-2030

Power S (2015) *Annexing Energy: Exploiting and Preventing the Development of Oil and Gas in the Occupied Palestinian Territory*, Al-Haq, Ramallah, Palestine.

Pysar N and Dergacheva V (2018) 'Determination of parity price for gas and electricity in terms of estimation of household incomes and energy costs', *International Journal of Energy Economics and Policy*, 8(5):342–346.

Rai S, Hoskyns C and Thomas D (2014) 'Depletion', *International Feminist Journal of Politics*, 16(1):86–105.

REACH (2017) *Ukraine: Analysis of Humanitarian Trends-Government controlled areas of Donetsk and Luhansk Oblasts, 5km Zone*, REACH, accessed April 10, 2025. www.slideshare.net/slideshow/anlysis-of-humanitarian-trends-in-ukraine-september-2017/89356310

Revutska T (2023) *Key Legal Developments in Ukraine's Energy Sector – IV*, Vasil Kisil & Partners, accessed April 10, 2025. https://vkp.ua/en/publication/key-legal-developments-in-ukraine39s-energy-sector-ndash-iv

Rosen R and Moghli M (2025) *Israel's War on Gaza Is Deliberately Targeting Children – New UN Report*, The Conversation, accessed April 5, 2025. https://theconversation.com/israels-war-on-gaza-is-deliberately-targeting-children-new-un-report-252398

Roy S (2016) *The Gaza Strip: The Political Economy of De-development*, 3rd ed., Institute for Palestine Studies, Beirut.

Rozwalka P and Tordengren H (2016) *The Ukrainian Residential Gas Sector: A Market Untapped,* Oxford Institute for Energy Studies, accessed April 10, 2025. www.oxfordenergy.org/wpcms/wp-content/uploads/2016/07/The-Ukrainian-residential-gas-sector-a-market-untapped-NG-109.pdf

Shoman H, Ajour A, Ababneh S, Jabiri A, Pratt N, Repo J and Aldossari M (2025) 'Feminist Silence in the Face of Israel's Genocide Against the Palestinian People: A Call for Decolonial Praxis Against Complicity', *Gender, Work & Organization*:1–8, doi:10.1111/gwao.13258

*South Africa v Israel* (Order) (2024) ICJ Rep 192.

State of Palestine WASH Cluster (2023) *Explainer: Water Supply & Fuel Relationship in The Gaza Strip,* The Applied Research Institute, accessed April 10, 2025. www.arij.org/latest/explainer-water-supply-fuel-relationship-in-the-gaza-strip/

True J and Hozić A (2020) 'Don't Mention the War! International Financial Institutions and the Gendered Circuits of Violence in Post-Conflict', *Review of International Political Economy*, 27(6):1193–1213.

Tzouvala N (2024) *Genocide and Political Economy: Reconstructing the relationship,* LPE Project, accessed April 10, 2025. https://lpeproject.org/blog/genocide-and-political-economy-reconstructing-the-relationship/

UN Women (2024a) *Gender Alert: Voice of Strength*, UN Women, Cairo.

UN Women (2024b) *Scarcity and Fear: A Gender Analysis of the Impact of the War in Gaza*, UN Women, Cairo.

UNESCWA (2023) *War on Gaza: Weaponizing access to water, energy and food* [online]. UNESCWA, accessed April 10, 2025. www.unescwa.org/publications/war-gaza-weaponizing-access-water-energy-food-land

United Nations (2017) *Gaza: Ten Years Later*, United Nations, Geneva.

UNOCHA (2018) *Humanitarian Needs Overview: Ukraine 2019*, UNOCHA, accessed April 10, 2025. https://reliefweb.int/sites/reliefweb.int/files/resources/ukraine_2019_humanitarian_needs_overview_en.pdf

UNOCHA (2021) *Humanitarian Needs Overview Ukraine*, UNOCHA, accessed April 10, 2025. https://reliefweb.int/sites/reliefweb.int/files/resources/hno_2021-eng_-_2021-02-09.pdf

Von Joeden-Forgey E (2017) 'Genocide', in Pető A (ed) Gender*: War,* Gale, Michigan:71–85.

Whyte J (2024) 'A "Tragic Humanitarian Crisis": Israel's Weaponization of Starvation and the Question of Intent', *Journal of Genocide Research*:1–15, doi:10.1080/14623528.2024.2339637

Winter Y (2015) 'The Siege of Gaza: Spatial Violence, Humanitarian Strategies, and the Biopolitics of Punishment', *Constellations*, 23(2):308–319.

Wolczuk K (2016) 'Managing the Flows of Gas and Rules: Ukraine between the EU and Russia', *Eurasian Geography and Economics*, 57(1):113–137.

Women's International League for Peace and Freedom (2017) *The Effects of Intervention by International Financial Institutions on Women's Human Rights in Ukraine* (CEDAW Committee, Geneva, 66th Session, 13 February–3 March).

World Bank (2022) *Relief, Recovery and Resilient Reconstruction: Supporting Ukraine's Immediate and Medium-Term Economic Needs*, World Bank, Washington.

World Bank (2024) *Note on the Impacts of the Conflict in the Middle East on the Palestinian Economy*, World Bank, Washington.

World Bank and ESMAP (2016) *Securing Energy for Development in the West Bank and Gaza*, World Bank, Washington.

World Bank, European Union and United Nations (2024) *Gaza Strip – Interim Damage Assessment*, World Bank, Washington.

World Food Programme (2023a) *Food Security Update: For Internally Displaced Populations in Southern Gaza Strip*, WFP, accessed April 10, 2025. https://docs.wfp.org/api/documents/WFP-0000155014/download/

World Food Programme (2023b) *Gaza Food Security Assessment,* WFP, accessed April 10, 2025. www.wfp.org/publications/gaza-food-security-assessment-december-2023

World Food Programme (2025) *Market Monitor* – Palestine, WFP, accessed April 10, 2025. https://docs.wfp.org/api/documents/WFP-0000165508/download/

Yergin D (2006) 'Ensuring Energy Security', *Foreign Affairs*, 85(2):69–82.

Youssef H (2023) *How a Gaza Marine Deal Could Benefit Palestinians, Israelis and the Region*, United States Institute of Peace, accessed April 10, 2025. www.usip.org/publications/2023/08/how-gaza-marine-deal-could-benefit-palestinians-israelis-and-region

# 11

# REMAPPING GENDERED CIRCUITS OF VIOLENCE

## A social reproduction perspective

*Elisabeth Prügl, Raksha Gopal and Luisa Lupo*

Over the past decade, feminist political economists have developed a rich literature on social reproduction, shifting the dominant focus of attention from the production of goods and services to what they have called the "production of life itself" (Elias and Rai 2019:202). The notion has inspired theorising about the relationship between production and reproduction, about the way social reproduction is governed, and has invited a methodological shift to study everyday care labour. Some feminist IR scholars also have begun to apply the concept to military households and post-war reconstruction. Inspired by this literature, in this chapter we seek to explore how social reproduction can help us think about gendered circuits of violence and war economies, the core topic of this book.

In their landmark 2020 article, Jacqui True and Aida Hozić introduced the notion of gendered circuits of violence, emphasising that it is not only capital that circulates globally but also bodies – such as those of migrants, refugees, military personnel, care workers, and development and humanitarian professionals. As these bodies move across borders, they carry with them the harms and violence they experienced and witnessed, enabling violence itself to circulate. This circulation connects violence in zones of war to the structural violences that persist in zones of alleged peace. International financial institutions play a central role in this process, distributing "harm and comfort" to transnational households (True and Hozić 2020: 1194). Through mechanisms such as austerity and post-conflict development, these institutions reproduce violence within the "interstitial post-conflict spaces created by remittances, care and debt" (True and Hozić 2020:1193).

The concept of gendered circuits of violence allows connecting themes of political economy to violent conflict in a specific way. First, it invites an ontological shift from seeing the world as made up of units to highlighting spatial connections and flows, and from privileging a static present to foregrounding temporal

DOI: 10.4324/9781003571667-14

linkages into the past and prefigurations of different futures. This understanding recalls the feminist concept of continuums of violence (Cockburn 2004), which suggests that sexual and gender-based violence does not just happen during war but precedes and follows times of war. It also suggests that such violence is not limited geographically to households (as in *domestic* violence) or territories at war but echoes beyond them. Second, the concept implies a feminist understanding of violence as not just a singular act, but as structural and, thus, pre-existing the rights-bearing individual. Seeing violence as *intrinsic in* economic and political structures (rather than as *effects of* these structures) broadens our understanding of what the phenomenon encompasses beyond bodily pain and the destructions of war: the "imploded homes" resulting from land grabs, un(der)paid labour, and austerity (Gago 2020:20) and the "slow violence" of poverty, environmental degradation and colonial erasures (Vorbrugg 2022). Third, the concept understands violence as gendered – to which we would like to add racialised – in the sense that it has different effects on differently situated people; moreover, gender impositions and racialised othering themselves need to be understood as violent processes (McNeilly 2014). The concept of gendered circuits of violence thus recognises the multiple and intertwined economic, political, and epistemic forms that violence takes in our globalised world, the way these forms circulate and impact people unequally, and the way they provide the conditions of possibility for war (Cockburn 2004; Wibben 2019).

True and Hozić (2020) gesture towards the importance of a social reproduction approach for understanding circuits of violence, and given the centrality of social reproduction in contemporary feminist political economy, we want to further develop this insight in this chapter. Scholars have applied the concept to a multiplicity of issues and contexts, and have brought to it different theoretical commitments, including historical and new materialisms, theories of governance and governmentality, and practice theory starting from everyday life. In these various applications, they have made social reproduction the core concept of new theories and approaches centred on life-making and the multiple, mutually reinforcing ways in which life-making is undermined by capitalism, state policies, coloniality and planetary destruction (Bhattacharya 2017; Elias and Rai 2019; Mezzadri et al. 2025). The topic of violence is more or less explicitly dealt with in this literature, and our purpose in this chapter is thus to tease out different interpretations and employ them for a better understanding of the connections between economies and war. To do so, we are staging an encounter between different writings that link social reproduction to violence. The concept of circuits of violence leads us to look for flows and movements of violence through different arteries, identifying specifically those of global capitalism, transnational biopolitics, and colonial epistemes of mastery. Together they provide one possible understanding of contemporary political economies and feminist foundations for theorising war economies.

Defined as the production of life itself, social reproduction seems logically opposed to violence, and much of the literature emphasises the way circuits of violence obstruct social reproduction. Yet, there is also a strong current in the literature that recognises how the labour and politics of social reproduction are complicit in perpetuating capitalist exploitation and militarism. The labour of social reproduction is implicated in capitalism by producing its labour force, and the politics of social reproduction drives the anti-immigrant policies of the welfare state and justifies the counterinsurgency operations of the security state by appealing to the welfare of populations transnationally. Following Rebecca Hall (2023), we thus approach social reproduction as a liminal practice that, on the one hand, is entangled in the deployment of gendered and racialised violence to secure the lives of some, while, on the other hand, gestures beyond such violence and towards the valuing of life. In the words of Hall, social reproduction is "both inside and outside the logics of capitalism, at once working for and against, and differentiated from yet integral to, the perpetuation of dominant modes of producing and understanding the world" (Hall 2023:327). This liminal character of social reproduction becomes visible in people's everyday negotiations and struggles for survival; it leads us to point to the potential of social reproduction practices as a locus of contention over futurity.

In the following analysis, we identify three interlocking circuits of violence reflecting differences in the ontological commitments in the scholarship on social reproduction (see Table 11.1). They open up different avenues for understanding gendered and racialised violence and the forms they take in processes of social reproduction. They describe how violence circulates geographically and temporally through the operations of capital, biopolitics, and mastery, coalescing in and generated through everyday practices. Within these circuits, social reproduction is conceptualised differently, reproducing different objects (e.g., life, population, the biosphere) and thus entailing different practices (e.g., labour, biopolitics, earth care). In *Circuits of Capital*, social reproduction enables accumulation, but is also put in jeopardy by the gendered and racialised violences of labour exploitation and primitive accumulation, supported by neoliberal economic orthodoxies and post-war reconstruction policies. In *Circuits of Biopolitics*, social reproduction becomes the task of governance in the form of social and securitised policies, but also emerges as complicit in othering. *Circuits of Mastery* suffuse the first two circuits and provide their worldview; they seed and legitimise the combined

**TABLE 11.1** Circuits of Violence and Social Reproduction (SR)

| | *Violences* | *Object of SR* | *Practice of SR* |
|---|---|---|---|
| **Circuits of capital** | Exploitation<br>Primitive accumulation | Life | Care<br>Labour |
| **Circuits of biopolitics** | Othering | Population<br>Society | Securitisation<br>Household rule |
| **Circuits of mastery** | Extractivism<br>Epistemic violence | Biosphere<br>Body-territory | Earth care |
| *Interlocking circuits negotiated and struggled over in everyday life* | | | |

epistemic and material violations of the earth and feminised bodies, but they also embrace social reproduction as something to be struggled for, seeding a politics of counter-mastery. We conclude by discussing the interlocking nature of these circuits, especially as they manifest in everyday life, and explore their relevance for understanding war economies.

## Circuits of capital: exploitation, primitive accumulation, and crises of social reproduction

The literature on social reproduction has long been concerned with bringing to light the gendered violences inherent within capitalist circuits. Early formulations outlined exploitative processes of surplus appropriation and primitive accumulation of women's labour facilitated by patriarchal norms. Neoliberal globalisation in addition brought into view how the policies of governments and international financial institutions facilitated these processes, including in post-war reconstruction. In this literature, social reproduction emerges as necessary for the continuation of capitalism, but also as threatened, and capitalist circuits as hostile to life.

Early social reproduction debates can be traced back to European and North American feminists writing on housework in the 1970s. Their distinctive contribution was to bring into view women's unpaid labour and to argue that doing this work was not simply a matter of love, but integral to the organisation of capitalism. Housework was necessary for the reproduction of the capitalist labour force, itself a commodity when exchanged for a wage in the market. It was thus implicated in the capitalist system of production, albeit in a subordinate manner. The debates over whether housework was "productive" or not, whether it was work or labour,[1] centred precisely on its relationship to capitalism. Whereas some argued that there was no evidence that housework increased the value of (waged) labour for capital, others highlighted the way in which it indirectly subsidised the accumulation process. If the surplus that could be extracted from the labour force hinged on the cost of the reproduction of that labour force, women's unpaid work reduced this cost for capital. Patriarchal oppression thus facilitated capitalist exploitation; the exploitation of the working class was buttressed by the oppression of women (Seccombe 1974; Molyneux 1979; Dalla Costa and James 2017). In other words, the violence of the capitalist system vis-à-vis the housewife lay in the way it employed patriarchal norms to further the extraction of surplus value.

An important modification of this argument was Mies' adoption of the notion of "primitive accumulation" to bring into view the violent dimension of the appropriation of women's work in a different way. In the writings of Marx, primitive accumulation referred to the dispossession of peasants from the land which "freed" them to sell their labour power and become available as workers in capitalist factories. Based on her research with lace makers in India, Mies argued that the appropriation of women's unpaid labour in the home is akin to primitive accumulation in Marx's sense in that it entails a violent extraction of value. And, going beyond the focus on labour, she identified a family resemblance between the extraction of value from women's unpaid labour, the subsistence economy, and nature. Capitalism needed these non-capitalist circuits and violently appropriated value from them. The "housewifization" of women was thus akin to colonisation; it redefined women's work as non-labour just as the subsistence economy was understood as a part of nature, ready to be taken (Mies 1986, 2012; Mies et al. 1988).

With other scholars (e.g., Federici 2012), Mies argued that including women in capitalist development was inherently violent. This was the case for the European witch hunts, which achieved the subordination of women – their housewifisation – in parallel to the proletarianisation of men. It was also the case for policies to integrate women into "development," which never made them simply into "free" wage labourers or proletarians, or into "free" entrepreneurs. Instead, they were subjected to "the use of structural or direct violence and coercion" in order to ensure their (super-)exploitation (Mies 1986:145). Violence against women, from sex-selective abortion to rape, was thus conceived as enabling the primitive accumulation of capital in an ongoing manner. Not confined to the origins of capitalism, it constituted a necessary element of capitalist accumulation.

The spread of neoliberal policy orthodoxies in the 1980s amounted to a geographical expansion of the violences of capitalist exploitation and primitive accumulation, also bringing into view the role of international financial institutions. Federici described globalisation as a "war that capitalism launched against women" (Federici 2012:10). For instance, structural adjustment programmes, promoted by the international financial institutions to modernise agriculture for commercial and export purposes, resulted in the displacement of subsistence farming largely performed by women across Asia, Latin America and Africa, jeopardising their livelihoods and those of entire communities. Similarly, the establishment of "global assembly lines," particularly in export manufacturing, largely relied on young women and the cheapening of their labour, exposing them to indecent working conditions and health hazards. In Europe and North America, neoliberal globalisation was associated with cutbacks of the welfare state, which Bakker (2007) characterised as "new enclosures," entailing a re-privatising of the social commons (including education and health). Finally, neoliberal economic and migration policies established transnational care chains, circuits of migration that solved the problem of care in the global North while establishing care deficits in the global South (Kofman 2012; Elias and Gunawardana 2013; Kofman and Raghuram 2015; Elias 2020).

Saskia Sassen has characterised these developments as "brutality," encompassing expulsions of people from the labour market, from land that is being grabbed for various purposes, and from the resources and wealth of nature (Sassen 2014). Other scholars have identified in neoliberal globalisation instances of unfree labour, epidemics of incarceration and debt – sometimes reviving the notion of primitive accumulation. Thus, Genevieve LeBaron and her collaborators have studied unfree labour in global supply chains, arguing that such labour cannot be understood without recognising the intermeshing of the logics of production and social reproduction (LeBaron 2015; Gore and LeBaron 2019). Adrienne Roberts has shown the interlinking of state welfare with criminalisation, identifying the violence of the law as a form of primitive accumulation (Roberts 2017). LeBaron and Roberts have developed the notion of "capitalist relations of carcerality" in order to describe incarceration, the "debt prison" as well as the prison of the household for domestic workers – all as an aspect of the shifting relations of production and social reproduction and as entangled in logics of primitive accumulation (LeBaron and Roberts 2010; Arat-Koç 2018).

Feminist writings going under the label of Social Reproduction Theory (SRT) have revisited the relationship of capitalist and non-capitalist economic circuits and brought them into a dialectical relationship (Bhattacharya 2017). Proposing an integrative ontology to account for the contradictory nature of capitalist processes, they have diagnosed a "crisis of social reproduction" as an intrinsic outcome of the contemporary organisation of capitalism. Whereas capitalism depends on social reproduction as the basis for creating value, and in this sense should give priority to reproduction over commodity production, it is at the same time sustained by a logic of accumulation that leads to an undermining of efforts at social reproduction (Ferguson 2016). In line with this view, Nancy Fraser suggests that capitalism systematically destroys, or cannibalises, its own conditions of possibility: "capital's accumulation dynamic effectively eats its own tail" (Fraser 2014:24). Picking up on this logic, Shirin Rai has developed the concept of "depletion" to describe the human costs of maintaining and reproducing social life, focusing on how these costs are unevenly distributed, particularly impacting women, households, communities and their environments (Rai 2024). Therefore, SRT surfaces a new kind of violence; it adds to the gender-based violences associated with labour exploitation and primitive accumulation the harms of depletion and social reproduction denied.

Feminist security studies have begun to relate these insights about gendered circuits of capital to situations of violent conflict and war economies. On the one hand, they have highlighted the way in which households participate in processes of militarisation. Thus, analysing the protracted armed conflict in Myanmar, Hedström (2020) has argued that social reproduction co-constitutes militarisation. As government resources are diverted to the military and the war effort, women's unpaid labour is mobilised in different ways to support this effort, including by reproducing the military labour force and providing emotional support, but also by symbolising home and hearth and legitimising the armed conflict. Similarly, Aharoni et al. (2021) identify how the discourse of "security as care" in Israel draws on gendered and national narrative to frame Israeli women's care labour as a strategy of warfare against Palestinians. Others (e.g., Basham and Catignani 2018; Rashid 2022) also have explored the central role of military families and intimate relationships between soldiers and their female kin in enabling war.

On the other hand, these studies bring to light the ways in which social reproduction is undermined both during and in the aftermath of war. For example, Rai et al. (2019) theorise social reproduction during war as entailing an intensified form of depletion embedded in layers of structural and physical violence, while Lingham and Johnston (2024) argue that depletion is not just a result of social reproductive labour but is intensified by war itself. Other research focuses on post-war reconstruction and the way the economic orthodoxies of international financial institutions ignore social reproduction. Along these lines, Cohn and Duncanson (2020) argue that women's care labour and subsistence activities are often invisible in these policies, and care is treated as a form of consumption rather than an investment. Moreover, the encouragement of extractivism for economic recovery fails to repair the harms of wars; instead, it often produces communal tensions, entrenching old inequalities and generating new ones, thus perpetuating the structural violence and inequalities that are known to fuel violent conflict, an issue that we examine later in this chapter under circuits of mastery.

A number of detailed empirical studies confirm these outcomes, emphasising in particular the pernicious effects of land policies. Thus, Hedström and Olivius show that post-conflict liberal economic reforms in Myanmar led to a disproportionate loss of land for women, generating "physical, material, and emotional depletion" (Hedström and Olivius 2020:379) and jeopardising social reproduction. Martin de Almagro (2022) observes a similar phenomenon in Liberia, where land reform was sensitive to gender relations, but still produced unequal outcomes in the context of a neoliberal global system and local patriarchal norms. Not surprisingly, states move to the centre of attention in this literature, and feminist scholars propose policies that focus on social infrastructure, participation and accountability during peace negotiations, advocating for what Rai and her colleagues term a "regenerative state" (Rai et al. 2019).

In sum, the concept of social reproduction brings into view the gendered violences embedded in capitalist circuits, which materialise through extractivism and the appropriation of women's labour. It also surfaces how the global circulation of capitalist processes endangers survival and human flourishing. While armed violence and war do not figure centrally in this literature, the idea of a "war against women" disrupts the war/peace binary and has invited scholarship that documents a temporal continuum of violence in post-war reconstruction. Moreover, the literature also alerts us to the implication of women's care labour in both, the militarisation of households and the reproduction of capitalism.

## Circuits of biopolitics: securitisation and othering

Much of the feminist political economy literature approaches social reproduction as the production of life through women's care labour. However, recent scholarship in feminist security studies also brings into view life as an effect of the exercise of biopolitics, that is, of the governance of populations (Foucault 1980). There is thus a family resemblance between the concepts of social reproduction and biopolitics in the sense that both are concerned with life and populations. However, while the social reproduction literature focuses on producing life, the topic of the biopolitics literature is managing life. In the words of Repo (2015:11), following Foucault, biopolitics is about "the strategies, techniques, knowledges, and regulatory discourses deployed to regulate life." Biopolitics includes a determination of how different bodies are valued or marginalised, and what types of violence are legitimised towards which populations. In postulating gendered and racialised circuits of biopolitics, we want to engage with literature that shows how violence is produced and reproduced transnationally through national and international efforts intended to secure life. And, as in the case of circuits of capital, we want to highlight the liminal character of such efforts, the way in which social policies intended to safeguard life also produce violence, including armed conflict.

In order to highlight the link between social reproduction and biopolitics, we find it useful to draw on Patricia Owens' theorisation of "household rule" which projects the patriarchal governance of households onto contemporary forms of government. By household rule, Owens means the despotic management of households under a male head "related to the fundamental human activity of managing basic life needs," which has historically involved hierarchical structures of power (Owens 2015:2). Owens thus introduces the household not just as a site of the production of life, but also a site of patriarchal politics. She argues that modern societies have externalised household management, producing the realm of "the social" as the arena for the management of life needs. This has become the task of the biopolitical state, which engages in household rule through its welfare policies, but increasingly also through its foreign and security policies. States perform what Owens calls "armed social work," that is, a kind of liberal welfare governance geared towards managing the life of populations across national borders, at times, through violent means. Policies of humanitarianism and counterinsurgency, such as the United States' counterinsurgency operations in Vietnam and its military campaigns in Afghanistan and Iraq, are thus motivated by the violent control of life and the domestication and management of others across borders (Owens 2015). In this way, household rule, as a form of biopolitical governance, imitates the liminality of social reproduction: it is motivated by securing lives and populations, while at the same time denying such security to some and directly fuelling armed violence transnationally.[2]

Importantly, the hierarchical logic of household rule and biopolitical modes of governance selectively support some population strata while jeopardising the daily and embodied security of undervalued, feminised and racialised others. This may take the form of deliberate and violent attacks on their social reproduction, for example, by limiting resources for some communities, fostering depopulation, or keeping some in concentration camps. But the effects of securing some populations may also be covert or inadvertent, circulating risk unevenly through the veins of the globalised economy as welfare states set up systems of social insurance for their own populations while expecting others to learn resilience (Duffield 2007). The ambivalent character of biopolitics and its uneven effects on social reproduction are thus visible in multiple fields beyond security. Three contemporary examples of foreign policy are illustrative of these effects: the securitisation of development policies, the neoliberal management of immigrant populations across various countries, and the global response to the COVID-19 pandemic.

First, under advanced capitalism there has been a shift in the foreign and security policies of states from a focus on containment to ensuring the sustainability and resilience of the life of populations globally. Accordingly, contemporary policies of developmental aid promote the security of individuals in vulnerable regions while also exerting control over various aspects of society, particularly social reproduction. For example, Jessie Clark (2016) illustrates how the Turkish government's gendered development initiatives, have the dual effects of securitisation and nation-building. She demonstrates how these initiatives enforce specific ideas around motherhood, marriage and family, reconfiguring the social reproduction of Kurdish communities in contested territories to align with the state's ethno-racial nationalist objectives. They circulate violence through the veins of the state by surveilling certain populations, disrupting their autonomy and reinforcing ethno-racial nationalist hierarchies and structural inequalities. And they do so in the name of development, often drawing on the circuits of capital described and turning projects of economic growth into a violent form of pacification.

Second, immigration policies are implemented in the name of national security and with the goal of protecting national populations from a number of imagined threats – including crime and competition for jobs. At the same time, there are also policies intended to safeguard migrants that discursively feminise them and construct them as vulnerable and in need of protection. Immigration policies thus reflect the liminal character of social reproduction, perpetuating violence against migrants in the name of biopolitical management: they seek to protect national populations against them while enacting paternalistic humanitarianism towards them. Crucial to this ambivalent operation is the sorting of populations into those needing protection, those deserving protection, and those constituting a danger because they assert agency or resist dependency narratives. The latter are threatened with biopolitical measures such as surveillance, detention, and deportation. For others, neoliberal and humanitarian management aims to foster "self-reliance" (Tazzioli 2024); yet paradoxically, they are often denied essential resources, such as work permits, social services, and confined in camps, which precludes their ability to sustain themselves independently. These forms of violence against immigrants are deeply gendered and racialised, and they are rooted in colonial modes of governance that reinforce global hierarchies among populations (Valiavicharska 2020). They circulate transnationally through international and national policies, through securitising discourses, and through the bodies of migrants as they move across various borders.

Our third example for illustrating the liminality of social reproduction within biopolitical interventions is the COVID-19 pandemic, which surfaced the profound contradictions of global health governance. While governments scrambled to protect one set of the global population, another was deemed disposable and, literally, left to die. Workers in the fields of healthcare, paid domestic work, food, transport and logistics were classified as "essential" to managing the emergency. Predominantly people of colour, women, and migrants, they remained undervalued while also being disproportionally exposed to disease, and experienced higher rates of illness and death compared to the rest of the population (Stevano et al. 2021). Racial hierarchies also played a key role in the global distribution of vaccines, which served as a conduit for the circulation of violence. Countries in the West secured early access through agreements with pharmaceutical companies, while countries in other parts of the world faced delays, higher prices and limited supplies, exacerbating inequalities in rates of illness and death (Mezzadri 2022). Efforts to safeguard the health of certain sections of the population thus led to neglecting and undermining the health of racialised and feminised others. The management of life normalised their disposability in the interest of national stability, security and capitalist accumulation. In this manner, disease, labour and vaccines became conduits for gendered and racialised violence circulating through intersecting spaces of the health sector, transnational supply chains, marginalised households and communities, borders, media and public discourse.

In the efforts to cope with the pandemic and its consequences, societies typically considered peaceful acquired the characteristics of war economies, demonstrating how the military and the health system are both in the business of securing populations and of managing life and death. This transformation was evident in the mobilisation of the military to enforce lockdowns, strict border controls, and the reorientation of industrial sectors toward the production of health equipment (Gibson-Fall 2021). In tandem with these measures, political leaders often used a rhetoric of war in reference to COVID-19, framing efforts to contain the virus through military metaphors and describing the labour of certain essential workers as a "front-line" combat (Sehran 2020). The circuits of biopolitics thus operated by securitising and militarising essential reproductive labour, and in the process perpetuated transnational economies of exploitation, insecurity and disposability that became visible in the exclusions they engendered.

In sum, like value creation through the labour of social reproduction, the management of social reproduction through biopolitics is not free of violence. It takes the form of governmental efforts to securitise populations locally and globally, including through counterinsurgency, humanitarianism, development initiatives, migration and health policies. These policies make up the circuits of biopower that transport gendered and racialised violence across geographies and across sectors.

## Circuits of mastery: extractivism and epistemic violence

Gendered and racialised violence moves not only through circuits of capital and biopolitics, but also through circuits of mastery. By mastery, we mean those material practices and discourses that reproduce exploitative and oppressive colonial relations (Barca 2020). Mastery adds to the economic and biopolitical violences we have described an episteme, thus rounding out an understanding of our capitalist and biopolitical worlds as shaped by violent ontologies of coloniality, patriarchal civilisation and modernity. Expanding notions advanced in feminist political economy and feminist security studies, and building on ecofeminism (e.g., Shiva 1988), we draw on decolonial scholarship to argue that circuits of mastery obstruct social reproduction by encouraging extractivism, such as landgrabs, mining and environmental destruction, and through the annihilation of indigenous cultures, knowledges and ways of life (Barca 2020; Gago 2020). Yet, circuits of mastery become sites of political contention, with social reproduction arguably a key focus. Epistemes entangle the material world, bringing into being bodies, our biosphere and with them forms of life. Therefore, epistemes of mastery encounter opposition in a struggle for social reproduction, so that it supports lives free of violence, dispossession, extractivism and war.

Circuits of mastery target bodies in conjunction with the biosphere, circulating knowledges that legitimize not only primitive accumulation but the destruction and appropriation of land and territorial wealth in conjunction with gendered and racialised bodies. Ecofeminist perspectives have long highlighted these connections and identified modernity and its misogynist discourses of mastery as central to environmental destruction, as obstructing the production of life, including the maintenance of the biosphere and ecological life-supporting systems (Plumwood 1993; Bakker and Gill 2019). This literature brings into relation the material violations of the earth and the epistemes that enable them, and it reads patriarchy as constitutive of such violations. Decolonial feminists remind us that modern epistemes also entail a categorical and racialised separation of the human and the non-human, and that, for the colonisers, the human made sense only in the binary form of woman and man. The colonialist project of civilisation thus required the imposition of gendered discourses, bringing about a unitary understanding of "women" as part of a heterosexual, racialised and hierarchical system. The diversity of gendered/sexed relations among humans and between humans and non-humans was thus erased, giving way to hierarchial subject/object relations. Gender surfaced as a tool in the circuits of mastery birthing a "high-intensity colonial-modern patriarchy" and enabling femicides and brutalities against women's bodies (Lugones 2010; Segato and Monque 2021).

Latin American indigenous feminists have proposed the concept of "cuerpo/territorio" or body/territory to push these insights one step further. Emerging from indigenous cosmologies, the concept, in Veronica Gago's words, "de-liberalises the notion of the body as individual property and specifies a political, productive, and epistemological continuity, of the body *as* territory" (Gago 2020:84, emphasis in the original). The historical and contemporary violations of the earth are thus theorised in connection with the introduction of heteronormative, neoliberal and patriarchal orders, and the scope of social reproduction is expanded to include human bodies in continuity with the territories they inhabit. Moreover, the concept informs a politics of resistance that combines the fight against extractivism and mining with the struggle against sexual violence and feminicides (Cabnal 2010, 2017; Falquet 2015).

The theorising of indigenous feminists can be adopted to provide a new language for describing the continuum of violence. As feminist political economists have argued, the extraction of natural resources, alongside the wealth and destruction it entails, is intertwined with histories of war, both fuelling and financing violence, while natural resources such as metals and minerals constitute the raw materials for military technologies and weapons themselves. During post-war recovery, international financial institutions often promote large scale, privatised natural resource extraction as a path towards durable peace, poverty reduction and socio-economic development. However, as Cohn and Duncanson (this volume) demonstrate, extractivism is antithetical to these goals. It leads to land dispossession, the undermining of livelihoods and social reproduction, physical violence and environmental destruction. It also undermines alternative measures to address inequalities, such as land reforms, and justice and reconciliation programmes.

The insights of indigenous feminists also inform new scholarship on reproduction, dropping the "social" and broadening the notion to encompass not just the social world and human bodies, but also the earth/territory as that which is in need of reproduction and care. We follow Barca (2020) to suggest that colonial worldviews, including binary constructions of gender, can be understood as discourses of mastery, and that their circulation enables the kinds of violence Latin American feminists and indigenous movements are fighting. Barca also argues for using the concept of reproduction to tell "other-than-master-stories" and counteract the ecological destruction that the "Anthropocene discourse" has wrought. Identifying the celebration of economic growth as violent, she calls for undoing this discourse, together with the extractive and oppressive relations it entails. She invites us to rethink social reproduction as "earth care," defined as care for humans, non-humans and the earth. This is the labour of the non-masters, including not just women, but also slaves, proletarians, animals and non-human nature, who provide the necessities of life for the masters, conceptualised not as a "species" but "a power system made up of material and symbolic relations" (Barca 2020:5). Thinking about the epistemic dimension of reproduction thus brings into sharp focus its liminal character as a site of politics.

In sum, seeing circuits of mastery entails an ontological shift and brings into view gendered and racialised violence against humans and the biosphere anchored in worldviews that propel exploitation, expropriation, extractivism and exclusion. The concept encompasses the processes described in circuits of capital and biopolitics, providing connections between different types of violence. It also invites a recognition of efforts at "counter-mastery," a politics of anti-violence arising from the invisibilised lives and epistemes of Others. Reproduction emerges here not as labour or population management, but as a political way of being, and life as a value to be struggled over.

## Understanding war economies through gendered and racialised circuits of violence

We are left with multiple understandings of the ambivalent connections between (social) reproduction and violence. Firstly, in the explorations of capitalist circuits, social reproduction emerges as under attack, in crisis, both intrinsic in and an alternative to logics of capital accumulation. Secondly, through the lenses of biopolitics, it is complicit in militarisation and violent othering while promising security, development, protection and health. Finally, within circuits of mastery, reproduction is modified to account for the multiple connected forms of violence of extractivism and colonial epistemes, together with resistances against them. Through our staged encounter of various literatures, social reproduction thus has emerged as a liminal practice and as a site of politics that engenders cooptation but also helps us imagine alternatives, allowing us to rethink political economies free from violence, dispossession, extractivism and war.

For heuristic purposes, we have presented the three gendered circuits of violence separately, yet they are entangled both in theory and in practice. Patriarchal and colonial epistemes of mastery have supported capital accumulation historically and continue to structure extractivism and associated violences, for example in the new rush for minerals enabling the green energy transition, in this way entwining circuits of capital and mastery. Moreover, inequalities aggravated by neoliberal capitalism fuel violent conflict and invite security and development policies to keep unrest at bay, thus enlisting racialised circuits of transnational biopolitics in circuits of capital. Gender and race – in intersection with other inequalities – provide the links between these circuits, links made visible through the lens of (social) reproduction.

How do these circuits of violence connect to war and war economies? A first take-away from our discussion is that violence inhabits everyday life to an extent that makes it difficult to separate war from non-war. In other words, today's political economies, which we have operationalised through our three circuits, are akin to war economies. For feminists this is not an entirely novel insight (see Cohn and Duncanson, this volume; True 2012); indeed, it is intrinsic to the concept of the continuum of violence. Starting from social reproduction, rather than gender-based violence, however, provides us with an expanded vocabulary to talk about violence, bringing into view its distinctive aspects. For example, making visible circuits of mastery adds to the temporalities of pre-/post-war a historical recognition of the colonial foundations of contemporary wars. Moreover, taking into account circuits of biopolitics, alongside those of capital, adds nuance to the way we understand efforts to safeguard the security of certain populations and their selectivity. Circuits of biopolitics also bring into view sectoral continuities (between health, migration, and development/economic and security policies) that may deserve more attention in feminist scholarship.

But denying the specificity of war and armed violence is a somewhat unsatisfactory move. For even if the war/non-war dichotomy is untenable, there is clearly a different quality to the experience of life in contexts of armed conflict. We are thus left with the question of how war economies enable war, how they provide its conditions of possibility, and how they work to escalate violence. The connection of neoliberal post-war reconstruction policies to the resurgence of war begins to provide a first answer to this question, centring the logics of privatisation and violent capital accumulation, together with a denial of social reproduction, as enablers of war. Framing counterinsurgency as a form of household rule offers a second answer, in which armed intervention becomes an extension of the management of populations, that is, of the political economy of social reproduction. Finally, the violence of extractivism provides a third answer, showing that armed conflict is often a manifestation of, or underwritten by racialised epistemes of mastery. A social reproduction perspective thus provides valuable theoretical tools for elaborating the relationship between violent conflict and war economies, that is, the intersectionally gendered circuits of capital, biopolitics, and mastery. Clearly, there is room for much more research on these connections.

An important insight from our discussion is the understanding of social reproduction as a liminal practice, one that coopts while also offering an alternative to war economies. We argue that social reproduction can serve as a beacon for a politics of life, one that recognises its complicity in violence, when it supports accumulation in the name of profit or militarisation in the name of biopolitics, and at the same time resists it. Bringing into view decolonial thinking and the operations of circuits of mastery encourages us to take the liminality of social reproduction as an opportunity for seeing it as a site of politics, where logics of mastery and counter-mastery meet. This has implications for our scholarship. It requires that we understand the three gendered circuits of violence as interlocked in the practices of everyday life, where they interpellate people to participate in exploitative economic structures and militarised biopolitics and where people negotiate and sometimes also resist these interpellations. Indeed, for many feminist scholars, everyday life has become the starting point to interrogate the different forms of gendered and racialised violence that constitute labouring and life-making across the world, including in post-war contexts (Mezzadri et al. 2025; Martin de Almagro 2022; Hedström 2021). This starting point holds great promise for a deeper understanding of how war economies work, how capitalism and biopolitical management foster armed violence, and how people are encountering the violent epistemes of mastery, including through a politics of resistance.

In sum, the concept of gendered circuits of violence offers a distinctive approach to war economies, emphasising continuums and the way violences flow through the capillaries of the capitalist system, biopolitics, and colonial epistemes. These circuits deserve empirical study, keeping in mind their entanglement and the way people negotiate them in their everyday lives. Social reproduction serves as a powerful lens for identifying and interpreting the often ambivalent experiences of people in war economies, and for guiding interpretations that acknowledge its liminality as a practice of both life-making and reproducing violence.

## Notes

1 Bakker and Gill (2019:507) explain that "work" is the broader category designating the activity of human beings as they relate to others and nature; in contrast, labour consists of a kind of work that is appropriated and controlled by capital. For a discussion of the dichotomy from a feminist perspective, see Bakker (2007).

2 In our reading of Owens, household rule is a form of biopolitics. But she criticizes the concept because Foucault does not take into consideration the household as a site of biopolitics (nor does he sufficiently link military and domestic power). So, in a sense, Owens expands biopolitics to make visible its origins in household management.

## References

Arat-Koç S (2018) 'Migrant and Domestic and Care Workers: Unfree Labour, Crises of Social Reproduction and the Unsustainability of Life Under "Vagabond Capitalism"', in Elias J and Roberts A (eds) *Handbook on the International Political Economy of Gender*, Edward Elgar Publishing. doi:10.4337/9781783478842.00038

Bakker I (2007) 'Social Reproduction and the Constitution of a Gendered Political Economy', *New Political Economy*, 12(4):541–556. doi:10.1080/13563460701661561

Bakker I and Gill S (2019) 'Rethinking Power, Production, and Social Reproduction: Toward Variegated Social Reproduction', *Capital & Class*, 43(4):503–523. doi:10.1177/0309816819880783

Barca S (2020) *Forces of Reproduction: Notes for a Counter-Hegemonic Anthropocene*, Cambridge University Press, Cambridge, UK.

Basham VM and Catignani S (2018) 'War Is Where The Hearth Is: Gendered Labor and the Everyday Reproduction of the Geopolitical in the Army Reserves', *International Feminist Journal of Politics*, 20(2):153–171, doi:10.1080/14616742.2018.1442736

Bhattacharya T (2017) *Social Reproduction Theory: Remapping Class, Recentering Oppression*, Pluto Press, London.

Cabnal L (2010) 'Acercamiento a la Construcción de la Propuesta de Pensamiento Epistémico de las Mujeres Indígenas Feministas Comunitarias de Abya Yala', in *Feminismos Diversos: El Feminismo Comunitario*, ACSUR-Las Segovias. https://porunavidavivible.files.wordpress.com/2012/09/feminismos-comunitario-lorena-cabnal.pdf.

Cabnal L (2017) 'Tzk'at, Red de Sanadoras Ancestrales del Feminismo Comunitario desde Iximulew-Guatemala', *Ecología Política*, 54:98–102.

Clark JH (2016) 'The "Life" of the State: Social Reproduction and Geopolitics in Turkey's Kurdish Question', *Annals of the American Association of Geographers*, 106(5):1176–1193, doi:10.1080/24694452.2016.1187061

Cockburn C (2004) 'The Continuum of Violence: A Gender Perspective on War and Peace', in Giles W and Hyndman J (eds) *Sites of Violence: Gender and Conflict Zones*, University of California Press, Berkeley, CA:24–44.

Cohn C and Duncanson C (2020) 'Whose Recovery? IFI Prescriptions for Postwar States', *Review of International Political Economy*, 27(6):214–1234. doi:10.1080/09692290.2019.1677743

Dalla Costa M and James S (2017) 'The Power of Women and the Subversion of the Community', in Aronowitz S and Roberts MJ (eds) *Class*, John Wiley & Sons, Ltd, Chichester, UK:79–86. doi.org/10.1002/9781119395485.ch7

Duffield M (2007) *Development, Security and Unending War: Governing the World of Peoples*, Polity Press, Newark, UK.

Elias J (2020) *The Gender Politics of Economic Competitiveness in Malaysia: Women on Board*, Routledge, Milton Park, Abingdon, Oxon; New York.

Elias J and Gunawardana SJ (eds) (2013) *The Global Political Economy of the Household in Asia*, Palgrave Macmillan UK, London. doi:10.1057/9781137338907

Elias J and Rai SM (2019) 'Feminist Everyday Political Economy: Space, Time, and Violence', *Review of International Studies*, 45(2):201–220. doi:10.1017/S0260210518000323

Falquet J (tran.) (2015) '« Corps-territoire et territoire-Terre » : le féminisme communautaire au Guatemala. Entretien avec Lorena Cabnal', *Cahiers du Genre*, 59(2):73–89. doi:10.3917/cdge.059.0073

Federici S (2012) *Revolution at Point Zero: Housework, Reproduction, and Feminist Struggle*, PM Press, Oakland, CA.

Ferguson S (2016) 'Intersectionality and Social-Reproduction Feminisms: Toward an Integrative Ontology', *Historical Materialism; Leiden*, 24(2):38.

Fraser N (2014) 'Behind Marx's Hidden Abode', *New Left Review*, 86(March/April):55–72.

Gago V (2020) *Feminist International: How to Change Everything*, Verso Books, London.

Gibson-Fall F (2021) 'Military Responses to COVID-19, Emerging Trends in Global Civil-Military Engagements', *Review of International Studies*, 47(2):155–170. doi:10.1017/S0260210521000048

Gore E and LeBaron G (2019) 'Using Social Reproduction Theory to Understand Unfree Labour', *Capital & Class*, 43(4):561–580. doi:10.1177/0309816819880787

Hall R (2023) 'A Social Reproduction Theory of Gender Violence', *Signs: Journal of Women in Culture and Society*, 48(2):321–345. doi:10.1086/722312

Hedström J (2020) 'Militarized Social Reproduction: Women's Labour and Parastate Armed Conflict', *Critical Military Studies*, 8(1):58–76. doi:10.1080/23337486.2020.1715056

Hedström, J (2021) 'On Violence, the Everyday, and Social Reproduction: Agnes and Myanmar's Transition'. *Peacebuilding* 9(4): 371–386. doi:10.1080/21647259.2021.1881329

Hedström J and Olivius E (2020) 'Insecurity, Dispossession, Depletion: Women's Experiences of Post-War Development in Myanmar', *The European Journal of Development Research*, 32(2):379–403. doi:10.1057/s41287-020-00255-2

Kofman E (2012) 'Rethinking Care Through Social Reproduction: Articulating Circuits of Migration', *Social Politics: International Studies in Gender, State & Society*, 19(1):142–162. doi:10.1093/sp/jxr030

Kofman E and Raghuram P (2015) *Gendered Migrations and Global Social Reproduction*, Houndmills, Basingstoke, Hampshire: Palgrave Macmillan.

LeBaron G (2015) 'Unfree Labour Beyond Binaries', *International Feminist Journal of Politics*, 17(1):1–19. doi:10.1080/14616742.2013.813160

LeBaron G and Roberts A (2010) 'Toward a Feminist Political Economy of Capitalism and Carcerality', *Signs: Journal of Women in Culture and Society*, 36(1):19–44. doi.org/10.1086/652915

Lugones M (2010) 'Toward a Decolonial Feminism', *Hypatia*, 25(4):742–759. doi:10.1111/j.1527-2001.2010.01137.x

Martin de Almagro M (2022) 'Building Feminist Peace: Gender, Legal Reforms and Social Reproduction after the United Nations Mission in Liberia', *European Journal of Politics and Gender*, 5(1):45–62. doi:10.1332/251510821X16363617184856

McNeilly K (2014) 'Gendered Violence and International Human Rights: Thinking Non-discrimination Beyond the Sex Binary', *Feminist Legal Studies*, 22(3):263–283. doi:10.1007/s10691-014-9268-y

Mezzadri A (2022) 'Social Reproduction and Pandemic Neoliberalism: Planetary Crises and the Reorganisation of Life, Work and Death', *Organization*, 29(3):379–400. doi:10.1177/13505084221074042

Mies M (1986) *Patriarchy and Accumulation on a World Scale: Women in the International Division of Labour*, Zed Books, London.

Mies M (2012) *The Lace Makers of Narsapur*, Spinifex Press, North Melbourne, Australia.

Mies M, Bennholdt-Thomsen V and Werlhof C von (1988) *Women: The Last Colony*, Zed Books, London.

Molyneux M (1979) 'Beyond the domestic labour debate', *New Left Review*, 116:3–27.

Owens P (2015) *Economy of Force: Counterinsurgency and the Historical Rise of the Social*, Cambridge University Press, Cambridge, England.

Plumwood V (1993) *Feminism and the Mastery of Nature*, Routledge, New York.

Rai SM, True J and Tanyag M (2019) 'From Depletion to Regeneration: Addressing Structural and Physical Violence in Post-Conflict Economies', *Social Politics: International Studies in Gender, State & Society*, 26(4):561–585. doi:10.1093/sp/jxz034

Rai SM (2024), Depletion: The Human Costs of Caring, Oxford University Press, Oxford.

Rashid M (2022) 'Precarious Attachments: Soldiers and Erasures of the Feminine in the Pakistan Military', *International Feminist Journal of Politics*, 24(4):544–563. doi:10.1080/14616742.2021.1995460

Repo J (2015) *The Biopolitics of Gender*, Oxford University Press, Oxford, New York.

Roberts A (2017) *Gendered States of Punishment and Welfare: Feminist Political Economy, Primitive Accumulation and the Law*, Routledge.

Sassen S (2014) *Expulsions: Brutality and Complexity in the Global Economy*, The Belknap Press of Harvard University Press, Cambridge, MA, USA.

Seccombe W (1974) 'The Housewife and Her Labour Under Capitalism', *New Left Review*, 83:3–24.

Segato RL and Monque P (2021) 'Gender and Coloniality: From Low-Intensity Communal Patriarchy to High-Intensity Colonial-Modern Patriarchy', *Hypatia*, 36(4):781–799. doi:10.1017/hyp.2021.58

Stevano S, Ali R and Jamieson M (2021) 'Essential for What? A Global Social Reproduction View on the Re-Organisation of Work during the COVID-19 Pandemic', *Canadian Journal of Development Studies / Revue canadienne d'études du développement*, 42 (1–2):178–199. doi:10.1080/02255189.2020.1834362

Tazzioli M (2024) 'Refugees' (In)dependency Conundrum: Obstructed Social Reproduction Activities and Unpaid Labour in Refugee Camps', *Antipode*, 56(4). doi:10.1111/anti.13020

True J (2012) *The Political Economy of Violence Against Women*, Oxford University Press, Oxford, New York.

True J and Hozić AA (2020) 'Don't Mention the War! International Financial Institutions and the Gendered Circuits of Violence in Post-Conflict', *Review of International Political Economy*, 27(6):1193–1213. doi:10.1080/09692290.2020.1732443

Valiavicharska Z (2020) 'Social Reproduction in the Making: Recentering the Margins, Expanding the Directions', *CLCWeb: Comparative Literature and Culture*, 22(2). doi:10.7771/1481–4374.3837

Vorbrugg A (2022) 'Ethnographies of Slow Violence: Epistemological Alliances in Fieldwork and Narrating Ruins', *Environment and Planning C: Politics and Space*, 40(2): 447–462. doi:10.1177/2399654419881660

Wibben ATR (2019) 'Everyday Security, Feminism, and the Continuum of Violence', *Journal of Global Security Studies,* 5(1):115–121. doi:10.1093/jogss/ogz056

# INDEX

Note: **Bold** page numbers refer to tables; *italic* page numbers refer to figures and page numbers followed by "n" denote endnotes.

For Product Safety Concerns and Information please contact our
EU representative GPSR@taylorandfrancis.com Taylor & Francis
Verlag GmbH, Kaufingerstraße 24, 80331 München, Germany